The Nurse Leader Handbook

The Art and Science of Nurse Leadership

By Studer Group
Nursing and Physician Leaders
from Across the Country

Published by:
Fire Starter Publishing
913 Gulf Breeze Parkway, Suite 6
Gulf Breeze, FL 32561
Phone: 850-934-1099
Fax: 850-934-1384
www.firestarterpublishing.com

ISBN: 978-0-9840794-2-1

Library of Congress Control Number: 2010923896

Printed in the United States of America

To all nurse leaders:

Thank you for choosing one of the toughest jobs in the world. You make a difference in the lives of many.

TABLE OF CONTENTS

Foreword i

How to Use This Book v

Section 1: Tactics to Manage and Lead Your Team

Introduction to Section 1 (by Lyn Ketelsen) 1

Chapter 1: Effective Communication 3

(by Debbie Cardello and Lyn Ketelsen)

- How clear communication aligns staff and moves culture forward
- The importance of connecting the dots to "why"
- Why leaders should embrace a variety of communication tactics
- "Best practices" leaders can adopt right now
- How transparency breeds accountability and facilitates behavior change

Chapter 2: Rounding on Staff 17

(by Lucy Crouch, Lyn Ketelsen, and Stephanie Baker)

- Power of the personal connection
- Looking for positives
- How to ask what's wrong (and make it right!)
- Capturing the wins and explaining the whys
- Helpful tools: rosters, rounding logs, and stoplight reports
- Recommended frequency of rounds

Chapter 3: Performance Management 35

(by Lyn Ketelsen)

- The nurse leader as change agent
- The Change Process: Believe > Decide > Act > Results > Understanding
- Four steps for managing negative performance
- The 3-to-1 Compliment-to-Criticism Ratio
- How to reward consistent high performance

Section 2: Tactics to Implement for Better Patient Care

FOREWORD

We at Studer Group® spend a lot of time with people in the C-suite at healthcare organizations. Like leaders in all industries, they face plenty of challenges and difficulties…and like all human beings, they become a little discouraged and overwhelmed at times. They might even think their job is very difficult, and they're right, it is. But is it really more difficult than the job of the nurse leader?

When I'm on site working with leaders or traveling around the country giving presentations, I often say to C-suite professionals: "If you are ever feeling sorry for yourself, just go into any patient care unit and visualize that you are the manager of that unit."

Yes, nurse leaders have a very full plate. First and foremost, your responsibility is to provide the best possible care to patients and their families. Care is the starting and ending point for everything you do. You must also manage quality and the expectations of your leaders and staff—and last but not least, manage the care teams who make nursing care possible.

Specifically, you are always trying to figure out:

- How to staff your unit 24 hours a day, 365 days a year
- How to deal with the individual complexities of every patient
- How to make sure patient flow is working well and all services that the unit is dependent upon are performing
- How to make sure that everything that is supposed to take place with the patient is taking place in the right way at the right time and by the right person
- How to manage relationships with a very high achieving group of individualists—physicians
- How to do it all while maintaining a flexible staffing schedule and managing labor costs

As the nurse leader, you know the ultimate goal is to make sure that every patient has a great experience, that every family member feels good about the care his or her loved one is receiving, that the staff members who provide the care are engaged and retained, and that every physician enjoys practicing medicine at your organization.

I find that after about 10 or 15 minutes of being in a nurse leadership office looking at the complexities of the role, the never-ending to-do list, and the many challenges, most people head back down to their offices very grateful for the jobs they have. I know I do.

As I have said in many talks, being a nurse leader is probably the most difficult role that currently exists in healthcare. At least it's as difficult as any role I've ever witnessed. I know some might disagree—but if you do, please send me the title of a job in healthcare (or any industry, for that matter) that's tougher.

I've asked nurses all around America why they went into this field. They tell me they went to nursing school because they wanted to take care of patients. Then, I ask them how they became a leader and I find that most of the time it was not their goal. What happened? Well, most say that one day somebody tapped them on the shoulder and asked, "Would you become a leader?" (Usually, the nurse was known for providing excellent patient care and an opening had suddenly become available.)

Often, nurses tell me they were asked to look at their mission to provide patient care and factor it into the family obligations they must balance. At this point they usually pause. Then, they were asked (perhaps in a pleading tone), "Would you try to help?" They tell me they then answered, "Of course." So, they were named the interim leader.

Then I ask them, "How long is *interim*?" They typically say, "I'm not sure." When I ask them, "Well, how much training did you receive?" the answer is "not enough."

And that's why we at Studer Group feel *The Nurse Leader Handbook* is so important.

After working for almost a decade and looking at Evidence-Based Leadership^{SM}, we believe the skill set of the leader is central to the process of creating a great organization. And, while plenty of books have been written about the general topic of leadership, we wanted to create one specifically for nurse leaders.

So in light of the great admiration we have for all healthcare leaders and our recognition of the unique challenges that nurse leaders face, Studer Group has pulled together a resource that we consider a "textbook with passion."

Written by a group of 29 experts, this book is a guide for leaders, and particularly nurse leaders, on how to 1) create better places for people to work, patients to receive care, and physicians to practice medicine, and, just as importantly, 2) create better places for the nurse leaders themselves to work. The goal is to give them the tools to continue to perform the important role of being a leader without being burned out…so they can go home to their loved ones as productive human beings and not worn out individuals.

And I think this is also important to note: We know that what is in here works. Studer Group doesn't publish anything based on theory, based on hypothesis, or based on thought (as in "We think this is true"). The book is basically the result of being out in the field, watching these tools being implemented, and observing and documenting the outcomes.

Jeanny Platt is a great example of the kind of leaders we want this book to help create. You'll find her story on page 361. Jeanny is a nurse manager for North Austin Medical Center, St. David's Health Partnership, in Austin, Texas, and was recently named our Frontline Leader of the Year. Jeanny is a type of leader who virtually anyone reading this book can relate to—one who faces a lot of challenges, but by implementing these tactics, has gotten great outcomes across the board in clinical quality, service, people, cost, and growth.

So this book is dedicated to Jeanny and to all the individuals in leadership positions. I know everyone reading these words has the will to succeed. This book will help them match the skill to the will.

Yours in service,
Quint Studer

HOW TO USE THIS BOOK

The idea to write this book emerged from Studer Group's experiences in working closely with nurse leaders across the country for upwards of 10 years now. As Quint describes in his foreword, being a nurse leader is not easy. One of the ways we can make it easier is to improve the skill sets of nurse leaders—to help them develop real fundamental skills and competencies necessary to succeed in an ever-changing healthcare environment. That's what *The Nurse Leader Handbook* is meant to accomplish.

The book is not designed to provide nurse leaders with an all-inclusive education in nurse leadership. Rather, it's designed to assist them in understanding the breadth of skills necessary to function in a leadership role—skills that are permeated with an unwavering commitment to serve patients and families to the best of their abilities. It's designed to give nurse leaders some practical guidance in how to improve their skills in these areas and perhaps understand where they might have opportunity to get further education.

Each year at our What's Right in Health Care℠ Conference, Studer Group® hosts hundreds of leaders from organizations around the country and the world. The idea is for attendees to learn about "best practices" presented by leaders and organizations that are getting results and making care better for patients and families.

At our 2009 conference, we conducted a breakout session targeted to nurse leaders. Some 300 people attended. Sixty-four percent of those attending were nurse leaders. Fifty-four percent of the nurse leaders had advanced degrees in nursing, 73 percent had more than five years of experience as a nurse leader, and over 40 percent had over 15 years of experience as a nurse leader. In other words, this was no rookie crowd.

During the breakout session, we presented some of the information contained in this book. We also had the opportunity to do some research with the group. While the results are not scientific, they are consistent with our experience as we travel the country working with organizations and leaders. That's why we found them so compelling and significant.

We discovered that nearly half of those nurse leaders in attendance were not familiar with basic business and financial terms and calculations such as net income. Neither were they able to articulate important concepts such as the connection between case mix and revenue. Findings like these have intensified our belief that a book like this one is needed.

The Nurse Leader Handbook provides a good working overview of financial management information. Through this book as well as through the supplemental information that appears on the Fire Starter Publishing website (www.firestarterpublishing.com/NurseLeaderHandbook), we hope to raise awareness of how important these skills are to the success of the readers' own futures and to those of their organizations.

Of course, financial matters are just the beginning. The book provides a vast amount of "big picture" information leaders need—from management behaviors to patient care tactics to knowledge fundamentals to professional development strategies.

In using this book, it might help to be familiar with a few terms from the Studer Group framework. The first one is *Evidence-Based Leadership*SM (EBL). This phrase refers to the importance of reducing variance in leadership skills and processes in order to produce a predictable and positive outcome for our organizations—in the same way that evidence-based clinical practices are designed to reduce variance and produce predictable positive outcomes for patients. The EBL framework consists of three components:

- Aligned Goals
- Aligned Behaviors
- Aligned Processes

Many of the strategies and tactics described in these pages fall within these three components.

Another term you'll see used periodically is *pillars*. This term is used to describe the foundational elements of an organization's overall strategy and typically identifies broad strategic priorities. Examples of these pillars or strategic priorities might include:

Service: Typically referring to patient satisfaction or improvement of the customer experience (a term that encompasses both patients and their families)

Quality: Typically referring to areas needing improvement, whether they're clinically related quality measures or performance improvement and process measures
Finance: Referring to specific measure of the overall financial performance of the organization
People: Referring to the focus on employee and physician satisfaction or retention and turnover
Growth: Referring to the organization's activities aimed at improving market share or growing volume
Community: Referring to measures that indicate the organization's commitment to those it serves

This is not an exhaustive list, and it can be customized to meet the strategic priorities of your organization. But one thing's for sure: Having a pillar framework allows an organization to consistently communicate a balanced approach to its priorities and thus to its subsequent actions and leadership.

Finally, you will see references to the Healthcare Flywheel®. Studer Group uses this visual analogy—which we developed to help organizations understand the journey to creating great places for employees to work, physicians to practice, and patients to receive care—to show how to create the momentum for change.

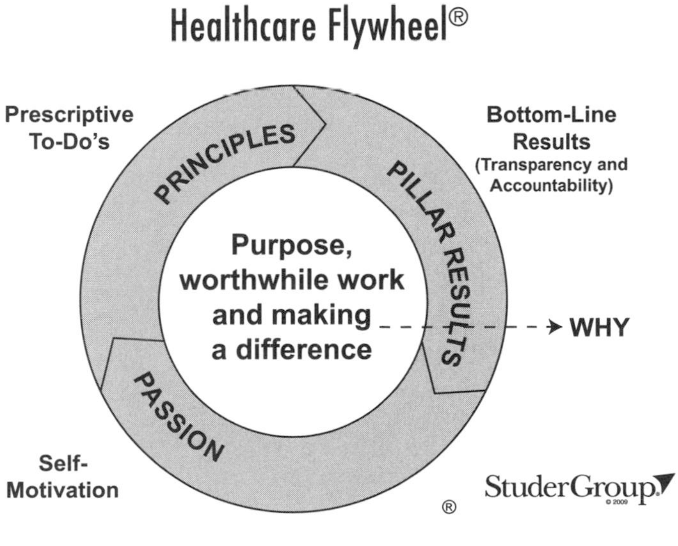

The first step to creating movement is to connect the dots to our hub (represented by the three words in the center of our flywheel), so that people truly believe that they can make a difference. This inspiration allows organizations to implement initial changes.

The second part of our flywheel represents the very prescriptive to-do's—called Nine Principles®—we give organizations to achieve results. From rounding for outcomes to implementing an objective performance measurement system to making discharge phone calls, these prescriptive to-do's—when implemented—will continue to turn the flywheel.

The third part of the flywheel process is when the organization starts to see results under the pillars, which provide a framework for prioritizing the desired results in step two. Instead of focusing on what *is not* getting done, the organization focuses on what *is* getting done.

In studying great healthcare organizations, we find that what motivates people is the accomplishment of desired results. By tying results back to purpose, worthwhile work, and making a difference, the organization is inspired to follow more prescriptive behaviors to achieve even greater results, thereby creating a self-perpetuating culture of excellence, fueled by the momentum of the flywheel.

When presenting the flywheel, we always make a dotted line from the words in the center that directs the eye outward to the word *why*. On the surface, this *why* refers to the leader's need to explain why a certain decision was made. But it's also an opportunity for leaders to explain to employees why what they do needs to be done and why it is important. It connects them back to purpose, worthwhile work, and making a difference...which is the big picture *why*.

To use this book most effectively, approach it as an opportunity to self-assess your knowledge and understanding of the topics covered in each chapter. In some cases you will come to understand that you need more education than this book is designed to provide. You can take semester-long courses in many of these topics. Of course, just reading the book will provide you with many valuable tips that you can start using right away.

Finally, think of *The Nurse Leader Handbook* as a handy reference work you can return to time and time again. Keep it on your bookshelf and pick it up again whenever a relevant question arises or when you just need a quick refresher in a certain topic.

We hope that this book will springboard your understanding of what competencies are going to be considered the basic foundation for the nurse leader of the future. Yes, it's a challenging role...but it's also one that has great impact on the lives of others, brings with it an inspiring sense of purpose, and provides the opportunity to do worthwhile work every day.

Lyn Ketelsen

SECTION 1: TACTICS TO MANAGE AND LEAD YOUR TEAM

Introduction

By Lyn Ketelsen

The initial section of *The Nurse Leader Handbook* focuses on skills that enhance your ability to lead. While the book is aimed primarily at nursing leadership, the competencies discussed apply to any leader responsible for single- or multi-department operations. If you are going to manage effectively, these are leadership skills you must practice and perform well.

In the pages ahead, highly experienced leaders and content experts offer practical advice on how to execute your role as a nurse leader based on the skills that led to their own success! They cover proven, evidence-based behaviors that will improve your performance. And they present time-tested tools and tactics to help you thrive in your leadership role.

In this first section, you will note that most of the topics focus on the team you manage or the "people" pillar. This is because as a leader, your impact depends on your ability to manage and lead staff. It involves ensuring that those who report to you have the capability, resources, and appropriate behaviors to do their jobs.

Want to know the best way to select and retain talented employees… manage their performance…communicate effectively…build individual and team development…and in general create the kind of staff that provides the best possible care for patients and their families? Then turn the page and start reading!

CHAPTER 1

Effective Communication

By Debbie Cardello and Lyn Ketelsen

For a leader, leading people is job number one. To be successful at this requires the ability to communicate effectively! After all, the team you manage impacts the lives of patients and their families daily. Communication, the exchange and flow of information and ideas from one person to another, is the very foundation of our functioning as human beings. Even the tiniest baby has a built-in communication system—it's called *crying*.

But the end result of communication—understanding—occurs only if the receiver grasps the exact information or idea the sender intended to transmit. This is why skillful communication is so important to you as a nurse leader: It enables you to coach, coordinate, counsel, evaluate, and supervise.

If there is one unifying theme that crosses all disciplines, it is the value of communicating information. It is rated by patients, employees, and leaders as key. In fact, Bruce Tulgan, the CEO of Rainmaker Thinking[1], says, "The day-to-day communication between supervisory managers and direct reports has more impact than any other single factor on employee productivity, quality, morale, and retention."

Furthermore, skillful communication empowers you to align staff behavior and move your culture forward. In order to improve performance, *everyone* in an organization must clearly understand the goals you're trying to reach and the actions required to most likely align their behaviors to your expectations. In other words, clarity of communication is the key to alignment, alignment is the key to good execution...and good execution is what will differentiate the winners in these challenging economic times. (See *Pillar Goal Management* sidebar.)

In the chapter ahead, we highlight a few basic practices to help you communicate well with your team.

Making Time for Communication

When communicating with employees, the biggest challenges are finding the most effective way to connect *and* the necessary time. Often, nurse leaders think that posting a policy on the communication board or announcing something during a meeting will suffice. (Then they

Pillar Goal Management

Defined Goals Lead to Excellence... and Clear Communication.

The pillars are used to align the entire organization toward the same defined, measurable outcomes. Not only does the pillars model provide a way to hold leaders accountable for outcomes, it also facilitates the free flow of information that ultimately leads to those outcomes. It provides structure and content for productive communication.

Goals are built within a framework. Studer Group uses the pillars (service, quality, people, finance, growth, and sometimes community) as the foundation for organizational goals. The pillars are populated with the highly specific measurable goals underneath them (Figure 1.1).

Once the goals are agreed to, widely communicated metrics toward progress support at least three important areas. First, they support the organization's goals and align desired behaviors. Second, establishing the metrics excites the organization. Healthcare professionals are by nature competitive and love the challenge of managing the metrics, particularly when the metrics matter—meaning that changes in the metrics have improved the lives of patients and those who take care of patients. Third, measurement across the goals by pillar provides a clear and unmistakable framework for holding ourselves accountable and communicating progress.

say in exasperation, "I don't know why it didn't get done! I told them in a staff meeting.")

Unfortunately, there is no silver bullet to effective communication. Nor is there ever enough time. As leaders, you will always have projects and priorities that compete with the time you're able to spend with staff. On the other hand, without efficient, creative approaches to communication, the ability to inform and engage your team is at risk.

Here's a simple rule to remember in communication: *Once is never enough.* We all need to hear something repeated numerous times and in many ways before we can clearly understand what is being asked of us, why it is important, and how to do it. Clarity and consistency are both important to effective communication.

The Art of Information Triage

Whether you work at a manager or director level, nurse leaders are typically referred to as middle management. By definition, being in the middle means there is someone over you and under you. In terms of communication, this is a tough place to be. You are typically passing information down from above and up from below. Not only must you know the science of communication, but the art of it as well—which in some cases means "triaging."

Because of the vast amounts of information coming at nurses at what feels like warp speed, it is not enough to be the funnel and just pass the information along. The real skill is in using your experience to convey to staff what is "need to know" information and what is "nice to know" information—and also to help nurses connect the message back to the "why."

Your staff is more likely to adopt behaviors if they understand "why" you are asking them to do something. For example, if you are in the process of teaching staff to use key words, they will be more responsive if they understand how it will make a positive impact on the patients they care for. Explain that key words translate to patients who are more satisfied and have the information they need, and that they also lead to higher employee satisfaction, fewer complaints, fewer call lights, and higher compliance with the treatment plan. You will certainly get your staff's attention with this approach.

> It's up to you to select the best method of communication to support the urgency of a given piece of information. It is when you have a "one-size-fits-all" approach that communication systems break down.

Tools and Techniques for Effective Communication

Gone are the days when nurse leaders could rely solely on the monthly staff meeting as a means of communication. For one thing, information is often dated in a month's time. Secondly, budget-conscious leaders try to avoid paying extra dollars for meeting costs. Finally, staff members work a variety of hours and shifts, which limits their ability to be in attendance. As a result, today nurse leaders supplement their monthly staff meetings using a variety of tools and techniques. Following are a few examples.

Communication Boards

Research tells us that open communication fosters employee satisfaction and retention. Communication boards placed in departments, units, and other staff-based locations throughout the organization can help us meet that need. The boards allow for consistent distribution of material based on the pillars or strategic framework.

Figure 1.1

Pillar Management:
Populating the Pillars with Defined Goals

The 5 Pillars of Healthcare Success™

Service	Quality	People	Finance	Growth
• Delighted patients • Reduce legal expenses • Reduced malpractice expense	• Improved clinical outcomes-decreased noscominal infections • Reduced length of stay • Reduced re-admits • Reduced medication errors	• Reduced turnover • Reduced vacancies • Reduced agency costs • Reduced PRN • Reduced overtime • Delighted A-Team members	• Increased bed turns • Reduced vacancies • Reduced agency costs • Reduced PRN • Reduced overtime • Reduced physicals and cost to orient	• Higher volume • Increased revenue • Decreased left without treatment in the ED • Reduced outpatient no-shows • Increased physician activity

For sample organizational and leader goals, go to www.firestarterpublishing.com/NurseLeaderHandbook.

Figure 1.2

Transparency:
Communication Board Example

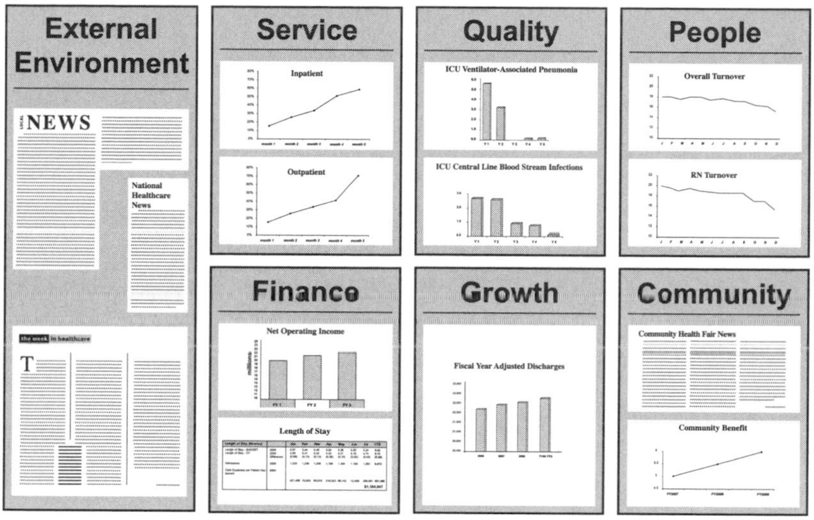

Often organizations provide standardized information for the boards—prepared by the Communication Team or the Marketing Department—designating what should be placed under each pillar or key focus area. If yours does not provide such materials, think of information that would be helpful to your team and create your own communication board structured under key focuses or pillars. Some examples are:

"Service" postings

- The most recent patient satisfaction survey scores
- HCAHPS scores and updates
- Examples of thank-you notes from patients and family members
- Specific service standards the hospital is celebrating or focusing improvement activities on

"People" postings

- Upcoming employee education events
- Benefits information
- Staff satisfaction survey results

- Employee turnover rate
- Stories that celebrate specific staff members/reward and recognition
- Information about new physicians

"Quality" postings
- The hospital's balanced scorecard
- Specific process improvement projects related to quality and safety, including results
- JCAHO continued readiness

"Financial" postings
- Data reflecting the organization's current financial state (income, expenses, and net income/bottom line)
- Department or unit budgetary concerns

"Growth" postings
- Information on new programs and services
- Ongoing or upcoming facility/campus renovations and additions
- Updates on progress towards the organization's goals
- Community impact projects

Make sure your communication boards are kept up to date. Some nurse leaders identify a unit secretary or any employee with a creative interest to assist with board keeping. This individual is responsible for updating information and ensuring material is properly placed, easy to see, and not overcrowded.

Department Newsletters

The department-specific newsletter is another effective communication tool. It's usually a simple Word document created by the manager or director and produced on a monthly or quarterly basis. Newsletters cover a variety of topics and can reinforce messages sent in huddles or staff meetings. (They are especially appreciated by any employees who might have missed these events.)

The newsletter can also be a great tool for recognizing deserving employees, as well as for highlighting the progress of initiatives within the department. Your staff members can get involved in creating and maintaining it.

Figure 1.3

Sample of Department-Specific Newsletter

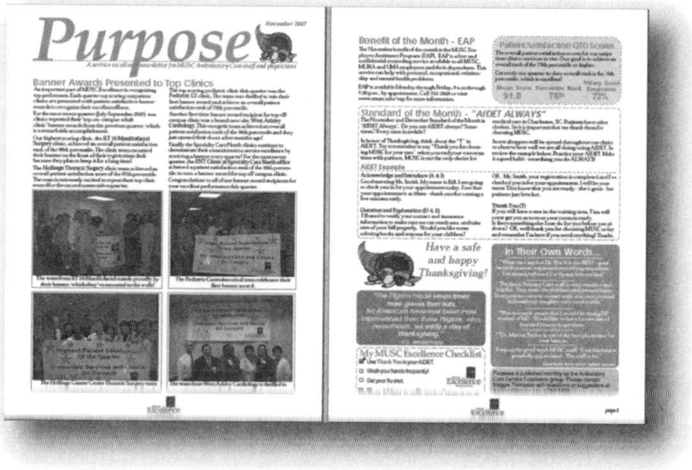
Purpose

Banner Awards Presented to Top Clinics

Benefit of the Month - EAP

Standard of the Month - "AIDET ALWAYS"

Have a safe and happy Thanksgiving!

In Their Own Words...

My MUSC Excellence Checklist

To download a complete example of this newsletter, go to www.firestarterpublishing.com/NurseLeaderHandbook under the resources section.

A "Tough Questions" Center

Employees probably have certain questions they're reluctant to ask. You as a leader need to know about these questions and be prepared with answers. That means giving employees a non-confrontational way to ask them. Consider designating a bulletin board in the employee lounge where employees can post these types of inquiries or provide a notebook where they can be documented. Then, you can answer these questions. The beauty of this system is that all staff members receive a consistent, "official" answer.

To learn more about this subject, read "How to Answer Tough Questions" by Bob Murphy at www.firestarterpublishing.com/NurseLeaderHandbook.

Daily Huddles

There are two types of huddles. The first is modeled after the famous Ritz-Carlton "line-up." The staff gathers at a prearranged time each day/shift (usually at the start of the workday/shift) at a specific location for a quick five- to ten-minute stand-up meeting. Employees take turns reading information prepared in advance and sent to the leader for sharing with staff.

Generally the information is thematic, focusing on one topic per week such as a particular Standard of Performance or positive behavior. This helps to deliver a consistent message as well as hardwire expectations. For example, Jeff Maton, the former CEO, and Larry Beck, the current CEO, of Good Samaritan Hospital—a partner of Studer Group® in Baltimore, Maryland—use e-mail to provide their leadership team with a week's worth of messages to be shared with staff in a daily huddle.

The daily huddle also fosters teamwork and offers nurse leaders an opportunity to reward and recognize appropriate people or share an inspiring story of high performance.

These daily, shift-to-shift huddles also allow nurse leaders to reinforce specific, unit-based areas of focus. For example, you might identify patients who are fall risks or deliver a reminder to document pain medication reassessments based on your last quality monitor. Selecting four to five quick key messages helps the staff "get their heads in the game" prior to charging off to take care of patients.

The second type of huddle is less formal. Nurse leaders pull small groups of staff together for a specific purpose. Perhaps the huddle is designed to share just-learned information about a patient, or to immediately recognize a staff member for going above and beyond, or to communicate shift-specific details. These are used as a way to convey time-sensitive information, address poor behaviors, and reinforce good behaviors immediately. At Good Samaritan Hospital in Baltimore, MD, leaders conduct daily huddles using scripted messages that are prepared for them. Using these carefully chosen key words ensures the consistency and accuracy of the message.

Rounding for Outcomes

In Chapter 2, you'll learn much more about the specifics of rounding on your staff, but we would be remiss if we did not mention it here as well. Rounding for outcomes is one of the most valuable tools in your communication toolkit. It offers you the opportunity to share verbal communication, but most importantly it provides a structured opportunity for receiving input and feedback from the staff. You might think of communication in terms of sharing information, but that's only part of the story! The most successful leaders are those who have a reputation for listening. The rounding framework, if used effectively, promotes listening first and foremost. When reading in Chapter 2, pay particular attention to the area referring to the use of the Stoplight Report. This is a great communication tool to close the loop with staff about what they heard and what actions they've taken as a result of rounding.

Storytelling

The art of storytelling is as old as civilization itself. Since the beginning, people have invented and handed down the stories that make us who we are and define our cultures. And yes, like every society, every organization has a culture, too. That's why stories are so valuable to leaders—they help us define, create, and understand our workplace culture.

Sharing stories about employees who modeled high performance, went above and beyond to deliver service, or made a huge impact on a patient or family member sets the tone for the work environment. These stories give life to the organization's vision, its very reason for being. These accounts also communicate expected behaviors, thus serving to sustain the performance standards of an organization.

> Hearing and telling stories during the daily huddle also helps healthcare professionals "connect the dots" between what they do and the outcomes that result. Thus, stories serve as one of the best ways to help employees understand the difference they can make. Stories inspire employees, touch lives, and create a shared sense of purpose.

Nurse leaders can harvest stories from discharge phone calls, from the rounding process, and from phone calls and letters. Sometimes we believe others may know about a particular good deed, but this often turns out not to be the case. So actively collect and share such stories. At Vassar Brothers Medical Center in Poughkeepsie, NY, leaders use "Spirit Stories" to reinforce the organizational values—service, pride, integrity, respect, improvement, and teamwork—and standards of behavior.

If you are trying to create or reinforce a standard of behavior, tell a story about someone who exemplified it. For example, if the standard is helpfulness, tell a story about how you saw a staff member accompany a lost family to their destination. Talk about the difference that person made.

There is so much "right" in healthcare. Our role as leaders is to harvest it and share it with others so they understand how they impact the lives of others. Storytelling is a powerful tool that you can use to recognize and reinforce desired behaviors and connect staff to purpose.

Staff Meetings

Monthly department or staff meetings continue to play an important role in communicating and educating staff. In Section 4 of the book, we will devote an entire chapter to conducting ***effective*** meetings. The goal of department staff meetings is to:

- Provide current updates and communication, especially that which is focused on alignment between department issues and organizational goals
- Provide an update regarding information received from senior leaders on the external environment and ensure that you connect the dots with staff about why this information is important to them and how it will impact your unit. (If you are unsure about how to message this, request help from your senior leader.)
- Communicate clear expectations to employees
- Offer a forum for small-scale education on timely topics—financial status, patient satisfaction results, rounding reports, and so forth
- Maintain contact and relationships with the department leader and peers
- Get input from staff on issues and topics
- Deliver reward and recognition

Meetings should follow the pillar structure to ensure agenda items are balanced across the important strategic areas. It is not uncommon for staff members or other department experts to present on specific agenda items; however, the department leader should be present for all meetings. Most departments will need to have multiple meetings—several times each month to make them accessible to all shifts and weekend staff—as they are generally considered "mandatory."

Yes, this is a big commitment for leaders. However, it is worth the investment. Since you need to come in during off-shifts and weekends periodically to round on employees, staff meetings may be an opportunity to do both. You might ask one or two staff members to stay after the meeting so you can complete their rounds!

Attendance is usually tracked and monitored, and staff are expected to know the content of the meeting. Even with great planning, some staff will not be able to attend, so it's important to keep good minutes. Also, keep a log so that employees can sign in to show that they have received the information.

The more effective you are at conducting these meetings the more credibility you create with your team. Being organized and running a well-planned staff meeting will set you apart from other leaders and ensure that your staff have great information to assist them in doing their work.

Employee Forums

Many organizations have "all staff" meetings on a quarterly basis, during which the CEO updates employees on the internal and external environment and provides other important information. They are often called forums or town hall meetings, and attendance is usually mandatory. Forums are usually scheduled at different times during the morning, afternoon, and evening shifts. A best practice at the unit or department level is to post the forum timetable in advance on the communication board and schedule employees to attend. It is often the leader's responsibility to have extra staff on hand during these times so that there is no gap in patient care.

Like information posted on the communication board, a forum's content is usually organized around the pillars or strategic framework of the organization. Thus the occasion provides an opportunity to communicate an open and consistent message to employees. Another value is the trust in leadership it inspires.

It's important to be familiar with the content of the forum so you are able to field any questions staff may have after attending it.

Innovations in Communication

Hospitals are implementing creative approaches to communication. For example, University Community Hospital in Tampa, Florida, uses communication relay assistants (CRAs) to convey organizational information to staff. The CRA is a unit-based delegate who is on the watch for e-mails, newsletters, and other information to bring back to team members and keep them informed.

And at Froedtert Hospital in Milwaukee, Wisconsin, a representative from each department plays a role called key communicator. These high performers ensure their area is kept informed of important communications and initiatives within the organization. Leadership meets on a regular basis with the key communicators to share information and get feedback.

Satilla Regional Medical Center in Waycross, Georgia, uses screensavers to share important information with staff throughout the organization. Subject matter such as new programs, new physicians, safety updates, and staff recognition is regularly communicated in this way.

The Power of Transparency

We can't do a chapter on communication without addressing this issue. *Transparency* refers to open communication that allows vital knowledge to flow freely to appropriate parties. When employees are better informed, they are empowered to make more engaged and thoughtful decisions.

> Historically, healthcare leaders have been opposed to transparency. Indeed, our systems were built on secrecy and confidentiality. Those days are gone forever. More and more is being shared publicly with regard to how well an organization performs on quality and safety issues. While we still protect the privacy of individual employee and patient information, transparency breeds higher levels of accountability for improving important processes.

One example of this kind of transparency is the use of rounding logs in patient rooms. By having a staff member sign the log after completing each hourly round, you are doing two things: Creating a promise to the patient that rounding will be done, and providing the transparent process by which he or she can see if you have honored that promise.

Transparency can be a powerful force in changing employee behavior. Quint Studer shares the story of how he corrected his leadership teams' behavior of chronically submitting late evaluations. He simply started posting at department manager meetings the names of leaders who had late evaluations. He explained he would begin sharing this list at each employee forum. (He considered late evaluations a matter of disrespect to the staff.) Well, you can imagine what happened. No more late evaluations!

Key Points in This Chapter

1. Patients, employees, and leaders all emphasize the value of effective communication. Sharing information in such a way that listeners grasp the exact meaning can help with the challenges nurse leaders face in aligning staff behavior and moving a culture forward.

2. To help get employees on the same page as partners in practice, use a variety of communication approaches. Remember, the more often people hear a message, the more likely they are to remember it!

3. The different ways that nurse leaders can convey information include communication boards, daily huddles, department newsletters, rounding, staff meetings, and mandatory attendance at forums. They should also share inspirational stories to help employees understand how they have purpose and do worthwhile work.

4. Transparency is powerful. It breeds accountability, creates patient trust, and facilitates behavior change—fast!

Pillars Affected by Communication

Service—Reduces risk and increases patient satisfaction.

Quality—Improves quality and safety.

People—Enhances employee engagement and reduces turnover.

Growth—Results in higher levels of loyalty and positive word of mouth.

CHAPTER 2

Rounding on Staff

By Lucy Crouch, Lyn Ketelsen, and Stephanie Baker

Nurse leader rounding is not a new idea. In fact, it's been a clinical activity for decades. Physicians have long made daily rounds to check on the status of their patients. And just as clinical rounding on patients has a specific purpose and a prescriptive process, rounding on staff has its own rationale and formula for success.

> Rounding for Outcomes, a tactic developed by Studer Group, is more than superficial "face time." It's meaningful. It shows employees that you care about and value them. It allows you to ask questions about equipment they may need or systems that may not be working properly. It provides opportunities for reward and recognition and for instigating discussions about professional development.

Basically, rounding for outcomes is the consistent practice of asking specific questions one-on-one of staff and patients to obtain actionable information. It's Evidence-Based Leadership SM at its best. In fact, Quint Studer in his bestselling book *Results That Last* writes, "Rounding for outcomes enables a leader to play offense, not defense."

Leader rounding on staff is the single best way to raise employee satisfaction and loyalty and ultimately attract and retain high performing employees. It helps employees feel they have purpose, worthwhile work, and are making a difference. It improves employee satisfaction by providing that which is important to them: strong relationships with managers who care about and value them, opportunities to provide feedback, recognition for what they're doing right, and more.

In the same way, rounding on patients improves clinical outcomes, promotes patient safety, and increases efficiency. (Rounding on patients will be covered in Chapter 10.)

In both cases, rounding for outcomes seeks to build relationships, help leaders learn what is working well, harvest "wins," identify areas for process improvement, repair and monitor systems, and ensure staff have the tools and equipment to do their jobs safely each day. Because it achieves all this, it's a foundational strategy and the first tactic to implement as you work to remove barriers to an excellent experience for employees and patients alike.

Most importantly, rounding gets tangible, measurable results. When practiced daily by the nurse leader, it yields such desirable outcomes as increased staff satisfaction and decreased turnover. The following graphs illustrate:

Figure 2.1

Employee Rounding
Employee Satisfaction Increase

Entity Comparison for % Excellent "As a Place to Work"

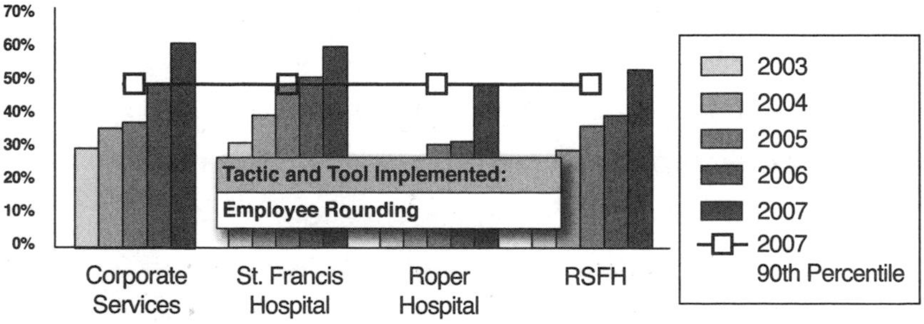

Source: South Carolina Hospital, Admissions=25,837 Total Beds=594, expanding to 644 in 04/08, employee satisfaction measured by PRC

Figure 2.2

Employee Rounding
Employee Satisfaction Increase

Employee Satisfaction Results

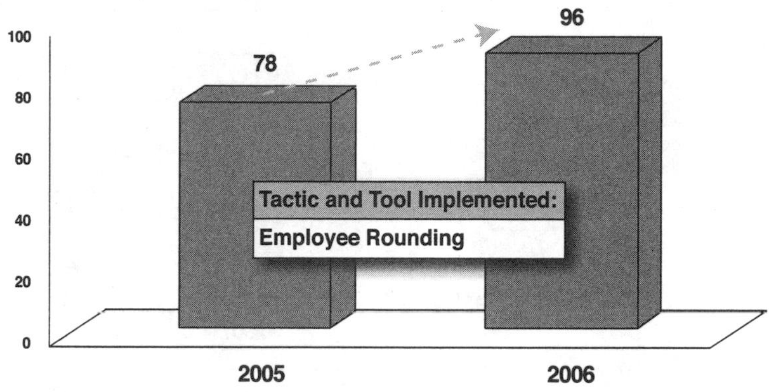

South Carolina Hospital, Total beds=109, Admissions=4,663, Employees=772

Why is employee satisfaction so important? For one thing, the reduced turnover that results saves the organization time and money. For another, it leads to better clinical outcomes. Nurses and other staff members who enjoy their work, who feel a strong sense of meaning and purpose, provide better care. It's that simple.

What's more, rounding creates more satisfied patients. When one organization implemented rounding in its Labor-Delivery Unit, it was able to dramatically reverse a downward trend in customer satisfaction:

Figure 2.3

Customer Satisfaction Results

Overall Quality of Care**

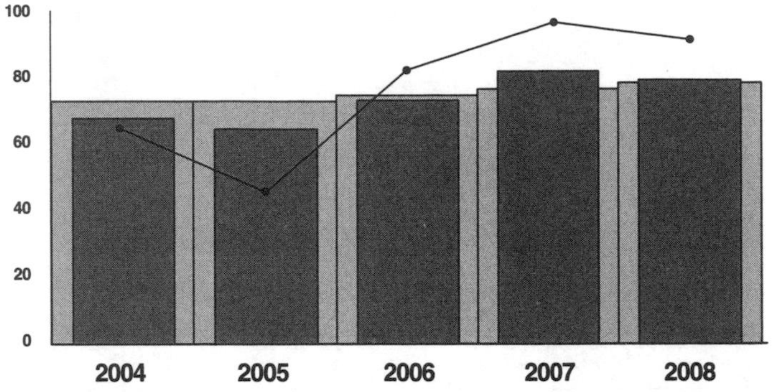

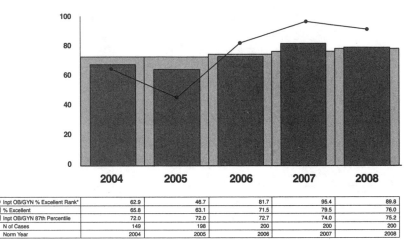

	2004	2005	2006	2007	2008
Inpt OB/GYN % Excellent Rank*	62.9	46.7	81.7	95.4	89.8
% Excellent	65.8	63.1	71.5	79.5	76.0
Inpt OB/GYN 87th Percentile	72.0	72.0	72.7	74.0	75.2
N of Cases	149	198	200	200	200
Norm Year	2004	2005	2006	2007	2008

* Rankings are based on PRC Norm data.
* The data in this chart has been filtered.

Questions to Ask During Leader Rounding

The number one reason employees leave a position—39 percent—is because they have a poor relationship with their supervisor.[1] What staff want in a leader is approachability, to work "shoulder to shoulder," tools and equipment to do their jobs well, appreciation, efficient systems, and opportunities for professional development. [2]

You can respond to these drivers of employee satisfaction by asking your staff these questions:

1. *What's working well today?* Consider opening with a relationship-building question (e.g., "I hear your daughter graduates tomorrow. What are her plans?"). Then, ask what's working well. Always begin with the positive. It's important to help staff remember that good things happen daily. Another way to ask is: "What's the best thing that happened this week?"

2. *Is there anyone I should recognize for doing great work?* Ask staff to be specific. You may have to break this question down more and ask, "Are there any individuals, departments, or physicians that I can reward and recognize?" This helps the staff think more

broadly and will help you harvest even more recognition. When you receive a general comment such as "Saul's great!" you need to dig deeper. Say, "Tell me more. Why is Saul great?" Then deliver the win. Say: "Saul, Lynne really appreciated that you came in and covered that sick call so they didn't have to work short last night. Thank you!" This allows you to carry the compliment to a coworker or physician to strengthen the relationship. Not only do they feel good about the leader who has given the compliment, they feel great about their coworker for recognizing them. This turns the flywheel, building momentum for better service, team

Leader Rounding on Staff

The number one reason we round on our staff is to build the relationship between the supervisor or manager and that employee. Leader rounding reduces employee turnover. That's because the number one reason employees leave an organization is because they have a poor relationship with their supervisor.[3]

Leader rounding delivers on this desire very specifically. And since happy employees lead to happy physicians and patients, it's the number one action you can take to raise employee, physician, and patient satisfaction.

When you round on your staff, you will stay close to what is working well in the ED, who should be recognized for exemplary work, and what opportunities exist for improving efficiency with systems and processes. You'll also learn what functional tools and equipment they need to do the job.

Because you're more connected with your staff, they will feel they have a voice at the table. You can validate positive staff behaviors so they become hardwired, manage up high performers, and identify trends and opportunities for improvement.

You'll even find that you're able to minimize the voice of the low performer by creating a more stable and cohesive voice for the whole department.

—Excerpted from *Excellence in the Emergency Department: How to Get Results*, by Stephanie Baker work, and higher clinical quality.

Rounding is a wonderful way to learn about the amazing things your staff are doing that would otherwise go unrecognized. Remember, what gets recognized gets repeated!

"That One Thing" That Makes a Difference

I tell leaders when I meet with them for the first time, that if there is one thing they need to do well, rounding on staff is that one thing. If you have conversations with staff and provide them with the tools and equipment they need, they will take very good care of the patient.

—Lucy Crouch

3. *Are there any systems or processes that need improvement today?* You might hear that the CT scanner will be down for several hours, which will require communication to staff and patients. However, you might also learn that the new self-scheduling process is working well. Having this information allows you to adjust and respond to both issues in real-time.

   How is that new process working? If you've recently implemented a new process, this is your opportunity to find out more. If you've just implemented discharge phone calls, for example, you can ask: "What is working well with the discharge phone calls?" "Do you have the forms you need to track the calls?" "Who's doing a great job making the calls that I should recognize?" "What have you learned from making the calls?"

4. *Do you have the tools, equipment, and information you need to do your job today?* This helps you identify barriers that can be immediately addressed. You might hear about simple fixes (e.g., "I've been looking for a blood pressure cuff/thermometer/pulse oximeter cable for 20 minutes!"). There may be times the barrier is more complex (e.g., "Can we add a field on the electronic health record?") and may require more time for follow-up. What's important here is to provide staff expected timeframes for completion. Let them know you will be providing updates as more information becomes available.

5. *Is there anything I can help you with right now?* You build credibility with your team when you are willing to assist when necessary.

Maybe your nurse has four patients to discharge and is feeling frustrated. A quick win is to say, "I've got a few minutes. Let me do one for you." A little goes a long way when trying to build trust, confidence, and collaboration. A bonus: You'll have an opportunity to spot check the patient's experience of care.

During the conversation centered on this question, you might want to bring up subjects like professional development—e.g., "I wanted to talk to you about applying for your certified emergency nurse certification" or "Let's talk about a development plan to orient you to the charge nurse role." High performers want opportunities for development and will appreciate your making this a priority.

New leaders might also want to ask, "What's the one thing I can do to be a better leader?" This shows approachability and willingness to accept feedback.

Figure 2.4

Communication Flow for Rounding on Employees

When you're rounding, your talking points should follow a specific flow. This keeps you on track, helps you manage the encounter, and encourages you to keep conversations consistent from employee to employee.

Rounding with Employees	**Concern and Care**
	What Is Working Well
	People to Recognize
	Systems to Improve
	Tools and Equipment
	Follow-up

Track Results from Rounding: Use a Rounding Log

Rounding logs are a tool to hardwire rounding. They are critical to the long-term success of rounding. In fact, Studer Group coaches frequently tell leaders they coach on rounding, "If you want incremental results, then don't use a log. If you want sustained results that accelerate progress, then logs are a must have to help you move faster."

As a leader, your staff are your customers in the same way patients are the customers of your staff. They deserve to hear back from you when they bring up a request, issue, or concern, so write it down on the log (Figure 2.5).

And when you write things down, connect the dots for staff by explaining why you are writing it down. You don't want them to think something unpleasant they said is going to be placed in their file. Say, "I'm going to take a few notes so I can follow-up on this for you."

Rounding logs also reveal key trends. When you hear that 10 of your staff are having trouble with Radiology, for example, you need to follow-up with that department leader. Items from rounding logs also roll up into your Stoplight Report (Figure 2.6) so you can report back accomplishments and the status of requests to staff.

What's Working Well Aids in Process Improvement

Posing this question also helps to identify *processes and systems* that are working well. Not everything is broken, and if you don't know what's effective, you may inadvertently change a valued process when trying to fix another problem.

This happened once when I was rounding with an Environmental Services (EVS) staff member. When I asked what was working well, her response was that she loved the new decentralized supplies because it was much more efficient. She now had a stock on the unit she serviced, which meant she no longer had to go down to the basement to refill her supplies.

Now, I was a pediatrics unit manager and I can tell you that managers on nursing units are always short of space. I could immediately see the handwriting on that wall. I would have gotten a new piece of equipment and gone scouring the unit for space. I would have come across a cabinet full of EVS supplies and called that department's manager to say, "You need to get this stuff out of here because I need the space." If I hadn't rounded to ask and learn what was meaningful to staff, I might have done the wrong thing, changed something that was working well, and in the process negatively impacted productivity!

—Lyn Ketelsen

Don't Forget to Capture the Win.

One of the best things about rounding is the fact that you get to help people get problems resolved. When people finally get the tools and equipment they need, or find their work lives improved in some other way, it creates good feelings. Take advantage of that positive energy by following up on what you did for them.

Let's say you've just helped staff members get the aforementioned field added to your hospital's electronic record system. Our advice would be to include a question about the system as you round over the next couple of weeks—in other words, to ask if the problem was resolved. Each time you do that (and naturally you'll be answered in the affirmative), staff members will be acknowledging that their leader has addressed an issue for them. And every time you get the acknowledgment, you're making a deposit in the staff's emotional bank account.

Tip: Make sure to communicate that the problem was resolved. We have found this is the part of rounding that nurse leaders tend to forget. We cannot emphasize enough the importance of always circling back to check on how the solution worked, thereby reminding staff that you followed up. Generally the only time we think about a problem is when it is irritating us. Once the problem is fixed, no more irritation; we forget about it and go on to the next nuisance. As a leader, you want to break this cycle, and you can accomplish that by checking back and capturing the win.

Recommended Frequency of Rounding

- A reasonable goal to set for yourself is rounding on at least two to three staff members per day, or 40 per month.
- If you have fewer than 40, you should connect with the entire staff every month.
- If more than 40, but less than 80, you should be able to accomplish a rounding conversation with each staff member every two months.
- If greater than 80, your goal should be to get to every staff member every quarter.
- To include night shift, you may need to come in early a couple of times a month; if you have weekend-only employees, you may also have to come in for a few hours on the weekend.

Reminding staff members that you "have their back" can yield long-term benefits for you as a leader. When you ask them to use key words, or utilize the new service recovery policy, they'll most likely be quick to respond. Because you're taking care of them, they will probably do whatever you need. This is what you can accomplish from consistent rounding on staff—a responsive, cohesive team focused on providing the best care.

Time Well Spent

Most nurse leaders find that as they get good at rounding, they can include additional items of interest in the process. For example, these conversations are good opportunities to share current patient satisfaction results and specific comments that patients have made on the surveys. They're also a good time to follow up on any specific departmental initiatives. For instance, if your department is in the process of getting ready for a JCAHO survey, rounding provides opportunities to discuss and prepare for the visit.

At one Studer Group partner organization, the process is used as part of the Patient Safety Initiative. Leaders ask as they round, "In the last month, did you observe any patient safety issues?" And, "If you do notice a patient safety issue, what do you typically do about it?"

Clearly, rounding is time well spent. As you get into the flow of these conversations and they become hardwired℠ into your routine, you can experiment with ways to make them even more productive. Everyone will benefit—you, the nurses you lead, and the patients you care for.

Tools to Maximize and Hardwire

Below are the tools Studer Group uses with organizations that have been successful at hardwiring (consistently using) rounding. We highly recommend these tools for effective nurse leader rounding on staff. These can be found at www.firestarterpublishing.com/NurseLeaderHandbook.

1. A **roster** identifying all of your staff members by name and space to indicate the date you rounded on each person. This tool will help ensure that no staff member gets left out.

2. A **rounding log** containing the questions you are going to ask, with space for you to take notes on the answers from staff. This will help you with follow-up. If you are like most people, the chances

of following up on something written down are very high, probably 99 percent (with a 1 percent chance of losing the notes and forgetting). We find that when we rely on memory, our follow-through is probably more like 65-70 percent.

The information you collect regarding reward and recognition, issues, and tools, is far too critical to risk not taking action. Interestingly, if your follow-up on information collected is poor, you actually risk decreasing employee satisfaction. (Employees will say, "I told her we needed new blood pressure cuffs and she never did anything about it!") The act of writing down what a staff member says during rounding also sends a great message: "You are a valuable person and what you're telling me is important."

Figure 2.5

Rounding for Outcomes - Staff

ROUNDING for Outcomes-STAFF UNIT__________________ Manager__________________

STAFF MEMBER/ DATE	Relationship learning	What is working well today?	Staff recognized and why	Departments recognized and why	Physicians recognized and why	Systems needing improvement & ideas to fix	Tools and equipment needed
1.							
2.							
3.							
4.							
5.							
6.							

3. A **stoplight report** is a great tool to help you "close the loop" with staff by reporting back to them the status of the issues you heard about during your rounds. The report, posted monthly in your department, has a section in green outlining what you learned,

what you were able to fix, or what you accomplished. The yellow section of the report outlines what is being fixed, but is a work in progress, and lists the next steps. Finally, the red section outlines those things that are not going to happen in the current environment: "So the answer is no, and here's why."

Figure 2.6

Sample Rounding Stoplight Report

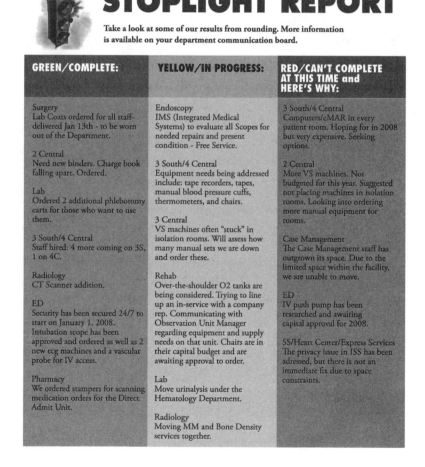

STOPLIGHT REPORT

Take a look at some of our results from rounding. More information is available on your department communication board.

GREEN/COMPLETE:	YELLOW/IN PROGRESS:	RED/CAN'T COMPLETE AT THIS TIME and HERE'S WHY:
Surgery Lab Coats ordered for all staff- delivered Jan 13th - to be worn out of the Department. 2 Central Need new binders. Charge book falling apart. Ordered. Lab Ordered 2 additional phlebotomy carts for those who want to use them. 3 South/4 Central Staff hired: 4 more coming on 3S, 1 on 4C. Radiology CT Scanner addition. ED Security has been secured 24/7 to start on January 1, 2008. Intubation scope has been approved and ordered as well as 2 new ecg machines and a vascular probe for IV access. Pharmacy We ordered stampers for scanning medication orders for the Direct Admit Unit.	Endoscopy IMS (Integrated Medical Systems) to evaluate all Scopes for needed repairs and present condition - Free Service. 3 South/4 Central Equipment needs being addressed include: tape recorders, tapes, manual blood pressure cuffs, thermometers, and chairs. 3 Central VS machines often "stuck" in isolation rooms. Will assess how many manual sets we are down and order these. Rehab Over-the-shoulder O2 tanks are being considered. Trying to line up an in-service with a company rep. Communicating with Observation Unit Manager regarding equipment and supply needs on that unit. Chairs are in their capital budget and are awaiting approval to order. Lab Move urinalysis under the Hematology Department. Radiology Moving MM and Bone Density services together.	3 South/4 Central Computers/eMAR in every patient room. Hoping for in 2008 but very expensive. Seeking options. 2 Central More VS machines. Not budgeted for this year. Suggested not placing machines in isolation rooms. Looking into ordering more manual equipment for rooms. Case Management The Case Management staff has outgrown its space. Due to the limited space within the facility, we are unable to move. ED IV push pump has been researched and awaiting capital approval for 2008. SS/Heart Center/Express Services The privacy issue in ISS has been adressed, but there is not an immediate fix due to space constraints.

When You Get Started, Tell Staff Why You're Rounding.

Don't just start rounding one day with no explanation. Let staff know up-front what you are doing and why. For example, "You will notice that my conversations with you are changing. I will be asking about what is going well, who I can recognize, issues to resolve, and what tools and equipment you need. I'm doing this because I want to be the best leader I can be, and provide you with a great work environment. Recently, I learned that these types of conversations can be very effective in accomplishing goals."

We've found that whenever a behavior changes, especially a very noticeable one, if there isn't an explanation, people draw their own conclusions. One leader learned this the hard way. Prior to being introduced to rounding on staff, he had implemented some cross training in his department to gain some very necessary efficiency. Initially, these changes were not popular with employees. About two weeks after the cross training began, this leader was introduced to rounding on staff. He immediately embraced the concept, and started the process without an explanation. As you can imagine, since rounding was occurring at about the same time the cross training was beginning, staff members interpreted rounding as the leader "checking up on them." Naturally, they resented it.

Fortunately, this leader figured out what was going on and was able to clarify his purpose. Still, we can let his experience serve as a warning to all of us to explain the why behind our actions loud and clear.

Leaders Don't Always Embrace Rounding.

Rounding is a proven leadership tool that gets fantastic results. However, leaders don't always welcome it with open arms. Here are a few reasons you might be feeling reluctant to round, along with what we hope are reassuring responses:

1. **You're worried that staff members will ask for something you can't provide.** Many nurse leaders hesitate to ask the questions about what systems/issues need to be addressed and what tools and equipment are needed. In drilling down, we learned the hesitation comes from the discomfort of thinking, *What if they identify an issue that can't be resolved?* or *What if they ask for equipment I know we can't provide?* Fortunately, most of the issues uncovered during rounding are small, easily fixable things. Still, there are those times when someone brings up a difficult issue or requests a piece of equipment that can't be purchased.

Remember, it's okay to say "no," as long as you include an explanation of the "why"—which is the part most nurse leaders fail to do. Maybe it's because we assume staff knows why; after all, it's obvious to us. Maybe we don't know how to explain it, or it could be we actually don't know (in which case we'd better find out!). We have never seen a situation where the answer was negative, and there wasn't a good reason. If staff members aren't given an explanation, they will make up something that is rarely accurate. Explain the "why" and people are able to move past their disappointment.

2. **You don't believe you have time to round.** Guess what? Rounding on staff shouldn't take more time. You are already having conversations with employees—it's doubtful that a day goes by that you don't speak to several of them. This is about taking that time and being more prescriptive in how you structure the conversation so as to get some tangible results—like increased employee satisfaction and decreased turnover.

Be aware that rounding does require you to have conversations with every single one of your staff members, and currently you may find that there are some you haven't spoken to in a while. This is particularly true of your night shift employees. We recommend keeping a roster with the names and date of your rounding conversations with staff members so that no one slips through the cracks.

3. **You don't like using key words.** Some nurse leaders simply are not comfortable with the practice of utilizing key words to accomplish outcomes. However, key words work. Please, rehearse them until they feel more natural. If you succumb to the temptation to change the questions you ask so as to make them sound less prescriptive, you are likely to lose efficiency. Even more importantly, you have lost the opportunity to role model the use of key words for your staff.

Advice for a New Nurse Leader

Note: On the following pages, Studer Group® partner Sherry Thompson, RN, BS, CCRN—Director Intermediate/Critical Care Units, Pekin Hospital (Pekin, Illinois)—shares what she learned during her "virgin years" as a new manager:

- First and foremost: Don't ever think you've seen it all…because you haven't and you never will.
- You need to keep a presence on your unit and not stay locked away in your office. (But it is acceptable to close your door and cry occasionally.)
- Get out into the trenches on a regular basis, all shifts, even weekends. I don't mean for you to do staff members' work by taking full assignments; rather, actually experience some of their functions. I will answer call lights, empty bedpans, start IVs, give a bath, answer phones if ringing too long, help physicians, help in a code, etc. My presence when they are "sinking" helps calm the storm, even if I don't do that much. The fact I'm present sends the message that I acknowledge their skills and respect what they do!
- Rounding on your staff means knowing your people and making yourself aware of their lives outside the hospital. No, you cannot solve all of their issues, but empathy goes a long way in helping them focus when they are at work! Learn about their families, pets, hobbies, about the current crisis in their lives, and remember to ask occasionally about what's important to them. I have over 80 employees and know at least one thing about each person, so it's not impossible! They have touched me, and I have grown!
- Accountability is the keystone to team morale. Early on in my career as a manager, I tried to be everyone's friend. It does not work! Start with communicating the expectations, use tough love, and if that fails, do what you have to do for the whole team. You can save some people, and some you can never fix. As you round and see positive behaviors, tell that person right then and there how much you appreciate them. If you see negative behavior, tell that person right then and there what is not right.
- Joy and laughter are truly very important! In the beginning, I was so serious and wanted everything to be perfect. But patient care is stressful enough; if we don't have joy and laughter in what we do, we'll burn out long before we should. Case in point: Upon

waking this morning, I made my usual phone call to the night supervisor to learn the census for my two departments. He told me, "Intermediate got killed last night; they got seven admissions in a four-hour span. They weren't too happy, but it did finally settle down." I hung up and my first thought was—maybe I'll go back to bed for awhile and go into work after night shift has left. NOT! This is what I actually did: The moment I arrived on the floor, I walked up to the group of night shift employees and said, "Has anyone told you lately what an awesome team you are? I heard you had a 's_ _ t storm' last night and I also heard you did a great job!" They actually started laughing, not complaining. Negative turned to positive by laughter.

- I believe that rounding on my staff is the most important and effective tool I have in my manager bag of tricks! Happy staff equals happier patients!
- Rounding on my staff with purpose, putting their needs first, is the one sure way to gain and retain their respect and commitment!

Key Points in This Chapter

1. The rounding process should start with a personal connection. Stay on a positive note by asking what is going well, and then inquire if there is someone you can recognize. Once the positives are harvested, ask if there are systems or processes that need your attention, and whether the staff member has the tools, equipment, and information to do the job.

2. Whenever you fix a process or purchase tools and equipment as a result of rounding on staff, it is important to "capture the win." This is accomplished by asking staff members over a couple of weeks during rounds how the new process or new tool is working for them. When they respond that it is working well, they are acknowledging you are a responsive leader.

3. Always explain the "why." As a result of rounding on staff, you will encounter issues or processes you can't change, or tools and equipment you cannot provide because we live in a world of limited resources. It is okay to say "no" to staff as long as you give an honest explanation for

why the process can't be changed or the equipment purchased.

4. The two recommended tools for rounding on staff are a dated roster and a rounding log. The dated roster will help ensure you get to every staff member. The rounding log communicates to staff members that what they're saying is important enough to be written down; it also helps you remember to follow up.

Pillars Affected by Rounding on Staff

Service—Enhances communication, resulting in better customer service.

Quality—Facilitates better clinical outcomes due to nurse leader's presence.

People—Fosters retention through higher staff satisfaction.

CHAPTER 3

Performance Management

By Lyn Ketelsen

One of the most important skills a nurse leader can have is an understanding of how to excel at managing staff performance. "Performance management" is a broad umbrella term describing actions taken by the nurse leader that result in employees making changes they sometimes don't want to make.

Let me clarify. I'm not implying that employees are being difficult and "refusing" to change. There are many reasons why it's hard for staff to incorporate new processes or behaviors. For the most part, it's about breaking old habits, which is incredibly hard for anyone to do without some compelling motivation. Therefore, our role as nurse leaders must be based on the understanding that we are first and foremost change agents.

When was the last time you conducted a staff meeting and said, "Guess what, everybody? There is absolutely nothing different. We have no changes and we can continue to do everything exactly the way we're doing it now"? I'm guessing your answer is "never." Our whole purpose as leaders is to ensure we are looking for opportunities for improvement and putting in processes that will change things for the better.

The Change Process

When nurse leaders are not successful in effecting change, particularly when they're trying to implement new tactics, it's often because they fail to understand the change process. They do things in the wrong order. Perhaps you've made the same mistake.

For example, if you're like many leaders, when you're implementing a new process the first thing you do is try to obtain "buy-in." In other words, you're looking for understanding. You desire for employees to know **what** you want done and **why** you want it done. So you take 20 minutes in a staff meeting to present the process, explain "why," and then tell everyone it starts on Monday. Perhaps you don't even tell people **how**. Then three months later you wonder why it hasn't happened the way you wanted it to.

To follow is a quick overview of how the change process really works.

The Phases of the Change Process

Figure 3.1

Understanding Change

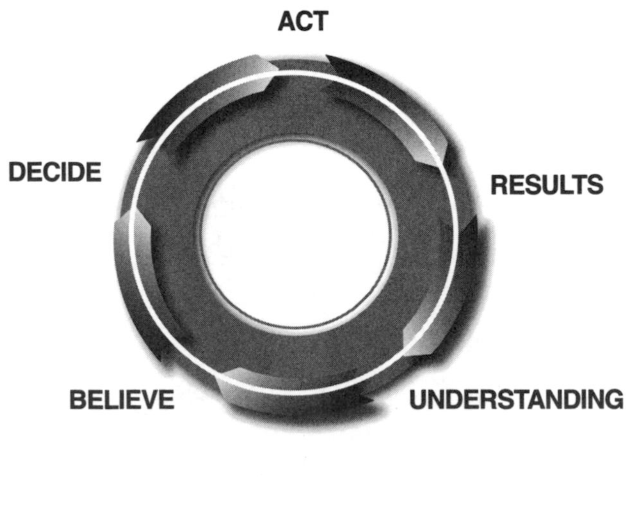

Believe: The change process does not *begin* with understanding (or buy-in) but rather *ends* with it. The first step of the process is to *Believe*. It is sometimes easiest to describe the step with an analogy almost all of us can relate to: a diet. If you've ever made a New Year's Eve resolution to lose 10 pounds, then you have probably gone through this process. Perhaps you step on a scale and see you're gaining more weight than you'd like. Maybe you notice a difference in the way your clothes fit. It could be that your physician has encouraged you to lose weight. You may even happen to see an infomercial describing how much better you would feel a few pounds lighter. The presence of any one of these circumstances may lead you to believe you need to lose the weight.

Decide: However, believing you need to lose weight is not enough. The next step of the process requires actually making the decision that you're going to do something different. So you investigate the available options and pick a weight loss method that will work for you.

Act: Many of us have been through the first two phases of the change process many times, only to learn that believing and deciding are not enough to make it happen. This is where we typically find the whole change process breaks down. The next step is the hardest: It's the *Act* step. If someone were to follow you around forcing the action in your new diet and exercise plan, success might not be so elusive. Unfortunately, this is seldom the case. You must count on yourself, and it's hard to do.

We use the term "force" for a reason. Many times when you're creating change, it feels like it's forced, requiring a tremendous amount of energy and willpower. (For example, if you're not used to exercising, you'll probably have to force yourself to get out there and do it. If you're addicted to sweets, you're going to have to force yourself to walk away from that box of delicious doughnuts lurking in the breakroom.) However, hard as it may be, the action must occur before you truly can move to the next step: *Results*.

Results: The correct action (diet and exercise) will get results; and when the results are what you're looking for (the scale reveals weight loss), you reach the final step: *Understanding*.

Understanding: The light bulb goes on! You have a true and meaningful level of insight. You decided to lose weight, took action, and got results. Those steps had to occur in sequence before you truly realized how the process of losing weight works.

In an organization, change is actually a little easier, and your authority as a nurse leader is the reason why. You can "force" action because you have the opportunity to set policy and expectations. Using your knowledge of the change process, along with learning some basic skills to "force" action more effectively, you can achieve the desired outcome.

But there is yet another thing to bear in mind regarding the change process. If staff members are to be accountable for their actions, they have to know what your expectations are. That's why clarity of communication is paramount. You must clearly articulate what you expect in the way of behaviors.

Fortunately, a whole range of expectations is usually found in the organization's written policies, procedures, competencies, and standards of behavior. These publications provide the basic platform leaders need to hold their staff accountable. But you must ensure that staff members are fully aware of these published expectations and have a clear understanding of the consequences of not meeting them.

The Performance Management Continuum

Performance management can be described as a series of actions executed in response to staff's behaviors. To drive positive change, a nurse leader must learn how to choose the appropriate action at the right time.

The continuum graphic on the following page lays out exactly what those actions are. The dotted line around the far right six boxes indicates options for low performers; the dotted line around the middle five boxes denotes middle performer activity; and the dotted line around the far left six boxes designates a leader's possible responses to high performers.

"I Absolutely Have Favorites."

One of my best bosses was once asked by staff if she had "favorites" or "teacher's pets." Her reply was classic: "I absolutely have favorites. I make no apologies for it. The difference is that every one of my staff has equal ability to be a favorite. All they have to do is be competent, follow the policies, and demonstrate the behaviors. They know exactly what the expectations are and make a choice every day to be a favorite or not."

—Lyn Ketelsen

Figure 3.2

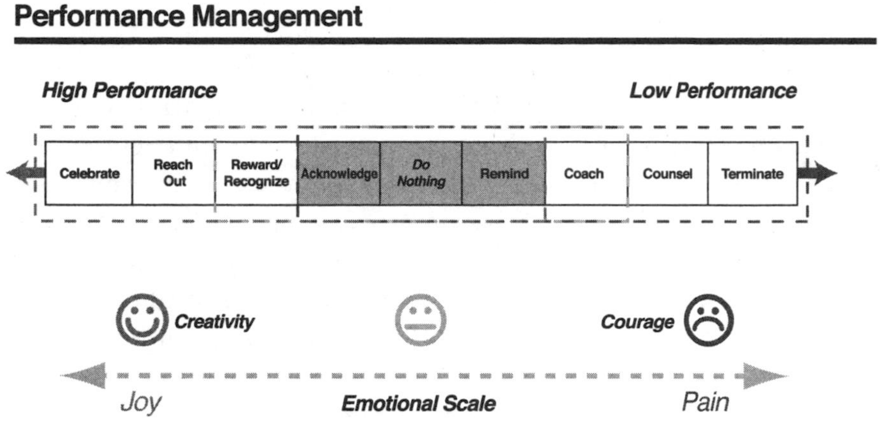

Do Nothing.

Let's start with the very center of the continuum. At any given point in time, when a staff member performs a process or enacts a behavior, the nurse leader has the option of doing nothing. And when the need to deal with problem employees arises, doing nothing can seem like the easiest way out.

In fact, this scenario is often the number one problem with new nurse leaders. Naturally they want to be liked as leaders (this is only human), and therefore they are reluctant to address performance issues. They fear that if they do take action, the result will be a "temperature drop" in their likeability factor. Obviously, doing nothing doesn't help the organization effect change.

There's another side to the "doing nothing" coin as well. Let's say an employee is performing well. She has embraced the process and is exhibiting new and desirable behavior. If the leader does nothing in this case, she is unlikely to see the positive actions continue.

Managing Negative Performance

Now let's suppose that staff has not performed the expected behavior. On the diagram, the continuum shifts to the right as you look at the choices of what to do when employees are not meeting expectations. Options move from doing nothing, to reminding, then coaching, proceeding on to counseling, and eventually to termination.

Step One—Remind

Most nurse leaders don't have a problem with this step. When staff are not performing to expectations, it's easy to remind them. As a matter of fact, if you were to take a tour of many nursing units in the country, you would see reminders all over the place. Look in patient rooms, for example, to see reminders of all kinds of processes: No BP in Rt Arm, Fall Precautions, etc. Go to the nurses' station and you can find them plastered everywhere in the form of Post-it notes, communication books, bulletin boards, and so on. Now enter the staff lounge and locker room: There are enough reminder memos and posters to wallpaper a gymnasium! We have even seen reminders posted in staff's restrooms (what better place to get their undivided attention!).

The problem is that employees become indifferent to all these reminders. Unfortunately, the "reminder" stage of the performance management continuum is where we see most nurses get stuck. Understanding when to move to more significant action such as coaching or counseling is a critical step in leadership.

Note that as you move to the right on the diagram, you'll see that parallel to the steps runs a relative continuum of courage and pain. The further to the right you go, the more courage you as a leader must have. Why? Because you are creating more pain on the part of the staff person involved. Moving from the reminder stage to coaching requires getting directly involved with an individual and openly discussing the person's opportunities for improvement. It's not easy…but it must be done.

Step Two—Coach

Coaching is a critical step in the continuum. It is pivotal because it takes the process of reminding, which is typically general, to the specific. This is when a nurse leader goes one-on-one with a staff person, identifying what the individual is doing well but also what needs improvement. This step should not be viewed as "negative" in any way, but rather as a juncture that unveils the full potential of the individual being coached.

When coaching a staff member who will eventually perform well, you'll find that person's reaction is usually positive. He'll readily accept feedback and take action on the coaching opportunities. There is a specific process to follow with these coaching conversations. In his book *Hardwiring Excellence*[1], Quint Studer refers to this process when discussing the middle performer. The concept is also covered in Chapter 5 of this book.

The format for this conversation is Support, Coach, Support (SCS). You'll start with what the person does well, then identify one thing he needs to do better, and finish by again supporting what he does well. In an SCS conversation, you'll have the opportunity to single out the area this person needs to focus on, and help the individual identify a specific plan to improve it. The goal in the conversation—at this step of the continuum—is still retention.

However, you also need to be aware that you cannot predict with certainty every person's response to coaching. That's why documenting these coaching conversations is a good idea. If things go as intended, you'll have a great record of reference for action steps to assist with continued development. On the other hand, if the staff person does not respond, you have the necessary documentation to go to the next step in the process: counseling.

Step Three—Counsel

This next step in the performance continuum is most often used when a staff person is overtly in violation of policy or displays inappropriate behaviors. It is best to consult with your Human Resources (HR) department prior to taking any action. Be sure you understand the organization's corrective action policy as well as its documentation requirements. Generally, it is a good practice to document all coaching conversations. It will be important to bring any documentation from previous coaching sessions with this employee. While your goal is to have the staff person improve, you must be prepared in case this doesn't happen. In fact, if you have not documented your coaching sessions, you may find that HR wants you to go back and repeat that step.

The low performer conversation should always be documented so the leader is on solid footing when progressing through the corrective action process. The format for this discussion, outlined in *Hardwiring Excellence* as the low performer conversation, follows the D-E-S-K approach. This will also be covered in more detail in Chapter 5 as it relates to moving organizations' performance.

The DESK model is as follows:

- <u>D</u>escribe the behavior that needs to change.
- <u>E</u>valuate/Explain how the behavior affects the performance of the department or outcomes for the patient/family.
- <u>S</u>how or tell specifically what you need the employee to do.
- <u>K</u>now the consequences—tell the employee what will happen if she fails to make the necessary changes.

During the *Know* portion of the conversation, it's important to provide an appropriate timeline upon which the consequences will take place. Very few organizations' corrective action policies dictate the timeframe in which the nurse leader needs to reevaluate employee behaviors. If you're like many leaders, you may be stuck in the "90-day plan" habit. But think outside that constraint. Determine a timeline that allows you full flexibility depending on the nature of the situation.

If the behavior you're working on is something that occurs frequently, you may be able to set a much shorter timeline and thus move the process forward more quickly. On the other hand, if it's something that rarely happens, you may have to extend the timeline to ensure you will catch the person if he repeats the incorrect behavior. Work with your HR department to determine the best period of time for the situation you're dealing with.

When you follow the organization's policies, include the DESK elements in conversations, and carefully document everything that happens, you will be well positioned if you have to execute the final step of the continuum.

Step Four—Terminate

As much as a leader dislikes doing so, it will occasionally be necessary to terminate a staff member. The goal is to be well prepared and show dignity and respect when dealing with that person. The DESK approach works well for this conversation too. Basically, you walk through the conversation you had before, but with a focus on knowing the consequences. You clearly state that because the employee did not follow through, you are now implementing the consequence. In some cases you may need to have a representative from HR present.

If you have been consulting HR as suggested in the previous steps, the department will be well informed when you get to this step and will be fully prepared to assist you in the process. When nurse leaders talk about HR not being supportive, it's often because they (the leaders) have failed to provide appropriate documentation. When you follow corporate policy, practice sound communication, and document faithfully, HR should have no reason not to support you in terminating the employee.

Managing Positive Performance

Now that you've seen how the continuum works for situations when expectations are not met, let's explore the other half of performance management. It's just as important—in fact, even more so—that you have solid skills for rewarding and recognizing people.

In the first place, those who accomplish goals and demonstrate behaviors consistent with the organization's values deserve reward and recognition. But providing it is not just a nice thing to do. It has a noticeable payoff. It is well documented in research that maintaining a three-to-one ratio of recognition to criticism will maintain a positive culture. Therefore, strong leaders who demonstrate competency in performance management should be spending three times more effort on the positive end of the continuum than on the other.

Figure 3.3

Compliment to Criticism Ratio

3 to 1	3 compliments 1 criticism	Positive!
2 to 1	2 compliments 1 criticism	Neutral
1 to 1	1 compliment 1 criticism	Negative

Revisit Figure 3.2 and you'll see that a leader needs creativity to move staff to the left on the emotional scale. The further left you go, the more opportunity there is to create joy for staff members.

Step One—Acknowledge "Jobs Well Done"

The first step is acknowledging a job well done. This can take many forms: a simple verbal comment passed along, an announcement at a staff meeting, or a mention in a unit newsletter. However, just as some nurse leaders get stuck on the "remind" portion of the continuum, some leaders get stuck on the acknowledgment step. Sometimes, acknowledgment is not enough.

> You know the phrase "The punishment should fit the crime"? I think the same is true of responding to a job well done: The reward should fit the deed.

> Therefore, use acknowledgment for those things worthy of a reinforcement message; but as the deed or behavior becomes greater or more consistent, it's time to get a little more creative.

Step Two—Reward and Recognize Via Formal Systems
The next step in the continuum addresses the reward and recognition systems most organizations already have in place. The basis of the various programs is usually staff to staff, leaders to staff, or patients/customers to staff. Typically developed by employee teams, each variation is designed to facilitate reward and recognition opportunities for leaders. These programs will be addressed in more detail with examples in the next chapter. The important message here is to make sure the programs are being maximized but also balanced—that the right tool is used for the right type of behavior.

Step Three—Reach Out to Consistent High Performers
Perhaps you've noticed that when you're harvesting recognition, certain people's names come to the forefront repeatedly and from many different sources: leaders, patients, other departments, other staff. As a nurse leader, you can send only so many handwritten thank-you notes to the same staff member before you start to wonder, *What else can I do for this person?* It is the right question.

This is when you really need to get your creative juices flowing. You need to reach out and do something special once in a while for those staff members who are consistently exceeding your expectations. They should know they are appreciated. In many cases these will be your high performers: people who are natural problem solvers and who like to be involved in the more strategic operations areas. Believe it or not, these staff members may like to participate on teams, take on new projects, or get more training. They view such options as rewards and appreciate the fact that you're investing in them.

It is also important to know your staff members on an individual basis so that you become aware of what "fills their emotional bucket" from a recognition standpoint. (The book *How Full Is Your Bucket?*[2], by Tom Rath and Donald O. Clifton, Ph.D., offers some great ideas on how to gather this critical information.) Studer Group recommends that leaders ask their team members individually how they would like to be recognized and personalize recognition for these consistent high performers. The idea, of course, is to create enough positive experiences with your consistent high performers that you build trust and loyalty. That way, when something doesn't go right or you ask them to implement something they're not quite sure about, they'll give you the benefit of the doubt.

Step Four—Celebrate Your Legends

Once in a while an individual or perhaps even a group will do something that has such a tremendous impact that it warrants special recognition. For example, an employee may coordinate a group of volunteers to build a wheelchair ramp at a patient's home. Or a staff member may personally take care of the laundry of new patients admitted so they will have clean clothes to wear home. (The book *What's Right in Health Care*[3] is a compilation of such stories; it serves as a magnificent testimony to the grand deeds of legendary performance.)

No doubt acts of "everyday heroism" take place in your organization. Our guess is, however, that many of these accomplishments go unrecognized because others didn't know about them. If you're a leader with a staff person in your department doing these kinds of deeds, make sure he or she is celebrated throughout the organization.

What About the Other Nominees?

I like to talk about recognition for legends because when I ask leaders what examples fall into this group, it is not unusual for them to mention some formal program that centers on nomination— "Employee of the Year" or "Nurse of the Year," for example. And while these are very worthwhile and meaningful awards, I often ask, "Then what was done for the nominees who didn't win?" The reply I get is a little like what you hear at the Oscars, "Well, it's an honor just to be nominated."

I don't think so. It is always better to win. So the real question is: What are we doing for the other nominees—those people who have done extraordinary things in difficult situations? As a leader, it is your obligation to make sure they get the recognition they deserve. The more creativity you apply, the more joy you create...not only for the individual but for yourself.

—Lyn Ketelsen

It's important to harvest high performance stories of self-sacrifice and heroism—they are inspiring and should be shared with others.

In Conclusion

This overview of the performance management continuum unlocks some important revelations in moving performance in your department. Regardless of the change implemented, understanding how to get your staff to execute boils down to clearly communicating the expectations and then following up with good monitoring. When you see people meeting the expectation, you use the left side of the continuum as reinforcement. Likewise, as you witness staff struggling to perform, you use the other end of the continuum to resolve the situation.

Yes, it's a simple concept—but one that can have powerful results when you diligently and consistently put it into practice.

Key Points in This Chapter

1. The change process does not begin with "buy-in," as many leaders assume, but rather ends with it. The stages are *Believe, Decide, Action, Results* and *Understanding.*

2. Change is foundational and requires us to "force the action" to gain eventual results and understanding. The performance management spectrum provides a guideline for how to accomplish this; it encompasses ways to manage both negative and positive performance.

3. Clearly defining expectations is fundamental to good use of the performance management continuum.

4. Spend three times more time on the reward and recognition end of the continuum to drive positive change.

5. Good performance management requires creativity and courage.

Pillars Affected by Performance Management

Service—Results in better quality of care.

People—Helps retain high performers and facilitates the process of low performers improving or exiting the organization.

CHAPTER 4

Motivating and Recognizing Staff (Reward and Recognition)

By Lauren Charles and Karen Cook

As nurse leaders, recruitment and retention of staff is a major part of our jobs. That means we need to be making sure our employees feel appreciated. And yet, with so many issues to deal with on a daily basis, it can be hard to find the time. Problem is, the minute we start taking people for granted, we risk losing them.

Sadly, this happens all too often in both our personal and professional lives. In the former, taking people for granted results in lost relationships, depression, and unhappiness. In the latter, it results in employee turnover, decreased productivity and efficiency, along with a sense of dissatisfaction impacting performance on many levels.

One way to avoid taking people **and** performance for granted is to practice consistent, fair, and sincere reward and recognition.

We all want to be recognized for a job well done...right? Recognizing staff members is one of the best ways to re-recruit high performers and reward desired behaviors. As Quint Studer says, "Rewarded behavior gets repeated." This is incredibly relevant when we're trying to build a positive work environment. Remember, studies show that to build a positive culture, your employees need at least three compliments to every criticism.

> Constructive rewards, whether verbal praise or other incentives, can be viewed as the consequences of behaviors that produce desired outcomes. If your high performers are not rewarded or recognized, they think nobody notices or cares. They feel devalued and perhaps taken for granted. Conversely, if you tolerate poor performance or behaviors, it could be said that by doing nothing you're "rewarding" the behavior and it will probably be repeated.

As nurse leaders, performance management is often where you will spend the bulk of your time and energy. But it's just as important to focus on building a positive culture of reward and recognition. Why? Because it fosters an intrinsic motivation in employees to perform at a higher level.

Of course, in the midst of so many competing priorities, it can be a challenge to hardwire recognition into your daily activities. This chapter will provide some simple solutions for doing just that! Wouldn't it be a better place to work if before leaving, every leader asked the question, "Whom did I recognize today and thank for doing a great job?"

But first, let's take a quick look at some hard numbers. What can reward and recognition *really* do for your organization?

Reward and Recognition Pays Off.

Rewarding and recognizing staff is hardly a soft, "warm and fuzzy" practice. It yields hard, measurable results. Through the use of rounding and thank-you notes, one hospital saw a decrease in employee turnover from 12.3 percent to 6.05 percent! During this same time, their employee satisfaction significantly improved to the 75th percentile! Imagine what results like these would do for your organization!

Another large academic center implemented rounding and thank-you notes in the Environmental Services Department. They focused on the positive during rounds and harvesting compliments rather than complaints. This is not to say they didn't get complaints; they did. They responded to them and provided service recovery. But they changed their managerial philosophy overall to proactively seek out the positive...and they have had fantastic results as well. Their turnover decreased from 26.7 to 10.4 percent in just one year. Imagine the return on investment when you factor in costs associated with recruitment, training, and orientation!

The Art of Written Recognition

One of the most effective ways a nursing leader can reward and recognize staff is by sending them regular thank-you notes. The notes that seem to have the biggest impact are handwritten and sent to the home address. We don't mean generic "thanks for a good job" notes, but ones that are very specific and tied to behaviors or results.

One transporter got a note from the nursing leader thanking him for "always making sure the patients' legs are covered before they are wheeled out of the room." "Thank you for protecting our patients' dignity and privacy," the note added. The employee was thrilled to have been recognized and he made a big deal of covering every future patient as well!

When you feel that someone outside your department deserves recognition, communicate that to his leader so that she can send the note. When she does she should mention in the note that you brought the recipient's good work to her attention. That way, he feels good about his boss for writing the note and about you (and by association, your department) for noticing. You will be surprised at how much a behavior can be reinforced when it is recognized with a note of appreciation.

As you begin to send out these notes, you will be surprised at the reaction from your staff! The vast majority of employees will tell you "thank you" for the thank-you note! Many will say that it "made their day" and they shared it with their family

A Thank-You from the Top

As a new graduate nurse, I received a thank-you note from my chief nursing officer for working two double shifts during a snow storm. In it, she related that my director had told her about my extra efforts and how much she appreciated it. She even included a free movie card as a small token. The note was completely unexpected.

I didn't even really know her at the time, but I thought she was just the best executive ever based on the fact that she took the time to notice my efforts. And I thought my director was even better for telling her supervisor about it! The lesson in this story is to manage up by including YOUR boss in staff recognition.

—Julie Kennedy-Oehlert

members. For special situations, a thank-you note from a senior team member, based on your recommendation, is a great way to WOW employees.

During your regularly scheduled meeting with your boss, take the time to manage up (i.e., "brag about") a staff member who's done an exceptional job. Again, make it very specific. Then ask your boss to send a thank-you note to that employee's home. You'll be amazed at the results!

> The truth is, good nurses are being recruited away all the time. The leader who sends a heartfelt thank-you note to a sought-after clinician can make all the difference in her decision to stay where she is appreciated and valued.

Remember to Thank Physicians, Too.

Before we leave the subject of thank-you notes, here's one more reminder...don't forget physicians. Send a note to a physician when you see a positive comment about her on a patient satisfaction survey. Or pen a "thank you" for timely dictation or the use of approved abbreviations. A handwritten note from a nurse leader to a physician is a wonderful way to build that all-important sense of unity and aligned purpose.

Focus your efforts on those doctors who come to work every day and just take great care of patients, even if they're not your top admitters. They're often the ones you count on to answer phone calls in a timely manner, treat nurses with respect, and quietly care for patients. They *deserve* recognition.

My First Thank-You Note

I will never forget the first thank-you note I sent out using this process. At the time I was a senior leader new to this particular organization and did not know many of the frontline staff. One of my nurse managers asked me to write a thank-you note to one of his unit secretaries, a woman I had never met. A few days later, as I was rounding on that unit, the secretary came up to me and gave me a huge hug and told me how much the note had meant to her! It was then that I realized the power of thank-you notes.

—Lauren Charles

And, yes, there are also those for whom we must look a bit harder to "find" a specific behavior to reward. One nurse leader tells the story of a physician new to his role as manager of the Operating Room (OR). He was diligent about sending thank-you notes to the top performers—those who always started their cases on time and treated the staff with respect. One particular physician was a bit cantankerous; he didn't do anything overly negative, but neither did he do anything to readily deserve special recognition.

The OR manager carefully observed his behaviors, looking for SOMETHING positive, and noted how he always cleaned up the lounge when he left. So the manager wrote a thank-you note saying he noticed and was grateful for this behavior. The surgeon's response was amazing. He came to the manager's office and told him how much he appreciated the note. A little later, the manager followed up with another note for a small behavior. Within a short time, the physician had turned from a scowling surgeon to one of the most congenial. He even brought in doughnuts for the staff, who then wrote him a big thank-you note signed by everyone.

A Few Tips for Hardwiring Thank-You Notes

1. Decide how often it makes sense to send them. If you have a large department, you might want to send three notes a week. If your department is very small, one a month may be fine. The idea is to create a system that gets results—and stick to it.

2. Target employees who go "above and beyond" the call of duty.

3. Be specific, not vague and general. You want the employee to know exactly what she did right. Remember, you're seeking to reinforce positive behaviors.

4. Handwrite your notes and mail them to employees' homes. E-mail is fine for a quick message of appreciation, but don't let it replace your "official" thank you. Follow up with a handwritten note.

5. Use rounding logs for follow-up. Note in the rounding log who you sent a note to (or who you asked a senior leader to send one to). Then, when you round you can ask the recipient about the note and again recognize the behavior.

So, while we're not suggesting you ignore negative behaviors, our advice is to try and find something positive in everyone. That's true of not just physicians, but of nurses and everyone else as well.

Create a Reward and Recognition Team.

Reward and recognition is so important to many organizations that they form an employee team whose role is discovering ways to make staff feel appreciated. Taking into account the programs already in place, the group helps identify HOW employees want to be recognized for reaching goals or demonstrating good behaviors. This team also ensures that recognition practices are hardwired℠ and executed at all levels, and it develops systems to ensure organizational consistency in implementation.

Staff recognition team members are usually high performers who are incredibly creative. They will develop some wonderful practices if given the opportunity. They also are the ones "closest" to the wants, needs, and desires of frontline employees.

At one organization, the reward and recognition team came up with the idea to have leaders give WOW cards to employees to recognize their accomplishments. The employees can turn in their cards for incentives like movie tickets or lunch in the cafeteria.

A team at another organization gave Almond Joy candy bars to all new employees at orientation with a note that said "Welcome—It Is a Joy to Work Here." This same team burst into orientation (typically at 2:30 in the afternoon, toward the end of the session) with ice cream and cake to celebrate the employees' first day on the job. This made an amazing impression and taught staff the importance of celebrating those joining the organization. This team, who represented the organizational value of "joy in work," also did a quick presentation on having fun at work, working with good people, and feeling like they made a difference…because they did!

The reward and recognition team may canvas staff members to learn new ideas to implement. They might ask employees, "If you were king or queen for the day, what would you do to make this a better place to work?" Often staff members reply that they want to be "thanked" for a job well done, which just emphasizes that a heartfelt, personalized, verbal or written thank you is most important. Other suggestions for rewarding employees include:

- Movie tickets or a meal in the cafeteria
- "On the Spot" bonus or recognition: *I saw what you did and appreciate it.*
- Pins or special recognition, visible to all, for accomplishments
- Employee of the month program
- Heroes or legends program
- Designation as a "mentor" or other prestigious title
- Additional training or development
- Being highlighted in the employee newsletters, forums, and board meetings
- Birthday, anniversary recognition
- Fun candy gram: *You are worth a MINT to us.*
- Traveling trophies like the "Ax" for those who helped break down barriers, or the "Helmsman Award" to the person who demonstrated leadership skills and has the designated "Captain" hat for the week
- Naming a day of the week after a special employee
- "Pass it on" coins—given to employees who were observed living the values or behavioral standards
- Traveling award—the recipient determines who gets it next and why
- Thanks a bunch—small bouquet of flowers
- Coupon for car wash

Clearly, the employee ideas are endless. So turn this team loose and let them have fun with it. You will find that they are usually very responsible with budget concerns as well.

Seek out Employees to Reward and Recognize.

As a nurse leader, you can't be everywhere. So how do you hear about the good things happening on your unit or department? At times, of course, you just happen to hear about a staff member who's gone above and beyond. Word usually gets around about your organization's "heroes." But you can't count on that happening. Sometimes it's necessary to actively seek potential recipients of reward and recognition.

There are two good ways to do this: ask employees and ask patients.

Hold rounding conversations with employees. The best way to identify deserving individuals is to simply round on employees. By their very nature, these conversations allow you to learn who should be rewarded and recognized. Sometimes great actions on the part of staff are so common, we take them for granted. Asking employees, "Who can I reward and recognize?" makes people stop and really think about it because they are uncomfortable saying "no one."

Sure, there may be weeks when there's no one to recognize, but generally employees will come out with a name. Tell them not to forget people in other departments and support staff. These individuals help us be successful. They deserve recognition too!

Ask patients: "Who provided outstanding care?" Rounding on patients (Covered in detail in Section 2) is another great way to harvest feedback for staff recognition. One nurse manager did this particularly well during her rounds by managing up the caregiver team. She also asked the patients or family if there was anyone who had made their care "special." Usually the patients would tell her about staff members who impacted their emotions. For instance, they might say: "Kate is so kind and explains things to me in ways I can understand."

Taking cues from what she was hearing, the nurse leader would go on to sing Kate's praises to other patients. She would glance at the whiteboard and then say, "I see Kate is your nurse today. She has worked on this unit for five years and I hear so many compliments about her care. I know you are in good hands." This enabled her to compliment Kate after rounds, telling her the many specific things patients said about her. Proactive rounding allows leaders to catch staff members at their best and find out great things they might never have known if they hadn't asked the right questions!

If You Don't Reward and Recognize...Why Not?

Staff members generally feel (and often rightfully so) that they aren't recognized enough. That fact alone should be enough to encourage nurse leaders to "up the ante" on expressing appreciation. Unfortunately, some may think to themselves (or even say), *I don't need compliments—why should they?* If you should fall into this category, perhaps you need a reminder that employees don't leave an organization; they leave their supervisor!

Thankfully, few leaders have such a negative attitude about reward and recognition. Usually their problem is time—too little of it, to be precise. Nurse leaders are constantly asked to do more and more in the same amount of time, which often makes reward and recognition a huge challenge. Still, you must make it a priority to reward and recognize and to role model a positive culture.

First, honestly evaluate what exactly you are doing that is MORE important than re-recruiting and retaining your valued staff? What is MORE important than rewarding and recognizing behavior we want repeated? If nurse leaders say reward and recognition is crucial, but don't follow through or don't act upon that concept, employees will not believe them. Actions (or lack of them) speak louder than words. Remember that staff is watching your every move.

Want to Get It Done? Put It on Your Schedule!

Next, commit to making reward and recognition part of your daily or weekly routine. Block time on the calendar to write thank-you notes or recognize an employee. Manage up: Commit to sending one name to YOUR director or boss so he can recognize this person as well. If the person being recognized is in a support department, send the note to her manager.

Always link reward and recognition to results or desired outcomes. For example, if your unit receives outstanding patient satisfaction scores one month, celebrate with staff members to make sure everyone knows you appreciate their going "above and beyond" to earn such great scores.

> Be aware that a consistent recognition process will actually save time. Look at it this way: Would you rather write a few thank-you notes—or would you rather have to find the time to interview and orient new staff?

It's important to realize generational differences when hardwiring a process for reward and recognition. Older managers may need a reminder because they may not think it's important or necessary to recognize someone "for doing their job." On the other hand, a younger workforce may expect and need more reward and recognition.

One final word of warning: Don't reward and recognize everyone equally. This practice will devalue your top performers and reward your lower performers. So refrain from global or generalized rewards unless for specific overall department achievements.

Remember what your mother taught you? "Thank you" truly is a magic phrase. Start putting it into practice in the form of rewarding and recognizing employees and you'll be amazed at the difference it makes.

Key Points in This Chapter

1. Recognize and reward behaviors you want to see repeated. This helps employees feel valued and creates a positive culture. It also pays off in measurable ways, such as decreased turnover.

2. Sending regular thank-you notes is one of the most powerful ways to reward and recognize employees. These notes need to be specific, handwritten, and sent to the recipient's home. Don't forget to thank physicians!

3. Harvest wins through the use of rounding on staff as well as patients.

4. Link reward and recognition to the performance you want. For instance, when a team reaches a desired milestone, reinforce their efforts with a celebration.

5. Recognizing everyone equally will de-motivate top performers and promote mediocrity. Single out those who truly deserve it.

Pillars Affected by Reward and Recognition

Service—Retains high performers who exceed service expectations.

Quality—Drives better outcomes and results due to quality staff.

Finance—Reduces costs associated with lower turnover.

People—Fosters higher employee satisfaction and loyalty.

Growth—Aids expansion potential due to better outcomes and results.

CHAPTER 5

highmiddlelow® Performers and Critical Conversations

By Beth Keane and Colleen Thornburgh

As a nurse leader, it's your responsibility to create and maintain a quality staff. You *have* to know how to re-recruit high performers, coach middle performers, and move low performers up or out. Yes, it sounds like a daunting task. But the good news is that there are specific techniques, conversation formulas, and other valuable tools that will help you be successful.

When we ask leaders what makes their job less enjoyable, many of them cite a "problem employee" (or maybe more than one). Oh, those dreaded low performers! You know, the ones you keep hoping will suddenly find irresistible career opportunities in another state. Unfortunately, your most challenging employees are also the least likely to leave—voluntarily, at least.

So what happens when you as a nurse leader don't have the energy or the courage to deal with your low performers? You'll most likely continue to spend 80 percent of your time with approximately 5 percent of your staff. And while you invest huge amounts of emotional and physical energy on employees who are fundamentally undermining your team, who are you **NOT** spending time with? That's right. The high and middle performers, who collectively form the "backbone" of positive outcomes. Perhaps saddest of all, while you're bending over backward to support underachievers, you're perceived as unfair by your top performers because you're not applying the Standards of Performance equally.

An Overdue Firing

Nationally recognized speaker and retired CNO Gail Boylan tells the story of when, as Chief Nursing Officer of Baptist Hospital in Pensacola, Florida, she finally fired a low performing nurse who had been there 25 years. She knew the staff would be upset, but she thought their distress would be focused on losing a long-term colleague. They were emotional, but the emotion was anger. They were angry at Gail for *not taking action sooner.* This makes sense when we think about it—if we leave low performers on our team, who takes up the slack for their laziness or poor patient relations? The high and middle performers do. We owe it to our good people to deal with inadequate performance. We owe it to our good people to spend equal or more time with them, offering them our mentoring and support.

—Beth Keane

The Impact of highmiddlelow Conversations

As the graphics below demonstrate, highmiddlelow conversations make a measurable difference.

The first one shows the impact of these conversations at two different organizations. As you can see, they resulted in substantial increases in inpatient, outpatient, employee, and Emergency Department satisfaction.

Figure 5.1

Impact of highmiddlelow®

Beds = 303, Admissions = 17,486, Employees = 2,500

Measure	Before highmiddlelow®	After highmiddlelow®
Employee Satisfaction	Month before - 65	6 months after - 81
Inpatient Satisfaction	2 months before - 74	4 months after - 87
Outpatient Satisfaction	2 months before - 86	4 months after - 98

Beds = 357, Admissions = 15,995, Employees = 1,788

Measure	Before highmiddlelow®	After highmiddlelow®
Inpatient Satisfaction	1st Quarter - 61	4th Quarter - 91
Outpatient Satisfaction	1st Quarter - 45	4th Quarter - 69
ED Satisfaction	1st Quarter - 50	4th Quarter - 83

The second graphic shows the results of a survey that demonstrates an increase in the staff's perception of how high, middle, and low performers are managed after highmiddlelow conversations were implemented.

Figure 5.2

highmiddlelow® Conversations & Organizational Results

How would you rate your organization's ability to:
(1 = Very Poor, 10 = Excellent)

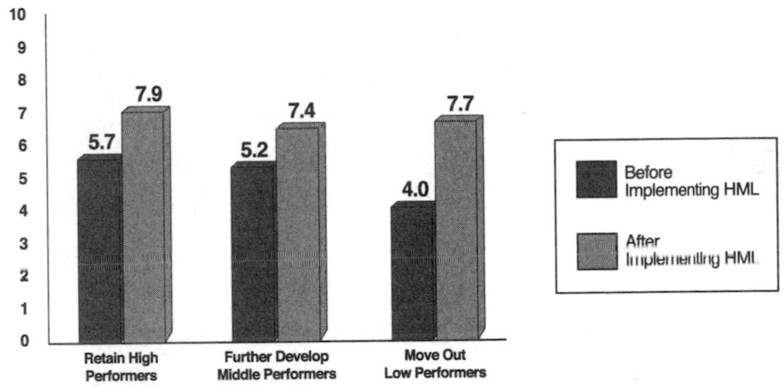

Source: highmiddlelow Research Study, 8/08
Before HML, N=26; After HML, N=25 for Retaining High Performers
Before HML, N=25; After HML, N=25 for Further Developing Middle Performers
Before HML, N=25; After HML, N=25 for Moving Out Low Performers

highmiddlelow Identification Strategy

Before you can implement the strategy to deal with highmiddlelow (HML) performers, you must first categorize each level of performance using your organizational standards to help guide you. What behaviors identify people as high, middle, or low?

High performers are people you trust. They are proactive and often come to you with solutions. They are good clinically, and they are also solid team members. They don't "manage down" anyone—including peers, physicians, senior leaders, or the organization.

Middle performers are employees you would hire again. With your help they can be developed to meet their full potential. They are dependable and reactive—when they see a problem, they don't necessarily develop or act on a solution, but they are there to help.

Low performers are employees you would not rehire. They often have a negative attitude and undermine the team. They are deficient in clinical skills or relationship building or both.

For more assistance in defining HML performers, refer to the Staff Differentiator and Leader Differentiator tools found on *The Nurse Leader Handbook* resource page at www.firestarterpublishing.com/NurseLeader-Handbook.

Next, create a list of all your employees and categorize them into the above performance groups. Get your leader's input on your decisions. Then arrange to meet individually with all employees, beginning with those you have identified as "high," then moving to "middle," and finally to "low." (You don't need to tell employees you are meeting with them in order of competence; they will figure that out!)

When doing this exercise for the first time, it's not unusual to get caught up in deciding who falls under each category. And don't be surprised if you get a list back from leaders creating two whole new categories: the high-middles and the middle-lows. These represent staff members who can't be conveniently placed in any one category.

Here's the most important thing to know about the HML activity: It's first and foremost a re-recruitment process for your high and middle performers. It's all about devoting time and energy to the staff you want to keep. It's also about greatly reducing the amount of time and energy we spend on the low performers who drag everyone else down.

Keep in mind that the only reason you're rating your staff is to determine which style of conversation you're going to have with each person.

High performers take responsibility for their own development. With them, you feel comfortable focusing solely on the things they do well and that add value to the team.

For the high-middles, ask yourself whether you feel the need to discuss development opportunities with them or help them with their growth plans. If you do, you're probably dealing with a middle performer.

If there's someone in your organization who you suspect is a low performer, here are a couple of good "acid test" questions to help you decide for sure:

1. If you could have it your way and do it all over, would you rehire him?

2. Are you working harder at his success than he is?

If you answered "no" and "yes," guess what? You most likely have a low performer and need to proceed accordingly.

Now let's take a look at the specific conversations.

High Performer Conversations

Recognition of your top performers is one of the most important benefits of highmiddlelow conversations. You have three objectives:

1. To **focus attention** on the majority of employees who contribute to the organization every day in a positive manner. Your goal

McMark's Recruiting Strategy

In college, a good friend of mine, Mark, aspired to own a franchise in a well-known restaurant chain. He took a lot of good-natured teasing from his fraternity brothers throughout college, being called McMark and other assorted fast food names, but that didn't deter him from pursuing his goal. After graduating from college, he took a job in corporate America while he and his wife, Sarah, saved to buy their first restaurant.

It's now 25 years later. Together Mark and Sarah have seven restaurants! Every summer, the fraternity brothers travel to Mark's house for a weekend of fun. He takes the group out to eat lunch, but not at his restaurants. Instead, they venture to similar establishments. You see, Mark is constantly on the look-out for talent. When he comes across a clean, well-run eatery with employees who appear to be enjoying their work, Mark introduces himself to the manager. He gives the manager his card with his phone number and asks him if he's ever considered a career with *his* major franchise. Mark knows that his most important asset is the great managers who run his restaurants.

Moral of the story: Your high performers can easily find other places to work, so you must constantly re-recruit.

—Colleen Thornburgh

is to formally "re-recruit" these high performers by rewarding and recognizing their efforts.

2. To **increase consistency** among department leaders regarding reward and recognition of star performers as well as their providing regular coaching and feedback.

3. To **move the organization** from good to great by focusing on the positives and building a strong emotional bank account with employees.

What happens when you ignore high performers?

Figure 5.3

Ignore Them?
High Performers:

- 47% are actively looking for another job, resumes, internet search and interviews:
    - Lack of recognition
    - Feeling under rewarded
    - Are the most unhappy
    - Even when unemployment is exceeding, have a pent-up demand to leave

- 55% said they were never or rarely thanked by their boss

Leadership IQ., Fall 2006
Maritz Incentives, St. Louis 2003

In most organizations, we find that about one-third of employees fall into the high performer category. Ignoring these individuals can be disastrous: Fully half of them will look for another job. Yet these are the very people who consistently deliver work at a high level, model the organization's values and behavioral standards, and are regarded as role models and respected by their peers.

High performers not only meet goals and expectations, but they also raise the bar on their own individual performance as well as that of the department. Who do you go to when you have a new project, committee, or fast-approaching deadline? Your high performers! They are motivated by achievement and willingly step up to the plate to help deliver on the objectives. Yet, how often and how well do you recognize your best contributors? Probably not as often as you'd like. It's time to remedy that.

Explain to the high performers that you are meeting with each employee individually for coaching conversations. Tell them how valuable they are (using specific examples of what they do well), and that you want them to stay. Then ask if there is anything you as their supervisor should be doing to ensure they are successful and remain with the organization. (Note: These staff members will likely ask for nothing, but instead will express thanks and appreciation.)

The key message for the high performers is to re-recruit them. "I value you. I do not want you to leave. Is there anything that might cause you to think about leaving? What can I do to help you and your department achieve your goals?" Spend 15-30 minutes with each high performer—starting with the person who role models the best leadership skills, obtains the best results, and contributes the most to the organization.

In summary, high performer conversations use the following model:

- Tell them where the organization is headed.
- Thank them for their work—use specific examples.
- Tell them why they are important—how they contribute to the department or organization.
- Ask if there is anything you can do for them.

> We start with high performers to build your confidence and skill in this process, but also to build an emotional bank account and set of supporters within the department. As a leader this also helps re-align your focus to those who are performing the best. Word will get out very quickly.

Middle Performer Conversations

Nurse leader conversations with middle performers—the largest group of employees—are not too different. For the most part, these employees aspire to work at high levels, but may lack confidence, experience, or skills—or perhaps they are new to their role.

Middle performers can sometimes be influenced by those around them. For example, when surrounded by high performers, middle performers raise their own performance level. When surrounded by low performers, they may find themselves dragged into the environment and mindset of that group. They lack the experience to consistently maintain or increase the level of their performance and need coaching from their leader.

Your goal with the middle performer is to reassure, re-recruit, and develop. Middle performer conversations use the *support, coach, support model.*

- **Support**—provide specific feedback on what they are doing well
- **Coach**—offer one specific opportunity for improvement and the benefit of growing in this area
- **Support**—reaffirm your confidence in their ability to develop and their current contributions

Start by assuring these employees you want to retain them (which you do), and that they are valuable members of the team. Give them some specific compliments about what they do well. Then point out the one or two things you would most like for them to improve upon, offering concrete examples of what you want them to do differently. It's important to make the coaching specific and provide no more than one or two development opportunities in order to keep it focused.

Use key words like, "As your leader, my goal is to help set you up for success. One development opportunity I see is…." Ask for their agreement and what they think they could do to improve. Do NOT begin this coaching segment with the word **BUT**—as in, "You've been doing a good job, **but**…" or you will lose the opportunity to help. Emphasize your role as a coach and mentor, as well as their potential. Close positively, getting their agreement to work on the development areas and reaffirming their value.

Low Performer Conversations

As you might guess, this last group of conversations will be the most difficult. These employees likely have been involved in a number of such discussions in their lifetimes and are skilled at redirecting the conversation.

Your goal with the low performer is to clarify expectations for improving a skill or behavior, and to communicate the very real consequences of not making these changes. In other words, you want to move her up or move her out. (Note: This is not a retention conversation. It should never begin with the words, "I'm glad to see you.")

> To some extent you must acknowledge that this conversation will be causing the low performer pain, but that is okay—pain is a motivator. And also, don't forget that this employee's poor performance has likely been causing some pain for others.

Our work in healthcare organizations tells us that around 8 or 9 percent of all employees will fall into the low performer category. Of those individuals, one-third will change their behavior as a result of the conversation. It's possible that low performers may not know what's expected of them; many times leaders are not clear or specific with what they want others to do.

Another third will notice you paying attention to their performance and will decide that they don't want to be held accountable to a higher standard. They may choose to leave the organization. This is desirable turnover, as these individuals are not contributing to the performance and the goals of the department or organization.

The final third won't change their behavior, no matter what. They will hold on until they are terminated.

Of course, it's not always possible to tell what any given low performer will do—who will move up and become middle performers and who will ultimately leave. That's why you need to plan to provide the entire group with continued coaching and feedback.

The most effective approach for low performer conversations is the DESK model outlined below.

Describe the behavior that needs to change. Begin the meeting by describing the behavior you have seen. For example, "Mary, I have noticed when you leave your work area, you leave it messy on a regular basis."

Evaluate/Explain how the behavior affects the performance of the department or outcomes for the patient/family. Connect the dots between the behavior and the consequence. "I'm very disappointed because when we met 30 days ago, you said this wouldn't happen again and you would improve. When your area is not clean, the next staff person has to spend time cleaning it. Most importantly, the chance for errors increases when the area is cluttered."

Show or tell specifically what you need the employee to do. "At the end of your shift today, Mary, I will clean up the work area with you to show you what I expect it to look like when you leave it."

Know the consequences. Tell the employee what will happen if she fails to make the necessary changes. "You need to know the consequences. Right now is a verbal warning. But the next time I see this happen, there will be a written warning. And if it should happen again, it will mean termination" (or whatever is appropriate for your situation and HR policies).

Your Human Resources Department can help you define the consequences, thus ensuring you've followed the correct process for formal corrective action. It's important to have strong follow-up to the low performer conversation to ensure the desired changes take place or that the consequences are implemented. All low performer conversations should be considered a part of the corrective action process.

> **Tip:** Keep a record of your counseling sessions and make sure you clearly define your expectations. As you repeat this process, often in rounding and periodically more formally, you will notice that employees start to internalize the standards you value and model them. As more employees develop positive attitudes and enhanced performance, the hospital will become a better place for employees to work, physicians to practice medicine, and patients to receive care. At that point, you are moving forward in the journey from good to great!

To Be or Not to Be? (Transparent, that is!)

The question is often asked, "Should employees be told whether they are high, middle, or low performers?" You should know that it takes a very mature organization to be able to do this with full transparency. Success hinges on the training and skill level of the leadership team. Poorly executed, this process can generate a lot of fear on the part of employees.

If you decide that transparency is for you, position the course of action as being a very positive coaching tool designed to help you clarify expectations and set everyone up for success. Stress that HML conversations are not meant to be an evaluation process. Involve staff in discussions about what actions exceed your expectations as the nurse leader and the expectations of peers.

Ideally, the process is executed mid-year between annual, formal performance reviews. Eventually, though, re-recruiting and dealing with low performers will become an innate part of your overall performance management platform. Just remember to always position yourself as a coach who wants every team member to develop best performance skills.

To Sum Up: How highmiddlelow Conversations Benefit Your Organization

- High and middle performers are recognized and re-recruited to the organization.
- Coaching to grow performance and development of the middle performer takes place.
- Expectations are clarified for the low performer.
- Leaders spend more time with the 92 percent of the employees who consistently contribute to the performance of the organization.
- Most importantly, the team's entire overall performance improves.

Figure 5.4

Improved Organizational Performance

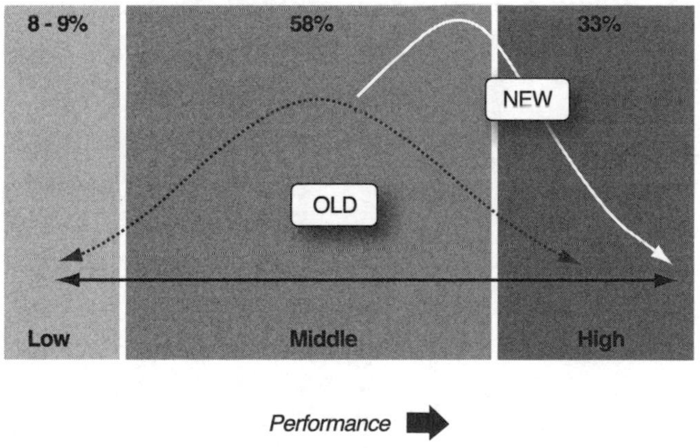

Key Points in This Chapter

1. Our high performers tend to leave if we don't reward and recognize their contributions.

2. Middle performers need mentoring and clear expectations if they are to reach full potential.

3. Low performers suck the life out of a team and undermine clinical quality. They must be counseled to move "up or out." Be sure to follow through on the consequences when low performers' behaviors/actions do not change.

4. If your employees don't understand expectations and see the link between behavior and consequences, it is your failure as a leader, not theirs as employees.

Pillars Affected by highmiddlelow Performers and Critical Conversations

Service—Improves patient satisfaction.

Quality—Generates continuous quality improvement.

People—Fosters employee satisfaction.

CHAPTER 6

Selecting and Retaining Talent

By Colleen Thornburgh and Beth Keane

Why Talent Selection Matters

The single most important asset in any healthcare organization is its staff—those men and women selected to deliver care to patients and families. In terms of performance, every aspect of an organization is affected by the caliber of employees hired and retained.

And as a nurse leader, it's important that you hire a high quality staff. Your decisions make all the difference between a good department and a great one. Do you want excellent clinical outcomes? Then hire staff with the skills to deliver those results. Do you desire an environment where everyone enjoys coming to work and functioning as a closely knit team? Then hire individuals who demonstrate the values of respect, communication, and teamwork.

In other words, determine the outcomes and work environment you aspire to achieve and choose employees with the skills, knowledge, and experience to deliver on those expectations.

The Impact of the Selection and Retention Process

We know it is difficult to attain patient and physician satisfaction results if the *right* individuals are not recruited to the organization and if the top performers are not retained. But consider also that when an organization hires employees who embrace the values and perform at high levels, then staff is more satisfied overall. A comprehensive selection process decreases turnover and increases the likelihood of retaining top talent.

Consider also that the cost of selection and orientation, depending on the position, can be 50-150 percent of the salary. The more skilled the worker, or more unique the skill set, the higher the price of replacement. Plus, if the organization is not viewed as an employer of choice, it can be difficult to recruit the talent necessary to expand and provide access, open a new facility, or offer extended hours.

Last but not least: Who is a more accurate representation of your organization than the employees who work there? What do community members see when they visit your facility and what do they tell

Hiring Right Pays Off

A woman checking me into a hotel in South Carolina asked why I was in town. When I told her I was visiting a hospital to speak about selection, she said: "That's so important. I always say, the only thing worse than a good hire that leaves is a bad hire that stays."

This summarizes the impact of selection. When we hire high performers, we increase retention by improving both morale and quality. According to a VHA study, when turnover drops below 12 percent, both length of stay and mortality decrease. This makes sense because stability on the work team enhances efficiency and productivity, resulting in better outcomes. Financially, high turnover costs dearly: the price of replacement, down time, recruitment, orientation, and precepting. It also undermines efficient teamwork.

The other cost is the one the South Carolina hotelkeeper mentioned: If you hire a low performer, at some point you have to deal with inadequate performance. Aside from the time you spend coaching, you have the additional stress of dealing with a non-contributor and shoring up the team. Hiring right saves us time, money, and energy.

—Beth Keane

friends and neighbors? Are they likely to recommend your hospital as the place they prefer to receive their care? There is no doubt—your most important asset is the men and women you select to work in your organization.

Figure 6.1

Quality Connection

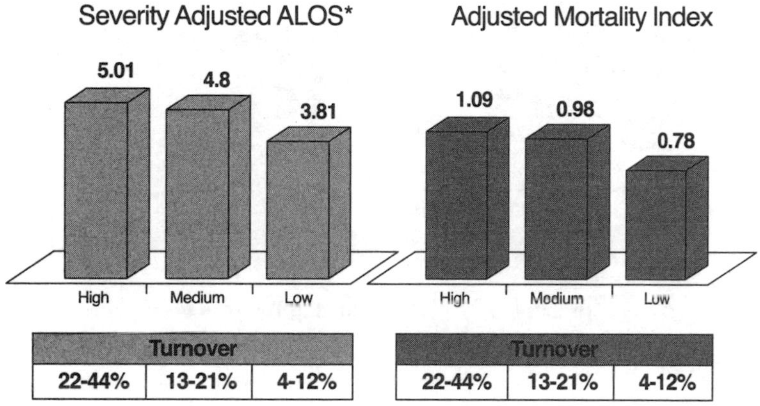

**Average Length of Stay*
Source: VHA, 2002, The Business Case for Workforce Stability

Figure 6.2

Cost of High Turnover

- Hospitals with high turnover (22% +) have a 36% higher cost per discharge than hospitals with turnover of 12% or less.

Source: VHA, 2002, The Business Case for Workforce Stability

Figure 6.3

Financial Impact
Overall and Nursing Turnover Reduction

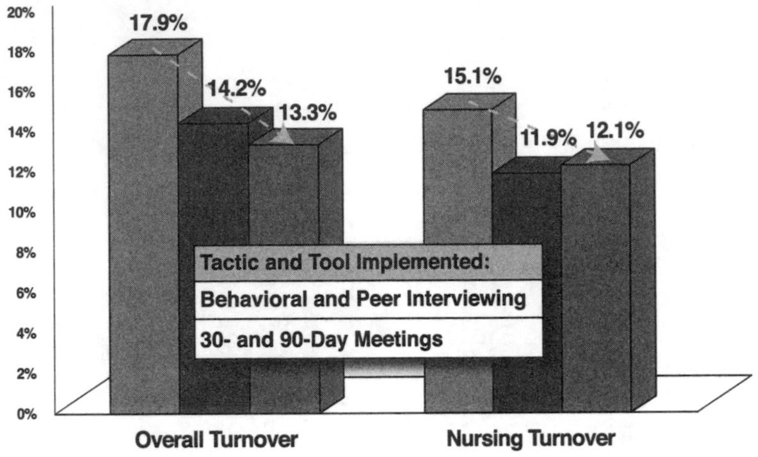

Source: Kentucky Health System, 42,000 discharges, Total beds = 1,900 beds

Figure 6.4

Interdependent Relationships
Quality Example

Relationship Between Employee Turnover and Patient Care

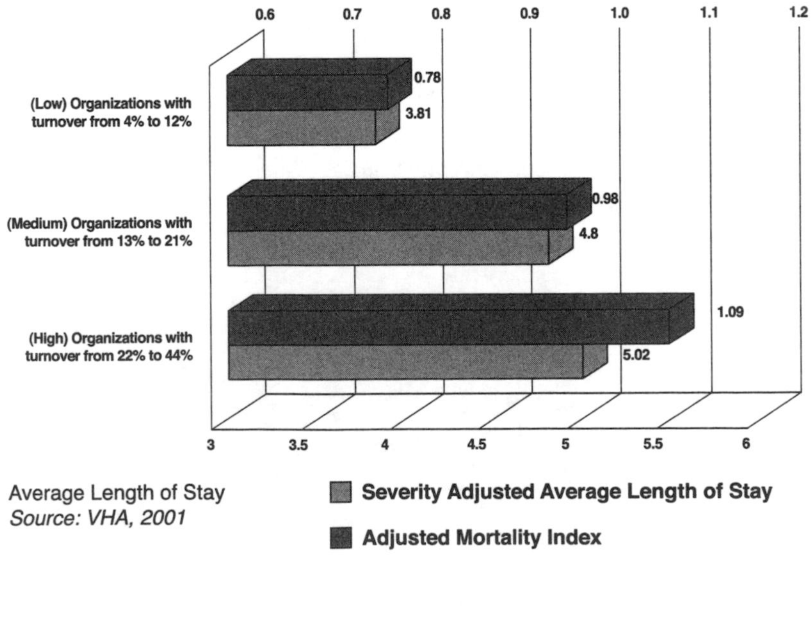

Average Length of Stay
Source: VHA, 2001

The Selection and Retention Process

Figure 6.5

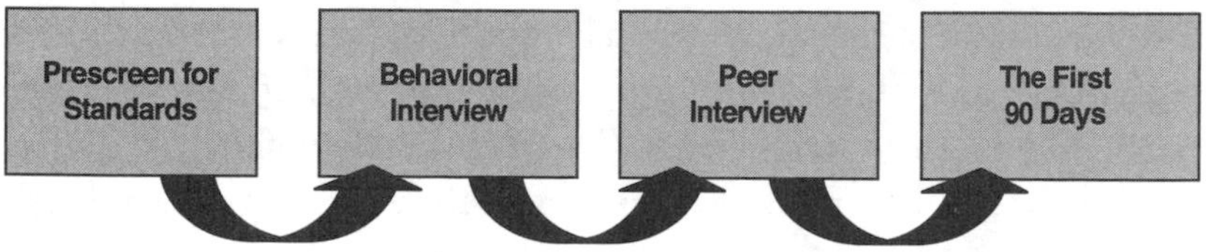

Step One: Prescreen for Standards of Behavior.

A typical Standards of Behavior contract addresses any and all aspects of behavior at work: from interaction with clients to phone etiquette to good manners (knocking before you enter a room or office) to positive attitude markers (smiling or saying "thank you"). If you don't already have specific, defined standards in your organization, create them. Think of these as the values you would expect of everyone working in your area.

Then, when hiring, show standards to any applicants. Make it clear: *If you don't feel you can sign the contract and abide by the standards, the selection process should end right now.*

Step Two: Conduct an In-depth Behavioral Interview.

Prior to the interview, use the job description to define the core competencies a candidate would need to possess to be a high performer. You can also work with your team to determine the essential skills and characteristics you need to look for during the interview. For instance, if you are hiring a unit secretary, then time management, the ability to determine priorities, and communicating effectively are qualities necessary for success. On the other hand, when hiring a clinician, competencies such as critical thinking skills, teamwork, and leadership are paramount.

You then conduct the interview using behavioral-based questions geared toward the key competencies you've identified. Behavioral-based questions are open-ended, requiring an example or story as the answer versus a simple "yes" or "no." Using them gives you far more ability to determine the extent of the individual's knowledge, skills, and experience. We often ask hypothetical questions in interviews, such as, "What would you do if…?" Or, "Walk me through the steps a patient care provider should take when…." These questions tell us what candidates think, not what they have done. Your interest is not in what applicants might know from a textbook. Rather, you want to see how they have applied themselves on the job and the experience level they would bring to the position. So a more effective and revealing question would be, "What **did** you do when…and what happened?" Or say, "**Give me an example of a time when you**…and tell me what the result was." Think about applying for credit or a mortgage. The bank asks about your credit history, not your assurance that you plan to send them a payment every month. They are interested in what you **did** do in the past, not what you think you **would** do in the future—because they know that actions speak louder than words!

> **Tip:** For additional help, go to www.firestarterpublishing.com/NurseLeaderHandbook for the Behavioral-Based Questions Sample. It provides examples to determine the candidate's qualifications in a particular core competency.

To get the most from a behavioral interview, you'll need to train yourself to listen carefully to the candidate's responses. You might think listening requires no effort, that it's a passive activity. The opposite is true. Listening is a process that requires your participation. Active listening means that you give full attention to the other person, putting aside your need to reply or ask another question, concentrating instead on what you're hearing. A good interviewer is in fact a very good listener!

Lend an EAR to the Candidate.

A tool to help you listen to and learn from how the candidate handled situations in the past can be found at www.firestarterpublishing.com/NurseLeaderHandbook. It uses the following "EAR" model to record the individual's answer after you ask a core competency question.

"E" refers to the event (or story) with which the candidate responded

"A" refers to the action the person took

"R" was the result or outcome of the experience

Keeping the EAR model in mind, read through the following candidate's response to handling a situation involving a family member.

"I had just arrived at the hospital when I came upon a woman pushing an elderly man in a wheelchair. She was very upset, so I asked her if I could help her. She mentioned that traffic had been particularly heavy and she was running late. She was taking her father to the hospital for tests but couldn't find any signage to point her to the Radiology Department. She was really worried. I told her that I would walk her to Registration, wait with her father while she registered him, and then escort them both to the Radiology Department. She was so thankful for the assistance and told me she would tell her friends about the great service she had at our hospital."

The candidate's response reveals how she handled a situation involving a dissatisfied family member (the Event). She took several Actions, including asking if she could help and walking them to the right department. The Result was a satisfied family member willing to recommend the organization. And, since we know that past performance is the best indicator of future performance, this candidate has the knowledge and the skills to handle similar situations when working for you.

Tip: An in-depth behavioral-based interview takes time—at least an hour to 90 minutes. However, it results in an excellent assessment of whether or not the candidate is qualified and will succeed in the position. You will also want to give that person time to ask you questions about the position and the department. The Studer Group℠ interview matrix can be used following your conversation to assess the skills of a candidate.

Figure 6.6

Interview Matrix

Date: ______________________ **Interviewer:** ______________________

Candidate: ______________________

Core Competency Area (Behavior Question/s)	Wt. 1 – 3	Score	Total	Comments
Competency:				
Competency:				
Competency:				
Competency:				
Competency:				

Weights:

1 – Preferred, but not necessary **2 – Moderately necessary** **3 – Essential**

Score:

1. No experience or example. Skills for position not evident.	2. Limited experience and example. Will require additional training.	3. Specific example and experience. Not all actions ended in desired results.	4. Solid experience and example. Can do.	5. In-depth experience and example. Can teach others to do.

Areas for further review by peer interview team or hiring manager:

Once you complete the interview, the next step is scheduling the candidate for a peer interview. **But it's critical that you move forward on only those candidates you would hire yourself!** You refer only your best candidates from your selection interviews to the peer team—applicants you can support hiring, and who are worthy of a "yes" from the group. Remember, you NEVER send a potential employee you could *not* live with to a peer interview!

Too many leaders make this mistake. They will short cut the interview process and end up undecided about how they feel about a candidate—but nevertheless will send that person on to the peer group for a final decision. Passing along a candidate you have not thoroughly screened is a waste of the team's time. What's worse, you may have even opened the door to hiring your next low performer, thus putting everyone at risk. When in doubt, sort them out!

Step Three: Schedule a Peer Interview.

Most leaders at some point in their careers have made a poor hiring selection. If you've done this, you know it's a mistake with lasting consequences. And when you look back on it, more than likely you recognized early on that you had made a mistake. And other staff members in the department probably saw that the new hire wasn't going to work out before you did!

> Chances are you prescreened for the organization's standards or values; you asked behavioral interview questions based on needed key competencies; and you confirmed that the candidate had good experience. However, most likely you failed to realize one thing: Job success is about more than skills and experience; it's also about "fit" in the work environment.

For instance, someone can be an excellent nurse in an Intensive Care Unit with a specific number of patients to focus on daily. Yet, she may perform poorly in a fast-paced, high volume Emergency Department requiring constant triaging and rearrangement of priorities. Hopefully, any serious shortcomings that would prevent her from succeeding will have been caught earlier in the behavioral interview, but if not, the peer interview will likely unearth them. It will also help ensure that the potential hire is the right team/culture fit—and if the peers select her to move forward, it will increase the likelihood that she'll be welcomed and mentored by them.

Peer interviewing is the process of engaging your high performing team members in the selection process. After all, who knows the job and environment better than those already working in the department? Yet many nurse leaders do not wholeheartedly embrace peer interviewing. They fear turning the hiring decision over to others in the department—and, yes, this is what you will be doing. But here are several reasons why and how the process works.

First, as a nurse leader, you fulfilled the important role of screening applicants thoroughly. You, yourself, are satisfied that the candidate is worthy of hiring. Generally, if anyone on the interview panel recommends that the candidate *not* be hired, the candidate is not hired. If you as the nurse leader have appropriately screened candidates, there will never be a time you need to disagree with the team's recommendation. Remember, your goal is not only to get the best employee for the job, but also a person whom everyone can set up for success. (Beware: Not honoring the recommendation of the peer panel is disrespectful of the team and will undermine it.)

Second, you pick and train only top performers to be part of the peer interview group. After all, high performers want to work with other such people and will have the greatest expectations and standards for the candidate. If possible, select peers who will be working most closely with the person or even staff from another department who will interact often with the potential employee.

Note that the nurse leader does **not** participate in a peer interview; this gives the candidate an opportunity to interact freely with staff and ask candid questions about the position.

Set your peer team up for success with training. They should know how to interview asking behavioral-based questions (just as you did), how to listen using the EAR model, and what constitutes illegal questions. The group should meet in advance and agree about critical requirements of the job. Plus everyone should have a copy of the job description from your Human Resources Department. At that time, the team also decides who will "own" certain behavioral-based questions during the peer interview. For example, one person might concentrate on communication skills while another chooses teamwork, and so on.

Training Peer Interview Team Members

You will want to instruct your peer panel on how to conduct a successful interview. Teach them the following steps:

1. First, establish rapport with the candidate and put the person at ease by smiling and making eye contact.

2. Explain that you will be taking notes so as not to forget any information.

3. Begin asking your pre-arranged behavioral-based questions about past performance and skills. These questions will explore how the candidate performed in real situations previously, so that team

members can evaluate how she will handle similar scenarios in their department.

4. If necessary, probe to clarify misunderstandings. Open-ended phrases such as the following are a great help.
   - Tell me about a time...
   - Describe a situation...
   - Tell us exactly how you dealt with...
   - It will help if you can describe in more detail...
   - Think of a specific time you...and then tell us step by step how you handled it.

5. After asking the question, actively **listen** and concentrate on the reply. Allow for silence if the candidate needs time to think. After all, behavioral-based questions can be difficult and she is most likely nervous. Resist the temptation to fill the silence and "help" the candidate.

6. If the individual is delivering a one-sided impression, try to strike a balance. Everyone has weaknesses as well as strengths, and the candidate should be encouraged to share both so that the team has the full picture.

7. Let the candidate ask questions. (We have found that potential employees who take the time to learn about the organization prior to the interview usually prove to be more successful.) Remember, the objective is to not only discover the right person for the job but also for the candidate to determine if the position is a fit.

8. Close the interview graciously. This is an important part of the process because you want to leave a good impression in the candidate's mind whether or not that person is hired. Remember, the applicant will be talking about your organization to friends and acquaintances, so be sure to include the following courtesies.
   - Thank the individual for taking the time to meet with you.
   - Be sure your closing comments don't imply that you definitely intend to hire the candidate.
   - Summarize what will happen next and when the candidate will hear back from you one way or another.

9. Complete your evaluation of the candidate immediately using the peer interview decision matrix and deliver the paperwork to the nurse leader.

Figure 6.7

Peer Interview Decision Matrix

Interviewer: ______________________ **Position:** ______________________

Core Competencies	Candidate 1	Candidate 2	Candidate 3
1.			
2.			
3.			
4.			
5.			
Total All Competency Scores:			
Would Recommend for Hire?	Yes/No	Yes/No	Yes/No

While it is preferable that the interview team meets the candidate all together, sometimes this is not possible due to shifts and schedules. Thus phone and individual interviews are sometimes necessary. Regardless, each candidate for a position (there are typically several to be interviewed) should be asked the same questions so as to ensure a level playing field. In addition, at the conclusion of the interview, team members should not consult one another and discuss their impressions. This could result in pressure to hire a particular person.

Legal and Illegal Questions

Prior to a peer interview, the nurse leader should ensure that team members are familiar with legal and illegal questions. Stress that the queries are always centered *on job performance*. The goal is to hire the candidate who possesses the core skills, one who will thrive in the organization's culture, and whose own needs are met by the job and the work environment.

In other words, the question is **not**, "You mentioned you have 28 children. How in the world will you manage to go to work every day?" Instead, "We work 7 a.m. to 7 p.m. shifts. Can you be here every day you're assigned during that time period?" Likewise, if your department is a relationship-oriented culture, tell the peer interview team that asking, "What year did you graduate?" may sound friendly, but could be used to discriminate on the basis of age; it *cannot be asked*. In general, any question not directly related to the performance of the job leaves the organization vulnerable to legal action.

Don't ask candidates:

- Age or anything that would indicate it
- Anything about marital status or sexual preference
- Whether they have children or the children's ages
- Whether they've ever filed for Workers' Compensation
- If they've ever been arrested
- Where they were born or live
- Questions relating to citizenship
- How long they've lived in a particular location
- Anything about their child care arrangements
- Whether they have a disability
- Anything about church or religion
- Questions relating to politics or organizational affiliations
- What kind of car they drive, or anything relating to their credit rating or financial status
- Their maiden name

A Few Tips for Engaging Staff

- Emphasize that the whole department's/unit's support is critical to the success of the peer interview team. After all, staff must cover for that group while it interviews and chooses the best fit for the job. In the end, everyone will benefit!

- Involve the peer interview team upfront in determining the competencies for each position.
- Make being a peer interviewer a reward and recognition opportunity.

Peer Interviewing Benefits Staff and Employees Alike.

Using peer interviewing in the selection process engages and empowers staff members. They "buy-in" to the process because you've shown them you value their perceptions and knowledge. In addition, the opportunity for staff to be involved in decisions affecting the work environment is one of the most frequently identified opportunities for improvement on employee satisfaction surveys. Peer interviewing also fosters friendships, team cohesiveness, and high morale.

Potential employees benefit, too. A candidate who is selected through the peer interview process gains built-in mentors invested in setting her up for success. Plus, applicants have the privilege of hearing firsthand about the job they are seeking. They learn about the position from those who are involved daily in providing care. They are able to ask specific questions and address concerns. In return, they receive answers from those in the best position to provide information. Finally, the peer interview process gives candidates an introduction to high performance team members and their diverse personalities. Thus, potential employees can judge for themselves whether or not they would be comfortable with future coworkers.

Peer Interviewing: A Quick Summary for Nurse Leaders

1. Select high performers to serve on the peer interview team.

2. Identify the key skills, knowledge, and expectations for the position.

3. Train the group on the behavioral-based interviewing technique, how to actively listen, and the steps involved in conducting a successful session. They should also be familiar with the organization's hiring process.

4. Instruct the peer team to meet prior to the interview to identify its behavioral- based questions; determine who will ask each question.

5. Provide team members with the peer decision matrix used to evaluate each candidate and rank that person based on responses received.

6. Extend a job offer to the applicant recommended by the peer interview team.

The First 90 Days

Once the best candidate is hired, the work of retaining him begins. The first steps in retention are to thank the employee for selecting your organization, make him feel welcome, and reassure him that he's made a good decision. Think about the last major non-work decision you made. Perhaps you purchased a car or signed the mortgage on a new home. If you were like most of us, underneath the excitement was the subtle yet nagging "buyer's remorse" thought, *Did I make the right decision?* Likewise, new employees often ask themselves, *Is this the right job for me? Will I like the work environment? My coworkers? My boss?*

Start your relationship with a new staff member by exercising a few key tactics. First, send a thank-you note to his home expressing gratitude for choosing your organization and conveying your excitement about working with him. This is a great way to begin your relationship!

Second, during the new employee's first day in the department, convey that you've scheduled a time for the two of you to meet af-

A Great First Impression

I remember accepting my job with Studer Group® five years ago like it was yesterday. I was still working for my previous employer and came home to a bouquet of flowers and a note from Quint Studer, CEO and founder of Studer Group, and BG Porter, president, welcoming me to the team and thanking me for making the choice to work for the company. As you might expect, I felt great about my decision and so did my family. This very simple and visible display created a great first impression and reaffirmed my choice to work for the group. You don't have to send flowers, but a note sent to the new hire's home conveying thanks for choosing your organization and your excitement about working with the new employee will do much for beginning your relationship.

—Colleen Thornburgh

ter the first 30 and 90 days on the job. Remember, new employees are an excellent source of heretofore unknown information and ideas. They also bring a fresh set of eyes to how your department operates. Spacing meetings at the 30- and 90-day marks is an excellent way to capture this valuable information as well as check in with new employees to see how they're doing. You'll be able to give and receive feedback, thus fostering a professional relationship of trust and communication.

Conducted casually in a private location, your 30-day meeting should be structured around the following questions:

1. Is the position/job what you expected? Did we clearly communicate the role and responsibilities during the interview process? (Identify win or process improvement opportunities.)

2. Who has been helpful to you these past 30 days? (Opportunity to recognize staff.)

3. Do you have the tools, information, and resources you need to successfully perform your job? Is there anything you need from me?

4. What ideas do you have from your past experience that might work here? (Gather new concepts; harvest intellectual capital.)

5. Is there any reason you would consider leaving our organization?

Why would you ask a new employee if there is any reason he would consider leaving? It's simple: If you don't ask, you don't know. Any opportunity to identify defects in your hiring or on-boarding process gives you the chance to be responsive and perhaps keep a good hire. Consider this an opportunity for service recovery; remember that a service recovery situation handled well is more likely to be positively remembered than just a good experience.

At your 90-day meeting, repeat your 30-day conversation, but also follow up on suggestions for improvement that were given at the first meeting and add one more question: "Do you know of any candidates you would recommend working at our organization?" After all, there's no better source of new talent than the employees working for you. And if the new staff member suggests someone, this presents the nurse leader with the opportunity to send a thank-you note to that staff person's home.

What is accomplished by the 30- and 90-day meeting technique? You create a pathway for open and honest communication, the first step in fostering a long-term relationship with a new employee. And ultimately you reduce turnover and raise morale, both of which not only benefit your organization financially but have a powerful positive impact on clinical outcomes.

> **Tip:** The 30- and 90-Day New Employee Retention Meetings template, available at www.firestarterpublishing.com/NurseLeaderHandbook, will help you structure your conversations.

So Why Don't We Do a Better Job of Selecting and Retaining?

Clearly, the selection and retention process we've outlined in this chapter pays off in tangible and often dramatic ways. So why don't more leaders embrace it? We find that quite often leaders believe the process is too involved. They are reluctant to expend the time to conduct in-depth behavioral interviews or train a peer interviewing team. However, in truth, the values far outweigh the time involved.

The nurse leader must ask herself, *Do I want to hire the right person the first time out, or spend even more time in the future re-hiring for the same position?* Quite simply, investing in the process upfront with the recommended techniques will bring success. You'll be pleased with the quality of your new staff person, and that individual will be loyal and meet all your expectations.

Key Points in This Chapter

1. Who you hire is one of the most important decisions a nurse leader makes. It has financial and clinical implications.

2. A comprehensive approach to selection and retention increases the leader's hiring success. By including peer interviewing in the process, a nurse leader can engage and empower staff members and help potential candidates determine if this is the right job for them.

3. Use a five-part approach:
    1. Prescreen for standards of behavior.

2. Conduct behavioral interview for knowledge, skills, and experience.

3. Use peer interviewing to confirm skills and ensure fit for work environment.

4. Start retention when the offer is extended…thank the candidate for selecting your organization.

5. Use 30- and 90-day meetings to build a professional relationship of trust and communication.

Pillars Affected by Selecting Talent

Service—The right staff fosters high patient and physician satisfaction.

Quality—Retention is associated with lower mortality and decreased length of stay.

Finance—Hiring costs are reduced with low turnover.

People—Selection process increases employee satisfaction and decreases turnover.

Growth—Enhanced recruitment of top performers enables program expansion.

CHAPTER 7

Developing the Healthcare Team

By Jackie Gaines and Lyn Ketelsen

The large string, woodwind, and percussion sections line the music theater's stage in anticipation of the arrival of their leader, who will guide them through another successful performance. The symphony orchestra is almost 100 musicians strong—each one counted on to do his or her part to exceed the expectations of the audience.

The curtain rises, and the conductor takes his place, baton in hand. Each musician finds individual focus and, with a wave of the baton, the combined skills of all these well-trained professionals bring *Beethoven's Symphony No. 5* to life.

The performance seems to go well to the untrained ear; however, the conductor is aware of challenges with the choral brass section, essential to the finale of Beethoven's historic symphony. He notes, "Rehearsals, more practice, and training are required. Precise execution is essential for excellence. It is the expectation for our performance."

Sound familiar? It should. In healthcare, we are counted on every day to execute the highest quality of care required to save lives, and to do so with the combined precision of many trained professionals. Effective leaders guide us in our processes and actions to achieve the targeted results.

And, like the audience who listens to a symphony, our patients also expect us to exceed their expectations for care.

Of course, a flawless performance is easier asked for than delivered! People enter our workforce with varying degrees of training and experience, and this diversity can often directly impact the precision of our execution and the quality of patient care. Development needs also evolve over time. What an employee needs early in her career may be very different from what's needed after 10 years of experience.

In terms of our orchestra analogy, the sheet music may be entirely different, requiring new skills of the musician. The instruments may change as well.

It is imperative for leaders to constantly evaluate the development needs of their workforce and offer guidance, training, and support. Like the conductor said, "Precise execution is essential for excellence." In healthcare, of course, the stakes are higher.

> A poorly executed symphony may bother the sensibilities of sophisticated audience members. A poorly executed medical procedure, on the other hand, can lead to serious illness, injury, or even death. When you hold patients' lives in the palm of your hand, poor performance is unacceptable.

This chapter will explore the importance of staff development and mentorship in nursing. It offers key strategies for nurse leaders to conduct their organization's healthcare orchestra.

Two Approaches to Staff Development

Nurse leaders can approach staff development in a variety of ways, both informal and formal. All approaches require the leader to actively engage with the workforce, constantly evaluating competencies and offering opportunities for professional development. This process can be ***proactive*** or ***reactive***.

Proactive Development

A proactive approach is preferred. This means the nurse leader looks ahead at the needs of the organization as well as examining the learning needs that best position employees for success. High performers in the organization will actually seek out professional development opportunities, often asking for mentorship or additional training to advance their careers. Middle performers will wait to be pushed toward the opportunity, and low performers don't think it's necessary at all. It's best for nurse leaders to focus resources on the high and middle performers for development and training. Very few low performers will turn the corner and see the benefit of growing.

Reactive Development

The reactive approach usually occurs after unacceptable performance on the part of staff, which forces a nurse leader to closely examine employees' skills. (Hopefully, this performance problem doesn't involve an untoward event with a patient.) However, we are all human and subject to times when our execution and delivery need improvement. Those open to learning will improve to the level of precision required. Still, if proactive development is practiced, the likelihood of reactive development being needed is greatly reduced.

Tough Decisions in Staff Development

An example of a proactive approach to implementing staff development came when I was managing the Neonatal Intensive Care Unit (NICU). We were in the process of changing from a Level I to a Level II and hiring an in-house neonatologist. We also were seeking to be accredited as a specialty unit by The Joint Commission.

This involved a big change for the staff: In the past, they were allowed to choose either NICU or the newborn nursery on a daily basis, but now they would be committed to one or the other. All of this was a huge undertaking, mostly because the skill level of the NICU staff was going to increase with more frequent ventilator patients and care of sicker babies. As such, their development plan needed to be in place and executed well. Some people were not selected for the NICU because overall we felt they didn't have the skill set needed in the new environment. While these decisions were hard and meant disappointing some of the staff, they were the right decisions for patient quality and safe care.

—Lyn Ketelsen

Lesson Learned the Hard Way

Early in my career, when I was working in a Pediatric Unit, I learned an important "reactive" lesson that shaped me as a future nurse leader. At the time, when a baby was admitted it was not unusual to rule out sepsis by administering the antibiotics Ampicillin and Gentamicin. The intravenous dose of the latter medication requires lab levels to be drawn to ensure therapeutic levels are maintained; toxic symptoms such as deafness can occur with overdose.

It was a very busy night on the unit and I failed to correctly measure the amount of Gentamicin I gave a baby, inadvertently resulting in an overdose. I didn't know it at the time. The next day my nurse leader called me in and confronted me with a litany of questions regarding the dosing of that infant.

I answered all the questions honestly. Mostly, I just admitted I had not maintained good medication administration practices. As you can imagine, I was devastated to learn that my error had the potential to cause harm. However, the good news was that while the Gentamicin level in the infant was high, there was no untoward effect. While this was comforting to the parents, it shook me to my nursing core. My leader had a full, one-page document written up of the corrective action plan I would undertake based on my error.

Interestingly, I was not involved in creating that plan; further, nothing on it would have prevented me from making the same mistake again. So I created my own plan. I asked a peer to double-check each medication I gave for the next 30 days to ensure I was focused on good administration practices. I was fortunate to work with a committed team willing to invest in my success, and I was smart enough to know that my embarrassment and pain would force me to learn better habits for the future.

Reactive lessons are learned the hard way. But I am proud to say I did not make another medication error during the rest of my clinical practice career.

—Lyn Ketelsen

The Benefits of Mentoring

Staff development and mentoring have a lot in common. They're both part of building a strong healthcare team, and they both involve helping individuals advance their careers. However, while the former is more an "official" path, the latter is more casual and, sometimes, deeply personal. Yes, mentoring does help the healthcare orchestra give a stellar performance, but it also helps the individual "musician" find a level of richness and fulfillment in his role that transcends what he would typically gain from a classroom.

What *is* mentoring, anyway? Here's an official definition:

"Mentoring is a process for the informal transmission of knowledge, social capital, and the psychosocial support perceived by the recipient as relevant to work, career, or professional development; mentoring entails informal communication, usually face-to-face and during a sustained period of time, between a person who is perceived to have greater relevant knowledge, wisdom, or experience (the mentor) and a person who is perceived to have less (the protégé)."[1]

As a nurse leader, it's your responsibility to intentionally mentor your direct reports. You can fulfill that role for staff directly or facilitate a connection to others with advanced knowledge. Even though the term "mentoring" is not always used, it is the foundation of staff development, preceptor programs, and the effective transmission of knowledge. Mentoring also fosters relationships that will lead to strong teamwork.

Mentoring takes time. And in the face of constrained staffing resources, it's often looked upon as an expendable activity. This is unfortunate, indeed. Research shows that employees who are paired with a mentor are twice as likely to remain in their job as those who do not receive mentorship.[2] And my guess is there isn't a nurse leader today who would deny the enhanced effectiveness of a staff that has received training or development. It's like making a deposit in your bank account and seeing the interest earned over time. Investing in employees yields a positive return.

New Hire Mentorship: Preceptors

As new nurses enter your organization, time should be allotted for their development and integration into the work culture. Even nurses who are experienced need a period of acclimation. Do you take the time to give clinicians the foundation they need for success—or are they thrown into the fire because they're desperately needed warm bodies? If it's the latter, please don't wonder why they leave within the first six months, or are not performing to your precise expectations.

> If you have invested resources into a new nurse for your department, it is imperative to set him up for success. Don't short-change the time needed for early mentorship; it will actually be more cost effective to retain the new hire than to start the recruitment process all over again. Pair your new nurse with a high performer who can offer information, good examples, and advice. This pairing will actually serve two purposes: a) mentorship and b) leadership development for the high performer. As a nurse leader, you should evaluate both roles in the relationship as it progresses.

The time frame for formal new employee mentorship programs will vary based on the needs of the employee and the department. Six to eight weeks may be the norm on a Medical/Surgical Unit, whereas Surgical Departments may require six months. Regardless, use a disciplined, objective approach in evaluating progress on expected competencies and offer ongoing feedback to the newcomer.

It's important to stay in constant communication with the mentor and new hire, offering your support and guidance as needed. The use of a unit-specific competency checklist during your conversations is the best way to review progress to date. It also gives new nurses the opportunity to see required expectations, to know where they stand, and to learn the most important areas of focus for improvement.

Don't assume all high performers automatically know how to be mentors. Having a job description for the role may help to define the expectations of the relationship. In addition, nurse leaders may need to guide mentors in their approach to the process.

At the end of the designated time frame, the mentor and mentee may decide to continue the relationship. They have discovered the value of working with each other in a collegial environment of learning. And together they have participated in developing a strong, vital, successful healthcare team. It doesn't get any better than that!

High Potential Mentorship

Throughout most of our careers and lives, we have had the privilege of having a variety of mentors. Often they were leaders of the organizations we worked for or community leaders who saw something in us long before we saw it in ourselves. It's safe to say we would not have achieved the remarkable success we've enjoyed in our careers without their foresight and encouragement. As a nurse leader, you can help others enjoy the same "leg up" that we did.

"High potential mentoring" is used to groom up-and-coming employees deemed capable of moving up into leadership roles. Here the employee (mentee) is paired with a senior-level leader (or leaders) for a series of career-coaching interactions. However, a mentor does not have to be a manager or supervisor to facilitate the process.

Nurse leaders are in a unique position to see the potential in their staff members every day. High performers who rise to the top are often already looking ahead to the next career phase. You could help clarify their goals, advance their skills, and open doors to their futures. You never know where your actions could take them. In addition, professional development and mentorship for high performers keeps them engaged and energized in their work. You can also help them become excellent mentors for middle performers.

We also can't end this section without discussing your role in identifying mentors for yourself and your own professional growth and development as a leader. This might be someone in your organization in the same role as you, but it could also be a person in a position you aspire to. As a leader—especially if you are high performing—you will need to take responsibility for your own development. Seek out others who can assist you in areas in which you feel you need additional training.

Tools for Staff Development and Training

So we've established that developing the healthcare team is of critical importance. But how, exactly, do you achieve that? It depends!

Staff development can mean offering forums to nurses for continuous quality improvement of patient care. It includes an evaluation of their individual competencies, assessment of learning needs, and actions to enhance their knowledge base. The end result is an improvement in daily practices.

Staff development might also mean promoting the pursuit of formal academic education or professional certification, both of which are vital to the department or the organization's operations.

Even in tough economic times, opportunities for staff development may be right in front of you. Most organizations have a wealth of talent within their own walls that goes untapped. Learning can come from a variety of sources; journal clubs, Nursing Grand Rounds, and case presentations from physician leaders can tide you over until resources become available for external experiences. All you have to do is ask.

Here are a few examples of tools nurse leaders can use to help develop their staff members:

Journey of a "Portland Trailblazer"

Initially it was my nurse manager who served as my mentor, offering me the opportunity to grow into a charge nurse role. As years passed and my skills improved, a nursing supervisor reached out to me with encouragement to apply for a nurse manager role. Unbeknownst to me, she had been following my career since my arrival at the hospital. After I was appointed to the nurse manager role, she offered continued support and guidance even though I did not directly report to her.

This scenario repeated itself on many different occasions. The one I remember the most is a board member who first encouraged me to advance to the CEO role at an area non-profit hospital. He assured me that one day I would be a CEO. I remember laughing and saying, "Nurses just don't make it that far up the food chain in healthcare." But he replied that I had what it took to be a leader in the healthcare industry.

In 2000, I was appointed the first minority female to ever run a hospital in Portland, Oregon. They called me a real "Portland Trailblazer." In 2007, I was appointed the regional president and CEO of a health system in northeast Pennsylvania. Wow… who would have thought! The fact is, somebody *did* think, and it was a leader.

—Jackie Gaines

The Selection Process

A leader should get a sense of a nurse's development needs at the very beginning of their relationship. Targeted questions during employee selection will offer a baseline of competencies required for the job. If that person is hired, the nurse leader should document her learning needs for future discussions and plan for how those requisites will be met.

Leader Rounding

Rounding on staff helps nurse leaders validate competencies in action. It also gives you the opportunity to intervene as appropriate, to teach, and to offer feedback in real time. Again, documentation will help you to track individual progress and look across your area of responsibility for trends. These trends could form the basis for staff in-services or other learning laboratories to advance the whole staff or to focus on a small group of individuals with special learning needs.

Thank-You Notes

When you take the time to compose and mail a thank-you note to the employee's home recognizing personal achievement, you will harvest several good things: a staff that "gets" the importance of professional development, employee engagement in further development opportunities, and loyal nurses who think highly of you for the recognition.

Annual Evaluations and Retention Discussions

Professional development goals can often be incorporated into annual evaluations. What better time to reinforce your interest in staff's success? Retention discussions are another vehicle for talking about the value of development. The opportunity to learn and advance is important to employees, particularly the high performers who often need re-recruiting. Remember, active and intentional development yields far better results than reactive efforts.

The Value of Team Building

Having a team that is mutually respectful of each other and genuinely enjoys working together is a real bonus for any leader. The energy is usually more positive and operational results soar. However, even though most of us spend 36 to 40 hours or more a week at work, there isn't always time to bond into a cohesive team. It's ironic that we sometimes spend more time with our co-workers than with our families, yet these relationships stay very close to the surface.

Usually, the most powerful bonding occurs off-hours in an informal atmosphere. Such events offer everyone involved a chance to learn more about their coworkers. Most employees enjoy the camaraderie that glues the group together into a real team. This social network helps to decrease stress and to increase teamwork. Nurse leaders cannot force these types of opportunities, since their staff are "off the clock." But, never underestimate the power of an annual team picnic or potluck dinner to take your team to a whole new level of engagement.

Of course, you don't have host a picnic to strengthen your team. You just need to integrate a few key principles into your leadership style:

- Role model cross-department collaboration. Silo thinking leads to waste and duplication of resources. For more information on this subject, read "Creating a Culture of Cross-Department Collaboration" by Jackie Gaines at www.firestarterpublishing.com/NurseLeaderHandbook.
- Facilitate discussions and activities that cultivate a shared vision for the work.
- Acknowledge that every member of the team is valued with an important role to play, even if those roles are different.
- Keep in mind that mutual respect is an essential element of an effective team.
- Insist that all members have input into team goals. When participation is encouraged, acceptance is greater, even if there is not unanimous agreement. Most of the time, people just want to have a voice and be heard.
- Be sure your team measures the outcomes as related to the goals, and identifies the processes that were or were not effective in reaching the outcomes.
- Always take the time to reward and recognize team success. This reinforces the desired behavior for the future.

Remember, it takes more time and energy to undo conflict and mistrust than to take the time to build an effective team.

Remember...Staff Development and Team Building Are Investments.

Budget constraints, shifting priorities, and available time can place staff development on the endangered list. Often, leaders are happy when they can send just one or two nurses a year to a conference or educational event. But in our rapidly changing environment, nurses must constantly be progressing and growing in the skills they need for success. Staff development cannot be expendable or viewed as extra, but rather as an investment. The results will be three-fold: employee engagement, staff satisfaction, and improved quality of patient care.

Team building efforts, likewise, should not be neglected. Fortunately, many team building tools are inexpensive or even free. Yes, it

Team Building Exercises for Nurse Leaders

Exercise 1: What's In, What's Out. Post two sheets of paper labeled "What's In" and "What's Out." Ask your team to give examples of what kinds of behavior will bring staff members together and help them accomplish team goals. Write them down.

Examples for "What's In" might include discussing issues directly with a person, rather than talking behind her back. Its opposite, gossiping, would go on the "What's Out" sheet. Later, you can keep these lists in your unit and display them in all staff meetings.

Have staff share examples of people who practice "What's In" behavior. The public recognition will reinforce the positive behavior and encourage others to adopt it as well.

Exercise 2: Put in a Good Word. Ask every member of your team to write his or her name at the top of a piece of paper. Then, ask people to pass the sheets around the room. Ask everyone to write something nice about the person whose name appears at the top of the paper. At the end of the meeting, everyone will leave with a list of all their good traits—and they'll feel better about themselves and their coworkers.

Exercise 3: Gratitude List. Ask each person to fill up a sheet of paper with a list of what he or she is grateful for. You'll find that most people run out of paper before they run out of gratitude. Keep in mind that back in 54 BC Cicero said, "Gratitude is not only the greatest of virtues, but the parent of all others."

takes time—and yes, time is in short supply these days—but there is no substitute for the power of an aligned, cohesive, engaged group of people who truly like and respect each other.

All of this underscores the importance of your role. You, the nurse leader, *are* the orchestra conductor for your department or unit of care. Their symphony is providing the highest quality of care possible for the patients served. You must seek the precision of skills from your team necessary for its success. You must always be on the lookout for exceptional talent to promote, additional learning needs, and those sour notes that have to leave the orchestra. You must make sure your team is as close-knit as possible.

Harmonious delivery is required in healthcare. Anything less is unacceptable. Investment in continuous growth and development of the orchestra is the essential sheet music. Conduct a symphony!

Key Points in This Chapter

1. Nurse leaders can approach staff development in a variety of ways, both informal and formal. Both approaches require the leader to actively engage with the workforce, constantly evaluate competencies, and provide opportunities for professional development.

2. Staff development can be both ***proactive*** and ***reactive***. A proactive approach is preferred. This means the nurse leader looks ahead at the needs of the organization as well as examining the learning needs that best position employees for success. Proactive approaches include: new hire mentoring, high potential mentoring, and staff development forums.

3. In our rapidly changing environment, nurses must constantly be progressing and growing in the skills they need for success. Staff development cannot be expendable or viewed as extra, but rather as an investment. The results will be three-fold: employee engagement, staff satisfaction, and improved quality of patient care.

4. Team building is critical. When people respect each other and genuinely enjoy working together, the positive energy benefits not only coworkers but the entire organization. Nurse leaders can hold after-hours social events, hold team building exercises, and infuse their leadership styles with principles that reduce conflict and create trust.

Pillars Affected by Staff Development and Team Building

Quality—Enhances quality of patient care due to improved execution.

Finance—Improves the bottom line due to decreased turnover.

People—Fosters employee satisfaction, engagement, and loyalty.

SECTION 2: TACTICS TO IMPLEMENT FOR BETTER PATIENT CARE

Introduction

By Lyn Ketelsen

In Section 2 we will highlight various evidence-based practices that, together, provide an excellent foundation for nursing clinical practice. Over the years, these methods have proven to be extremely valuable in improving operational efficiency and patient outcomes for hundreds of organizations. They've also successfully improved the quality and safety of the care provided, as well as ensuring that patients and family members are satisfied with the healthcare experience.

It is your role as nurse leader to implement changes that will bring about the best results for the people you serve. The most successful nursing care model is one that meets the needs of patients and families and provides evidence of positively impacting outcomes. Consistent execution of the tools described in the pages ahead will give you and your staff an outstanding platform for success.

In this section you will discover four tactics that, when all are well executed, become a solid basis for nursing care excellence. They are Hourly Rounds, Bedside Shift Report, Individualized Patient Care, and Post-Visit or Discharge Phone Calls. Cumulatively, we call them the Patient Care Model. These tactics, when executed with the full participation and engagement of competent, professional staff members, will provide a strong framework for quality patient and "family-centered" care.

We'll describe each of the tactics and suggest a sequence for implementing them.

Please approach the implementation of these ideas with a "less is more" philosophy. As coaches, we all too often find that organizations have action plans with literally dozens of initiatives in various stages of execution. As a result, leadership resources are spread so thin that nothing is implemented well—and there are no results to speak of. As you read our book, keep this in mind and choose carefully what you feel will bring about the best results. Resist the temptation to implement too much at one time. Implement one to two things well and then move on to the next.

Also, please understand there is some benefit to executing the tactics in the sequence in which we've presented them. Still, there can be some variance, so don't worry about changing the order if you feel there's a compelling need to do so. As the leader, you have to determine the right sequence for your unit. Just be sure you focus on one tactic at a time. Less is more!

CHAPTER 8

Nurse Leader Rounding on Patients

By Lyn Ketelsen

As a nurse leader, you work hard to ensure the care provided is meeting the quality and satisfaction needs of patients. This is your primary role and is truly a noble calling. There is no better way to find out if you are serving patients well than to ask them directly! This is where the process of rounding on patients comes in.

In Chapter 2 you read about rounding on staff members. You learned how to ask staff members specific questions one-on-one in order to get actionable information. Rounding on patients works in much the same way.

This tactic allows you as a leader to connect with patients to reinforce care, verify nursing behaviors, and recognize staff members who go above and beyond the call of duty. Rounding is one of the most important actions you can implement. But make no mistake: It's far from easy.

At first it will unearth process improvement opportunities and require that you spend additional time rewarding and recognizing. It will also force you to deal with sub-par performers. In other words, rounding creates more work upfront. But once you've been at it for awhile—after processes have been improved, systems are working well, and sub-par performers have been dealt with—you'll find it takes much less time and becomes one of the most enjoyable parts of your job.

It will allow you to connect with patients, which is probably why you went into nursing in the first place.

The results below indicate the powerful effect that nurse leader rounding has on patients' perception of the care provided. In the first example, you see the difference in the percentile rank of patients who were rounded on during their stay versus those who were not.

Figure 8.1

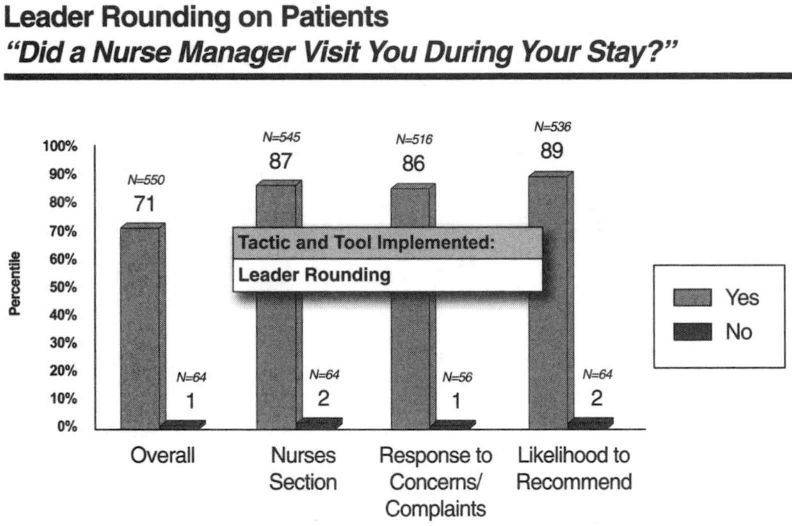

Source: Arizona Hospital, Total beds = 355, Employees = 4,000, Admissions = 10,188, 4Q08 Data

Figure 8.2

Leader Rounding on Patients
"Did a Nurse Manager Visit You During Your Stay?"

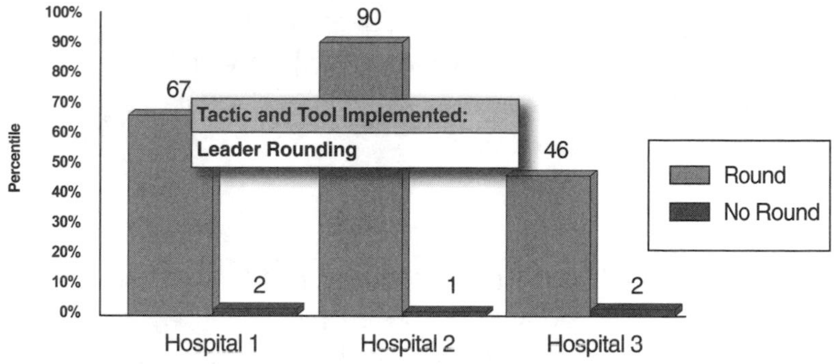

Source: Aug 2009, New York Hospital, Total beds = 1,094, Employees > 4,000 employees, Admissions = 65,908

Next, let's take a look at the improved results an organization saw in its overall ranking after implementing nurse leader rounding.

Figure 8.3

Leader Rounding
Customer Perception Overall Ranking

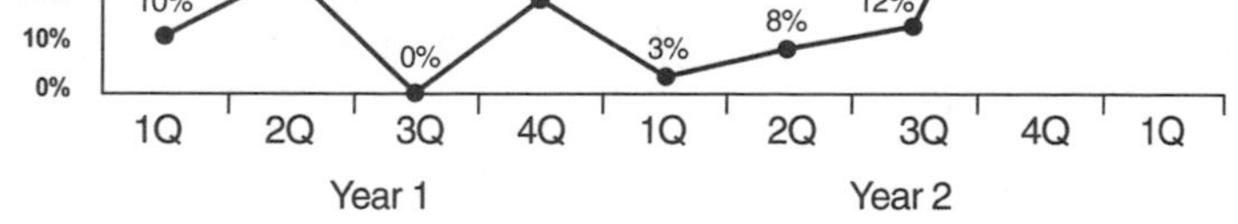

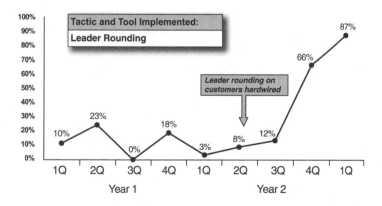

Source: Virginia Organization, Admissions: 16,776, Bed size: 330, >1,600 employees, Employees=1,652

And it's not just patients who benefit. Physicians also appreciate the impact of rounding. Because it enhances patients' perception of the care they're receiving, doctors receive fewer complaints and make better use of their time. They also see better clinical quality of care due to nurse leader interventions.

As a frontline nurse leader, you'll be the person "on the ground" implementing the rounding process. You will eventually be able to delegate this and get others involved, but it is best to start the process yourself and maintain an active role until it is well defined.

Establishing a Rounding Discipline

How do you establish a rounding discipline? The following sequence of steps will help you accomplish this.

1. Prior to implementing rounding, obtain buy-in by introducing its value to the chief executive officer (CEO) and senior team. The results they can expect to see include opportunities for employee recognition (which ups the potential for improved retention), heightened perception of care by patients, better quality outcomes, increased market share, enhanced safety, and reduced risk. Knowing the value this evidence-based tactic brings to the organization also reinforces what leadership needs to do when there is a lack of compliance. Let senior leaders know how you plan to introduce and hardwire rounding as well.

2. Work with senior nursing leaders on what to expect and how they can help in the process. This step is critical. They need to not only understand how they can be supportive, but also their bigger role as change agents to make it happen. By sharing information from rounding logs (See Step 5, on the following page)—for instance, by managing up good experiences and recognizing staff members who were mentioned favorably by patients—they can reinforce wins and manage up the value of this tactic to the senior team.

3. Implement "no meeting times." Many nurse leaders find that not having to attend meetings in the morning for a couple of hours eliminates the "time" barrier and sends a message about rounding's importance to the organization. Many leaders have found that initially their perception is, *How can we ever have the time to do this?* But it's very

short-lived; leaders quickly realize that nothing is more important than being with their patients and staff through rounding.

4. Review patient satisfaction results by unit level and post them. Educate staff on the elements of the measurement tool that rounding will have the most impact on.

5. Introduce the rounding log. Every day, senior nursing leaders should know the total patients in each unit and the number of rounds completed. Compile a weekly percentage of rounds completed by unit, as well as throughout the entire hospital.

6. The chief nursing officer (CNO) and CEO each receive a weekly report with the percentage of rounds completed by unit.

Don Dean: Lessons I've Learned About Nurse Leader Rounding

The following is excerpted from an email written by Don Dean, one of Studer Group's most seasoned coaches.

It's been 16 years since Quint and I began this journey at Holy Cross Hospital, Chicago, IL, and I'd like to share with you some lessons learned along that journey, a bit of history, and some must haves in hardwiring nurse leader rounding.

In 1993 Quint and I were looking at the service results at Holy Cross Hospital and noticed that one of the nursing units was much higher than all the other units. (Michelle Walsko was the nursing leader.) Quint said, "I wonder what Michelle is doing differently? One thing's for sure: We are not sending all the nice patients to one unit, so she must be doing something."

It was then that I received my first assignment: to follow Michelle for about a week and to see what she was doing differently to warrant the high perception of care by her patients. (I was very good at my job and I followed Michelle to the point that she said, "I am going to the bathroom now, so you can stop right here.") Anyway, I noticed that she went into every patient's room every day and said, "Hi, I am Michelle. I am the nursing director on this unit and my job is to make sure that we take great care of you." I also noticed that when she said that her patients relaxed and really began to open up.

Michelle didn't spend a long time in every patient's room—maybe about five minutes—but that was part of her daily routine. She went on to ask her patients, "How are we doing? Are we managing your pain? Is my staff doing a good job of keeping you informed about what's going on?" I also noticed that when she received good feedback about a staff member she went out and found them and complimented that person right away. She was also noticing and assessing the care that was being provided and coaching her staff to higher performance.

I also noticed how much her staff respected her and trusted her. My thought at the time was that her employees were very aware that Michelle was going to round every day, and they were almost beating her to the rooms to make sure everything was done well. My biggest lesson: When a leader is checking and monitoring performance, performance improves.

I talked with several physicians who visited Michelle's unit and they shared with me that they really liked it when their patients were sent to her floor. They knew their patients were going to receive great care—that Michelle was very visible and if they had an issue they could always go to her and it would be resolved. The docs appreciated and respected Michelle's visibility and responsiveness.

Overall, I noticed that there seemed to be a harmony on the unit. It just seemed to work like a well-oiled machine. People were happy—they were working hard but there was a general sense of happiness and there was a sense great care was being provided. We then tried what Michelle did on her unit on all the units, which led to our breakthrough performance at Holy Cross.

Getting Started: How to Round on Patients

When you begin rounding, it's important to remember what you're trying to accomplish right from the start. You want to connect with patients, make sure you're meeting their needs, and recognize staff members who are going above and beyond the call of duty (as well as those who are not).

When you first get started, you might set the goal of rounding on every patient once during his or her stay. Eventually, however, if you want to see the biggest returns, you'll want to round on every patient, every day.

Don't worry: Unlike employee rounds, which cannot be delegated, you can recruit others to assist with patient rounds. In many cases, charge nurses or supervisors can help you accomplish this task.

However, you shouldn't delegate something you've never done yourself; so it's best if you initiate this task first, gaining a solid understanding of the process and what's involved before asking others.

Prepare the Right Questions.

Before you begin rounding on patients, prepare by deciding what questions you will ask. Remember, your purpose is to ensure that expectations are being met and quality care is being provided. Yet you need to balance this goal with efficiency in the interest of time. Build your questions based on the patient's needs and concerns and also to verify nursing skills.

For example, if I'm an orthopedic nurse manager speaking with a patient who has had total knee replacement, I will focus on pain management as opposed to food or housekeeping. These patients care about pain above all else. If I'm the OB nurse manager, I know patients are worried about going home, so I will ask about any questions or concerns they have about caring for the baby once they are home.

> **Tip:** Prior to rounding on patients, a nurse leader should first talk with staff. Let them know that you are going to round on patients and ask if there is anything you should know. This will help you be better prepared and will demonstrate teamwork. If the patient has just suffered terrible news, for example, it is helpful for a nurse leader to know of it ahead of time. It will also reduce patient anxiety and increase her confidence to feel that her nurses and the nurse leader are on the same page regarding her care.

Being specific in how you word questions is the key to getting actionable and valuable information. Too many times nurse leaders fall into the trap of asking age-old, "nurse-y" questions like, "How are you feeling?" or "How has the care been?" You're opening a Pandora's Box when you do this! You have no idea what you're going to get, and once you ask the question, you have to respond to whatever the patient says. This is when your efficiency—and, in many cases, your effectiveness—goes out the window. So be strategic in the way you ask for feedback; this guarantees you get really good information and still manage to complete rounds.

Use Questions Strategically.

The framework of your questions should be dynamic—that is, designed around the initiative you're focusing on to improve care for patients. Ask questions designed to test whether the things you have asked the staff to do are actually being done and having the impact you would expect. Many nurse leaders ask, "Why focus on only one or two things?" This is where the philosophy of "less is more" plays out. You should be implementing just one or two projects at a time, thus allowing you to make the most of your resources. That's where real hardwired success comes from.

For example, if I am working on managing pain, I introduce myself, then ask the following questions:

> Greeting: Hi, Mr. Johnson, I'm Renee Clark. I'm the nurse manager on this unit. I'm going to write my name and number on your whiteboard so you can access me at any time. We want to make sure that while you are here you are very satisfied with your care. If there's anything we can do to make you more satisfied, let us know.
>
> Question One: Mr. Johnson, I see Sara is your nurse today and has her name on the whiteboard. She is an excellent nurse and will take great care of you. She has been with us for 10 years and is one of the best. (Note that by doing this I'm managing up staff members.) "We want to make sure that your pain is managed. In the last 24 hours have you needed to use your call light to request pain medication?" This question is designed to test whether the staff is effectively addressing the three Ps, one of which is pain (potty and position are the other two). If nurses are proactively asking about pain, patients shouldn't need to call for medication.
>
> Question Two: Is there any staff person you've interacted with who's done a particularly nice job that I should acknowledge? I would love to share it with him or her personally. This question allows me as a nurse leader to reward positive behavior. It also focuses the patient on the positive care he has received.
>
> Closing: Thank you for your time, Mr. Johnson. Is there anything I can do for you right now? I have time. We have learned that if you don't say you have the time, patients will assume you are too busy. However, they'll hit the call light later. When you say you have

time, you reduce call lights by up to 40 percent. This closing statement also reinforces to the patient that your time and your team's time is focused on his care.

It's important that your "talking points" flow in this particular order. Structuring the conversation the same way every time will keep you on track and help you effectively manage the encounter. Also, of course, it will ensure that every patient gets a consistent experience.

Figure 8.4

Conversation Flow:
Nurse Leader Rounding on Patients

Rounding on Patients	Greeting/Introduction
	Manage Up Staff
	Question Regarding Team Focus
	Ask About Outstanding Staff
	Thank You
	"I Have Time" Closing Question

After you have completed rounding on the patients in your unit, you have two very important questions to ask yourself:

1. What have I learned about the care of my patients?

2. What must I do with this information?

You may have learned that care is being delivered at the highest level. This is a great time to immediately reward those behaviors you were verifying. Remember, rewarded behavior gets repeated. Alternately, you may have learned that there is an opportunity to improve the care being provided. There is no time like the present to coach the staff involved! Finally, you may have learned that you need to contact a leader in another department to address concerns, or add a topic to your staff meeting agenda because you are seeing a consistent gap in performance across many staff members.

Leader rounds on patients are your opportunity to get close to the action. Use these conversations with your patients to make lasting changes that will improve the care of all patients to come.

Four Goals for Leader Rounds on Patients

1. **Manage the Patient's Expectations**
   "Good morning, I am Faye Sullivan, manager on this unit. I stopped by to visit you. Is this a good time? I want to check in and make sure that you are receiving very good care. That is my expectation for all of our patients." Goal: Establish empathic, compassionate rapport.

2. **Service Recovery**
   "How well are we doing in providing care?"

3. **Harvest Recognition/ Manage Up**
   "I see XXX is your (nurse, nursing assistant, or physician)." (Manage up this professional.) "Is there anyone who stands out as having provided very good care?" If the patient says everyone has been great, then ask, "Can you give me an example of how we have provided you very good care?"

4. **Manage Staff Performance**
   Observe for/question patient about:
   Quality of care: Is the patient clean, comfortably positioned, pain free? Is staff rounding hourly? Does patient know plan of care for day? Does patient know staff members' names, etc.?
   Other shifts: Ask about nights, weekends, etc.
   Safe environment: Make sure side rails are up, floor is clear, arm band is in use, IV tubing and labeled meds are left at bedside, and whiteboards are complete. Also make sure Hourly Rounding^{SM} logs are complete and staff and MD hand washing is observed by patient.

Daily Public Recognition

"Karen, I've rounded on three of your patients today. All three know your name and their plan of care for the day. Every room is safe and clean, and whiteboards are filled out. **THANK YOU** for making it happen!"

Deal with Negative Feedback.

It would be great if all patient responses were positive, but of course the reality is they're not. In cases where you receive negative feedback, you must be prepared to switch gears depending on the strength of the reaction from the patient. If it's a minor complaint, then you apologize, convey that you'll follow up, and still proceed with the rest of your rounds. However, if the complaint comes with strong emotion and the patient is very upset, you need to switch gears from proactive rounding to service recovery. The latter will be covered in a later chapter of this section.

The key is to follow up with the patient and also address the issue. If the issue is a low-performing nurse, there are tactics covered throughout this book to help you address it. If the issue is around a process, fix it if possible, and it is likely you'll improve care for more than just this patient.

Hardwire Rounding.

Consistency, consistency, consistency. Rounding has so much impact that it is important to hardwire it into your daily routine. The best tool to manage this is the rounding log; remember, if it's not documented, it's not done. Utilizing the log is important for two reasons: staff accountability and a system to ensure that you follow up with any information gleaned during rounds. All that recognition has to be delivered, so be sure to note which staff person is deserving and then decide the form of acknowledgment you wish to use. (Note: This is a great source to help you maintain that necessary three-to-one ratio of positive to negative communication.)

Figure 8.5

Rounding on Patients Log

Parameters

- Inpatient: 100% of patients each day
- Critical Care: 100% of patients and/or families each day, 100% of patients prior to transfer from unit
- Outpatients: 25% of patients daily and 100% of new patients to episodic care settings
- Medical Practice: 100% of new patients and 100% of patients in waiting room more than 30 minutes

Key Word (excellent, very good, completely satisfied)

Area of Focus (behavior that is being hardwired)
Example: Hourly rounding, AIDET, pain management

"Our goal is to provide you with very good care, which includes rounding on you each hour to manage your pain, assure you are comfortable, and offer assistance to the bathroom. How well are we doing?"

Patient	Type	Feedback on Area of Focus Working Well (WW) or Needs Improvement (NI)	Staff	Actions		Notes
				Recognize	Coach	

Total Number of Patients: ________ Total Number Rounded On: ________ % Compliance: ________

Name: ______________________________ Date: ____________

To download a usable version of this rounding log, go to www.firestarter-publishing.com/NurseLeaderHandbook.

It also helps to hardwire rounding when you share the results of your rounding in staff meetings. Being able to say, "Last month, as a result of my rounds, I was able to deliver 47 compliments because of the great work many of you are doing" has a lot of impact. Just stating a raw number is powerful. Also be sure to share some of the great things employees have done, along with stories of positive patient feedback. This helps connect the importance and purpose of rounding to its impact on patients' lives.

Plus, if you have a low performer in the group, that employee can no longer think you don't appreciate people for the work they do or you never say "thanks." It will become very obvious to the person that it's not that you don't value staff; it's that you haven't recognized him personally. And that, of course, should ideally lead the person to ask himself what he's doing wrong.

Trust, But Verify: Certifying the Quality of Nurse Leader Rounding

If something is worth doing, it's worth doing right. And it's worth putting in a system to ensure that it's being done right. This doesn't just apply to staff. If there is an important skill leaders need to demonstrate—and rounding qualifies—then that competency needs to be validated. This means arranging for someone to shadow you and provide feedback in terms of what you did well, and what opportunities there are for rounding improvement.

Here's a best practice process for certifying the quality of nurse leader rounding:

1. Introduce skills station, with a "patient" (staff member) in the bed.

2. Leaders do the assessment and provide feedback to resource nurse or manager who rounded.

3. Another leader waits outside the room. As the person being assessed leaves the room, the evaluating leader asks her what she learned (requiring her to process the feedback and repeat it) and then asks her what she knows about the care of the patient (assessing her ability to assess the patient and the environment). Last, the leader asks what she is going to do with the info she gathered (i.e., who gets recognized and who gets coached).

4. Make it fun. In one hospital, the evaluators took "clappers" to use for the positive feedback and a buzzer to push when they gave coaching. Anyone deemed an expert was named in the hospital newsletter.

5. Nursing leadership continues to shadow leader.

Final Thoughts: The Many Reasons to Round

As with many evidence-based tactics, rounding has two elements: skill and process. If you round every single day, but fail to ask the right questions or follow up on what you hear, you will not get results. On the other hand, you can be the most skillful rounder in the world, but if you do it only once a month, you won't see an impact on your patients. This is sometimes called the "skill and will" equation. Both need to be present to achieve results. In addition, building effective accountability systems requires evidence that skill *and* process have been validated.

Rounding on patients helps you round on employees. You'll harvest reward and recognition opportunities and hear great stories you can share. Processes or systems that patients perceive as not working will also come to light.

Rounding on patients will also provide you with great information to help coach your staff to higher levels of performance—which will ultimately help you improve the quality of care being provided. Each time you walk out of the room after rounding on patients, ask yourself these questions: What did I learn about the care of this patient? How can I use this information to coach and mentor the staff involved?

But rounding also makes a great difference in attitude because it helps nurses stay connected to the purpose and joy in their work! In today's complex healthcare environment, some nurse leaders have become frustrated and feel that they no longer have adequate time to spend with patients. They may complain that they're always in meetings or holed up in their offices doing some project with a deadline, or putting out fires on the unit and not achieving important goals.

A strong rounding framework that positions you to be proactive reduces the number of fires to be put out. You will, over time, fix broken processes and systems that in many cases created all those meetings. But most important, you will increase your time with patients. I find that's where nurse leaders who are successful with rounding really find joy.

The Joys of Rounding: A Clarian Nurse Speaks Out

The following is a blog entry posted by a nurse at Clarian Methodist Hospital in Indianapolis, Indiana.

Nurses Rounding for Outcomes...How Fun!

Monday, July 6, 2009, by Tracy Davis, BSN, RN, CCRN, Pediatric Critical Care

As part of our approach to improving patient and family satisfaction, we "round" on our families in the Pediatric Critical Care Unit daily. Every family, every day. I have found that it is one of my very favorite things to do. Anyone who knows me would not be surprised to hear this, as a part of rounding involves talking. But an even bigger part involves listening. It is really an underrated skill, and often an underused skill.

I have found with most of our families, after I introduce myself and ask a simple question such as, "We always want to provide the very best care possible for your child. How well are we doing with that?" I just need to stop talking and start listening. I have said many times that there is no time that parents feel more helpless than when their child is critically ill or injured.

Having a person listen to their fears, perhaps listen to the story of how their child came to be in our care, and to show the genuine care and concern that we have, is invaluable. Often there are tears shed, and a hug is needed, or perhaps an arm around a shoulder. Parents are often pleasantly surprised that we come in to round on them, to just check in on them and make sure their immediate needs are being met, as well as those of their child. They are always grateful. Even when they know we may not be able to tell them what they really want to hear…that the beautiful child lying in that bed will be fully restored to the same child they previously were. They do know that we will give every effort we have to try and make that happen, though.

After they have seen us the first day, they look forward to a return visit the next day, as I tell them I will see them tomorrow. I suppose it is the promise that not only will I keep my word, but it is the opportunity for them to tell me of their child's progress, and share the ups and downs of this ride they did not ask for. Rounding is just one more great opportunity to make a lasting connection with our families. If by doing it we improve our patient satisfaction, what an outstanding bonus!

—Tracy

Key Points in This Chapter

1. There is no better way to ensure the care provided is meeting the quality and satisfaction needs of patients than by nurse leader rounding.

2. Before implementing the process, obtain buy-in and support by communicating rounding's value to the senior team: recognition for employees, heightened perception of care by patients, better quality outcomes, increased market share, and enhanced safety with risk reduction.

3. Your eventual goal is to round on every single patient every day.

4. Prepare by defining the questions you want to ask patients based on the current initiative you are in the process of hardwiring.

5. Trust but verify by checking rounding logs in each patient's room to ensure staff's accountability.

6. Nurse leader rounding significantly impacts the patient's perception of care as proven through measurement tools. It increases physician satisfaction, and it helps you connect with the joy and purpose in your work!

Pillars Affected by Nurse Leader Rounding on Patients

Service—Improves the patient's perception of the care being provided.

Quality—Improves safety and quality of care due to nurse leader interventions; decreases length of stay.

Finance—Reduces expenses related to quality and length of stay.

People—Brings about opportunities to reward and recognize, thus heightening employee engagement.

Growth—Improves physician satisfaction with the care staff is providing.

CHAPTER 9

Pre- and Post-Visit Patient Calls

By Regina Shupe and Julie Kennedy-Oehlert

It doesn't take long to make a phone call. But the benefits of those two or three minutes can be astronomical. Just ask any healthcare professional who has made pre- and post-visit patient calls.

These calls may not only reduce costs and generate revenue for your organization—and those reasons alone are sufficient to justify their implementation—they may save lives. That, of course, is the best reason of all. Pre-visit calls ensure that patients show up for what could turn out to be lifesaving appointments. Post-visit calls help ensure that people are following the physician's instructions and that no life-threatening complications are developing.

Once you realize how critical pre- and post-visit calls are—and once you have a system in place for making them—they will become a part of your culture and an extension of your care. As Quint Studer often says, your values won't allow you *not* to make the calls. Read on to learn more about both.

Pre-Visit Calls: Lots of Bang for Very Few Bucks

In areas such as Outpatient Surgery, Radiology, and Lab—anywhere scheduled admissions take place—a pre-visit call can greatly impact care to the patient and productivity of staff. Ask yourself: *How often do patients miss or arrive late for a scheduled appointment? How often do patients show up having eaten when the test required fasting? How much overtime are we paying due to these events or delays?*

A pre-visit call can reduce no-shows and tardiness, which in turn improves access by creating more capacity for patient care. It can also greatly improve patient compliance. Likewise, it can increase patient perception of care, increase patient safety through explanation of pre-procedure protocols, and increase revenue. The graphics below illustrate some of the impact of pre-visit calls.

Figure 9.1

Pre-Visit Phone Call Results

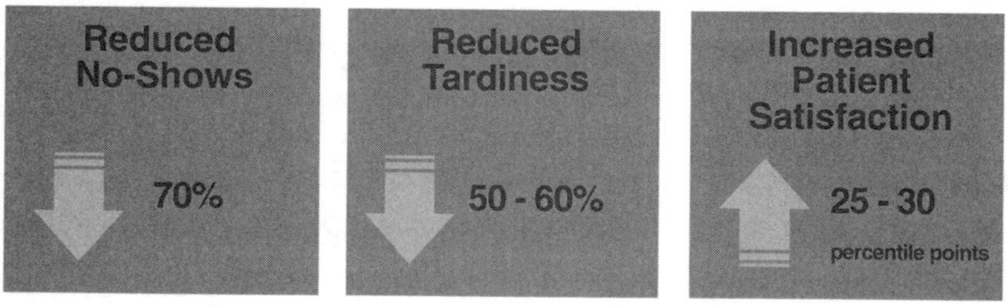

Figure 9.2

Pre-Visit Phone Call
Outpatient Procedure Results

	Historical	Current
No-Show Rate	12% - 15%	4%
Late Arrivals	11% - 14%	8%

FINANCIAL IMPACT = $750,000/YEAR

As Figure 9.1 shows, when one organization implemented pre-visit calls, patient no-shows decreased 70 percent, and late arrivals were reduced by 50 to 60 percent. In addition, patient satisfaction scores rose 25 to 30 percent.

What does all this translate to in dollar signs? Take a look at Figure 9.2. The financial impact of these phone calls turned out to be a staggering $750,000 a year!

What makes pre-visit calls so valuable? Well, consider what happens when a patient doesn't show up or cancels an outpatient test or procedure. Open appointments must be rescheduled. And even if every lost appointment could be rescheduled, the rescheduled visits come at a cost because they result in lost staff productivity, additional staffing, and associated overtime. Pre-visit calls are an opportunity disguised as an expense problem to serve patients better while increasing access, productivity, revenue, and volume.

The lesson is clear: Make pre-visit phone calls.

How to Implement Pre-Visit Calls

A basic pre-visit phone call format:

- confirms the appointment,
- reviews instructions,
- provides directions to the facility,
- asks the patient to arrive early, and
- reaffirms the necessity of the procedure.

A "next level" pre-call also:

- explains the patient's financial obligation,
- asks the patient to arrive prepared to pay his or her co-pay, and
- asks the patient to write down any questions for the doctor and bring them to the appointment. (This helps physicians run on time by avoiding last-minute questions.)

When effective key words are used, patients perceive this explanation as a value-added service provided by the hospital. It also increases revenue by ensuring early collections before the procedure.

A Basic Pre-Call Script

"Hello, Mrs. Smith, this is Sally from St. Vincent Mercy Medical Center in Toledo, OH. I am calling to remind you of your MRI appointment on Wednesday, July 6, at 10:00 a.m. *(Tell how long it will take and explain any special requirements.)* I see Dr. Jones ordered the MRI, so he must feel it is a test you should have. Have you been to St. Vincent in the past? Do you need directions? Do you know where our MRI Department is located? *(If not, give directions.)* When you come in for your test, could you please bring a list of your current medications? If you can arrive 10 minutes early that will help us make sure the hospital runs on time for other patients. Is there anything else I can do for you today, Mrs. Smith? Thank you for choosing St. Vincent for your healthcare needs."

An "Advanced" Script Also Addresses Co-pays

"I see you are covered by Blue Cross-Blue Shield. Under the provisions of your 80/20 policy, there will be a co-pay on this particular procedure of 20 percent. The total cost is $1,000, so please come prepared to pay $200 when you arrive. That will take care of it so we won't need to bill you later. It will make things more convenient for you."

These calls do not have to be long. In fact, in two to five minutes you can remind a patient of the time of her appointment, share specific instructions, and check that she has the proper directions to get her to the appropriate area. The graphic on the following page demonstrates the flow of this call.

Figure 9.3

Pre-Visit Phone Call Sample

- Confirm appointment
- Talk about test and why procedure is important
- Explain procedure and pre-visit requirements
- Give directions
- Request patient bring a list of current medications
- Review co-pay
- Answer questions

These calls are also a way to begin to build a relationship with your patients—a relationship that can be strengthened during the appointment and enhanced even further with a post-visit call.

Post-Visit Calls: Why They're Worth the Effort

Nurses just feel better when we know that patients understand their discharge instructions. Unfortunately, research tells us this is often not the case! One study found that 81 percent of patients requiring assistance with basic functional needs failed to receive a home care referral, and 65 percent said no one at the hospital talked to them about managing their care at home.[1] In another study, the findings showed that many patients had very little understanding of their medication and its effects.

Figure 9.4

State University of New York Study
Mayo Clinic Proceedings, August 2005

- Only 28% knew medication names
- Only 37% knew purpose of medication
- Only 14% knew side effects

It seems clear that many healthcare organizations and their patients could benefit from implementing post-visit calls.

Statistics show heart failure—a manageable condition affecting five million Americans—is also one of the most common reasons for readmission. The data seems to support the need for aggressive use of post-visit calls:

- According to the Agency for Healthcare Research and Quality (AHRQ), heart failure (HF) represents $25 to $35 billion of healthcare expenditures each year; readmissions have tripled in the past 25 years and are expected to triple again over the next 30 years.
- According to AHRQ, the high rate of re-hospitalization for HF patients results from patients' inability to adequately self-manage the condition:
    - National average readmission rate 30 days post-discharge ranges from18 to 20 percent depending on the region of the country.
    - Thirteen percent of these readmissions were "potentially avoidable," based on the IPPS rule, with major areas of concern including poor communication with patients at discharge, especially around medications, and inadequate post-discharge monitoring.
    - Prevention of these avoidable readmissions could save Medicare $12 billion per year. (Report on Medicare Compliance, Volume 17, Number 24, June 30, 2008)
- Using interactive care, such as post-visit calls, organizations have been able to achieve a 74 percent reduction in HF readmission rate 30 days post-discharge, resulting in an overall readmission rate of 5 percent.
- At the same time the organizations saw a 43 percent improvement in patient satisfaction.

In Studer Group's experience, our partner organizations that practice Evidence-Based Leadership℠—including post-discharge phone calls—perform 20 percentile points higher on HCAHPS than non-partner organizations that don't.

Clearly, post-visit phone calls have numerous measurable benefits. That's why Studer Group® is committed to this action. As the graphs on the following page clearly indicate, these calls greatly improve patients' perception of clinical quality and increase the likelihood they will recommend the organization to others.

Figure 9.5

Post-Visit Calls
Likelihood of Recommending-Inpatient

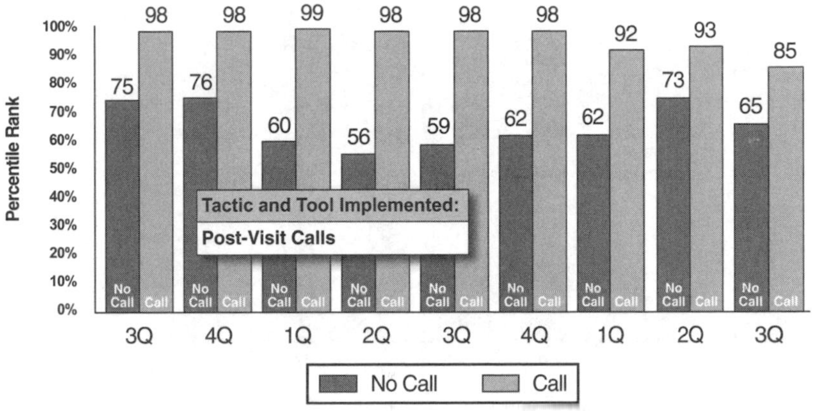

Source: New Jersey Hospital, Total beds = 775; 3Q2007 – 3Q2009

Figure 9.6

Post-Visit Calls
Likelihood of Recommending-ED

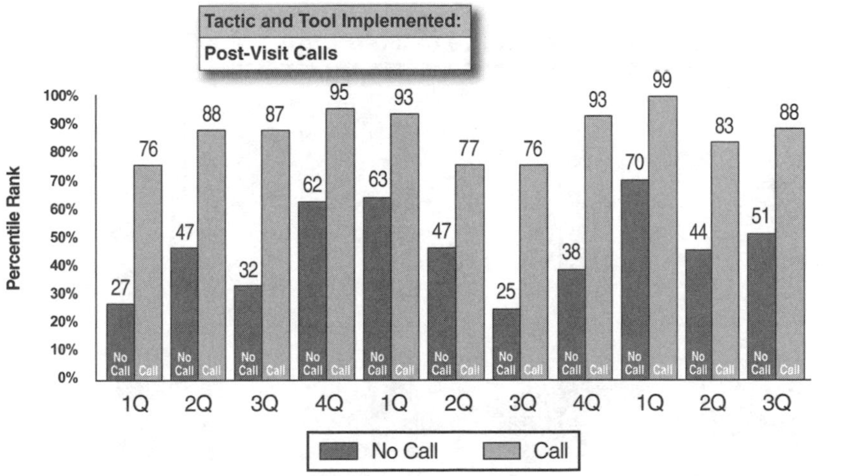

Source: New Jersey Hospital, Total beds = 775; 1Q2007 – 3Q2009

Figure 9.7

Post-Visit Calls
Clinical Quality

Instructions to Care for Yourself at Home

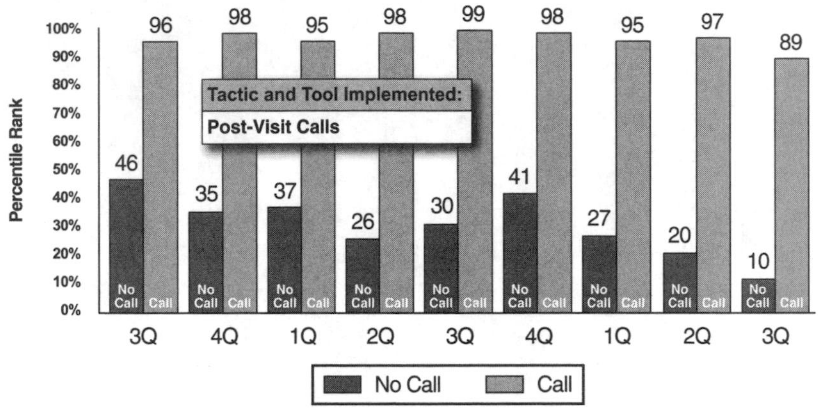

Source: New Jersey Hospital, Total beds = 775; 3Q2007 – 3Q2009

And take a look at what happened when one organization implemented post-visit calls:

Figure 9.8

"Did you receive a follow-up phone call after your stay?"

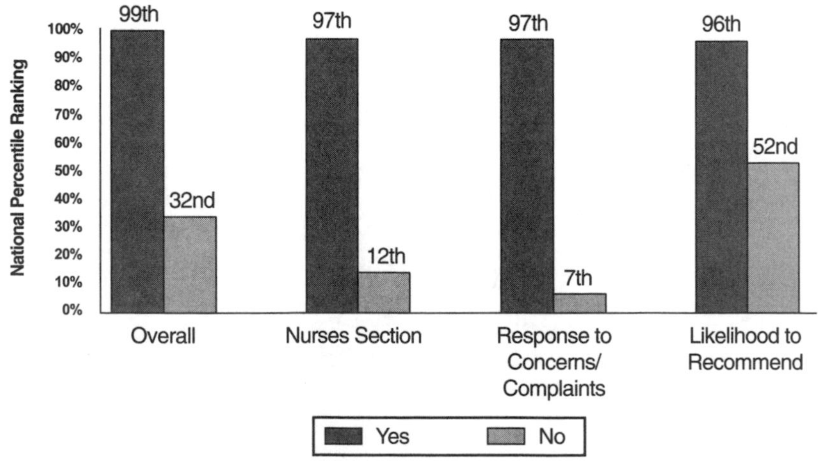

Source: Inpatient surveys received April 22-June 4, 2007
n=468 *surveys (52%=YES; 48%=NO)*

These post-visit calls are the best and most honest cycle of continuous quality improvement a nurse leader can be a part of: hearing about opportunities from your patients and their families; providing feedback to nurses, ancillaries, or unit council; making the necessary changes; and then asking the patients for feedback again. It should be a never-ending process. The feedback comes directly from patients; they're the best source of information regarding how the care in your area is being delivered and perceived. While it is wonderful to hear the positives, there is also tremendous value in hearing about opportunities from the patients.

Implementing Post-Visit Calls

Post-visit or discharge phone calls (along with pre-visit calls) are one of the first tactics to implement in Studer Group's Patient Care Model. These calls have proven to be a very effective way of ensuring that our patients are doing well after they leave our care.

> Post-visit phone calls are not a task to be "checked off." Rather they're meant to assure safety, quality, and service to patients and families served. The calls allow staff to hear firsthand the status of recently discharged patients, and confirm they have what's needed to return to wellness at home. These calls are also known to save lives!

How do you as a nurse leader put these post-visit calls into action when staff feels they already have enough to do with current patients? First, you need to plan your overall strategy. This includes evaluating the resources you have to devote to calls.

To maximize clinical outcomes, post-visit calls should be made by the unit's nursing staff, which shares the responsibility for calling patients discharged the previous day. It is valuable for staff to hear how the patients perceive their care. Ideally, calls take place within a 24-72-hour time frame (or until the nurse has made three attempts).

If the reason for doing post-visit calls is clear—and they go on to see the outcomes of these calls and the appreciation of the patient and family—staff will find value in making the calls. If your staffing situation does not allow for nurses closest to the patients to make the calls, consider non-traditional resources such as light duty or retired nurses to do so.

When clinicians are not available at all, find others to make the contacts—even if they're not healthcare professionals. Remember, a call is better than no call. The questions asked by non-healthcare professionals will need to be more about service and process improvement than clinical matters. The conversation is always meant to reinforce the caring factor.

Once the resource decision is made, you can move forward with planning the specifics of implementation.

My First Experience with Making a Post-Visit Call

Working as the nurse manager of a community ED, I was trying to change the patients' perception of care. We had already implemented several important processes, such as educating staff on key words and rounding on patients and employees. By becoming hardwired℠ to those tactics, our perception of care rose from the 5th percentile to the 43rd. But we'd set a goal to create an excellent environment for patients to receive care, staff to work, and physicians to practice medicine. It was time to start making discharge telephone calls!

So there I was...embarking on a whole new challenge: how to get staff to buy in to post-visit phone calls when their plate was already so full. I decided, as the nurse leader, that first I needed to understand what this would require of staff. I also wanted to test the waters and hear for myself what patients thought of our care. So I decided to begin the process by making the calls myself.

I initiated conversations by asking patients how they were feeling: Were their symptoms better, worse, or the same? It was with this question that I learned very early on the critical importance of discharge phone calls. Knowing I had begun the process, the day shift charge nurse would stack the charts with the highest level of acuity on top.

One day, one of the first charts was an older woman whose discharge diagnosis had been asthmatic bronchitis. The doctor wanted to admit her as an inpatient, but she was rather insistent about going home. He obliged and sent her on her way with family. She was my first phone call that day. When she answered the phone I could tell that she was wheezing and short of breath. I asked if there was someone else there I could speak to. There was no one. I told her I was extremely concerned with her present condition and the fact that she was so short of breath. I felt very helpless and almost panicked, but I knew at that moment I was her lifeline.

I instructed her to stay on the phone while I switched to another line to call 911. She agreed. I remained on the telephone with her until the squad arrived and informed me they would be transporting her back to our ED. Once she arrived staff worked to stabilize her breathing, a process that required intubation and eventual admission to the Intensive Care Unit.

Once she was stabilized, the ED physician sought me out and asked, "Why did you call her?" I responded that I was making discharge phone calls on all eligible patients released from the ED. He replied, "Your phone call saved her life." It was at that moment I knew, without a doubt, I was making discharge phone calls on ED patients to save lives! And if the calls improved their perception of care, then that was an added bonus.

—Regina Shupe

Once you know who will be making calls, it's important to gain your team's buy-in. Connect the dots to the impact of post-visit calls and share your plan to implement. They all may not be on board right away but they'll come around as calls begin to impact patients.

Convincing the Staff

To obtain staff's buy-in, talk about the "why" of post-visit phone calls. Share stories about when a call to a patient became a lifesaving intervention. Ask staff members, "What are some positive outcomes of calling patients after they're discharged?" and "If you were a patient discharged from our unit, how would a call from one of your nurses checking on you make you feel?"

Figure 9.9

Reality of Adverse Events Post-Discharge

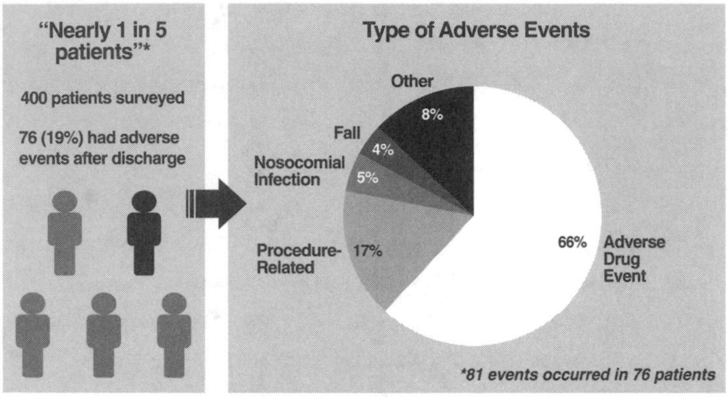

"Adverse Events After Discharge from Hospital," Annals of Internal Medicine, February 2003

If after they've heard all the benefits, staff members are still hesitant about making calls, it may be because they are worried about time. But once calls are scripted and the process is tried out and demonstrated (more on both of the subjects later), they'll see that the average phone call lasts only between two and five minutes. Connecting to the "why," as well as using a script and timing the calls, will help nurses see they get a lot in return for a few minutes of follow-up with the patient!

Finding the Right Words

The next step is to work collaboratively with your nurses to decide on the best **questions and key words** to use in the conversations. These tools are critical for success. Refer to your patient satisfaction survey results to identify the priority items or key drivers you can ask patients about. This information tells you what is most important to them and their experience at *your* organization.

Consider the following as you review the survey results while choosing what to ask:

- What do you worry about when you discharge patients home? Perhaps it's whether they understand their discharge instructions, whether their pain was controlled, and whether they made their follow-up appointment.
- What do you want patients to teach you with regards to your care? How frequently did you check on them (verification of Hourly Rounding^{SM})? Did you always wash your hands upon entering and exiting the room (verification of hand hygiene)? Did you introduce yourself? Did you keep them and family members informed of care?
- What aspects of service do you want feedback on from patients? Did they receive very good or excellent care?
- What aspects of quality do you want feedback on? Did you check their armband before administering medications? Did you explain procedures in a way they could understand?
- What other health issues did you address? Did you offer information on diet or smoking cessation?
- Who provided the patient with memorable care so that you can reward and recognize that person—a nurse, a physician, or some other caregiver?

It's also important to ask questions in a way that elicits the most information; often yes/no questions are not deep enough to give you the facts needed to improve your care. Instead, consider using a scale such as "always, usually, sometimes, never" or a few choices of answers the patient can respond to. In the interest of efficiency, use structured questions; open-ended questions often are more time-consuming and more difficult to capture feedback on.

A series of four to six well-constructed questions will give you good information in a timely manner. Remember, the purpose of these calls is not to repeat a mini satisfaction survey, but rather to drive clinical outcomes or demonstrate to patients you are thinking about them and their progress. Finally, using a solid script with key words as a guide fosters consistency in the calls, and assures that each nurse hits on the elements identified as important. On the following page is a post-visit call sample.

Figure 9.10

Post-Visit Phone Call Sample

Empathy and Concern	*"Mrs. Smith? Hello. This is <name>. You were discharged from my unit yesterday. I just wanted to call and see how you're doing today."*
Clinical Outcomes	• *"Do you have any questions regarding your medications or any possible side effects?"* • *"Is your pain well controlled?"* • *"We want to make sure we do excellent clinical follow-up to ensure your best possible recovery. Do you know what symptoms or health problems to look out for?"* • *"Do you have your follow-up appointment?"*
Reward and Recognition	• *"Mrs. Smith, we like to recognize our employees. Who did an excellent job for you while you were in the hospital?"* • *"Can you tell me why Sue was excellent?"*
Service	*"We want to make sure you were very satisfied with your care. How were we, Mrs. Smith?"*
Process Improvement	*"We're always looking to get better. Do you have any suggestions for what we could do to be even better?"*
Appreciation	*"We appreciate your taking the time this afternoon to speak with us about your follow-up care. Is there anything I can do for you?"*

The Hospital Consumer Assessment of Healthcare Providers and Systems (HCAHPS) survey as a quality indicator impacts post-visit calls. You must be sensitive to the survey guidelines set up by the Centers for Medicare & Medicaid Services (CMS). It's important to know you should not use any HCAHPS questions within the context or script of your follow-up calls. You must also avoid asking something in a way that entices a patient to respond to the HCAHPS survey in a certain manner.

This is relatively new territory for leaders, so you should keep close tabs on the guidelines either from CMS or your quality department director. It's important to be aware of any changes made. You can get more information at HCAHPS Technical Support via email at hcahps@azqio.sdps.org or via telephone at 1-888-884-4007. To learn more about the HCAHPS survey, please visit the HCAHPS website (www.hcahpsonline.org) and review the *HCAHPS Quality Assurance Guidelines V4.0* found under the Quality Assurance navigation button.

Set Goals for Post-Visit Calls.

Once you've settled on the right words, it's time to set an attempted goal as well as a contacted goal. Attempts are worthy, but what matters is actually talking to your patients! The attempted goal should always be 100 percent of the eligible patients. As a minimum, your connect rate should be the following: Emergency Department—60 percent; Inpatient—70 percent; and Ambulatory Surgery/Outpatient—80 percent. These connect rates take into consideration the challenges with incorrect phone numbers.

> When collating your data, attempts are counted by number of patients actually called, not by the number of times staff tried calling each person. In other words, if your goal is contacting ten patients and employees attempted to call eight of them, even if they dialed the number twice for each patient, your attempts are logged as eight, not sixteen.

Once the goals are set, it's time to determine the specifics of the calling process. For example, you will need to have the list of patients to follow up with. This can be compiled electronically if you have an electronic medical record or an electronic registration system. If not, a copy of each patient's discharge instructions and face sheet stapled together can serve as your call inventory.

This list is then "scrubbed" for certain types of patients typically not contacted, a process especially important if you are using electronic resources. For instance, staff does not call fatalities, transfers, and certain psychiatric diagnoses. Obstetric unit staff might not make contact in the case of a fetal demise. In the ED, you might not call sexual abuse patients.

This doesn't mean you don't care about those patients, it simply means that contact with them might come from different resources. Each unit needs to carefully consider which patients to call, and as the leader, you ensure that the right balance exists between appropriate and scrubbed.

Getting Started...and Keeping up Momentum

After you've settled on the words, it's time to get the ball rolling. A best practice is for you, the leader, to begin making the calls. Make them at the nurses' station or another location where staff can observe. As we mentioned earlier, when staff members see how long the calls take and how easy they are, their anxiety will be greatly reduced.

After you've set the stage by making some calls yourself, ask a few of the higher performing nurses to make calls and share their stories. This will further increase buy-in. After several weeks of you and the high performers making the phone calls, they can be transitioned to the rest of the staff.

Be sure to communicate to staff exactly what you are hearing from patients. You'll find there are opportunities to recognize employees for outstanding care. There will also be stories to share regarding lives saved by making the phone calls.

> **Best Practice:** Creating and sharing the wins obtained from discharge phone calls is essential to their success. At one community hospital in Ohio, during staff meetings different employees tell stories of calls they made. At the end of the month, staff votes on the great "story of the month." Then the manager shares that story with the hospital leadership team at its monthly manager meeting. Once the ED started this practice, it didn't take long until other departments got involved in story sharing as well! In addition, when the senior leadership team and managers round, they congratulate staff on their success and excellent care.

The feedback staff members receive from patients and the stories they share with the rest of the team keep the momentum going. It feels good to know for certain that these calls are appreciated—and that they work. You can tell people the theory behind post-visit calls all day, but nothing compares to seeing the results firsthand. Seeing is believing...and it's what will keep staff members dialing those phone numbers day after day.

Post-Visit Calls: A Powerful Tool for Nurses and Patients Alike!

Ultimately, all nurses benefit from speaking to patients after they have left the hospital. They get to hear the voice of the patient, note what needs and issues were not addressed, and then make necessary adjustments in future care practices. Sometimes these conversations actually save lives. Often the readmission rate is reduced.

The calls also offer the opportunity to perform service recovery—as well as reinforce a patient's perception of having received the very best care! These calls build a continuum of care for the patient.

In addition, nurses hear firsthand what a difference they make in the lives of their patients every single day. When these great stories are shared, the result is renewed motivation to connect post-visit and learn how to improve their care.

Never, Ever TOO BUSY to Save a Life

This story could have happened to you, in your practice, in your Emergency Department (ED), on your busy day.

I am the ED nurse leader, rolling out discharge phone calls under duress because my CEO wants them done. The ED battle cry is, "WE are TOO BUSY." I do not connect these calls to making a difference to our patients, to our profession. I don't want to do them.

In my community that summer, in the ED where I am the nurse manager, we had experienced the grave sadness of four cases of meningococcal meningitis. Each of the young patients died—college students who would never finish their degrees or make their parents proud. The fifth case had come to the ED the night before, as yet unidentified by us. He was a college boy who had been drinking alcohol and presented with a headache. He had been "treated and streeted" (put in a cab and sent back to his dormitory).

The next day I was rounding to assure discharge phone calls were getting done. I cannot say I am passionate about doing them; I cannot say I am being a good role model. I round in triage and remind the nurse to do her discharge phone calls. "Too busy," she tells me. "DO THEM," I instruct her.

She makes a few half-hearted calls, before getting the college boy on the phone who had been sent back to his dorm the night before. His headache is not better. He sounds frightened—he tells the nurse he has a funny rash and cannot lift his head up. The triage nurse suddenly knows who he is: the fifth case of meningitis, and she calls 911. In minutes, the boy is in our ED with intravenous tubes inserted. He does not die. He does not die.

Later that day, the triage nurse comes to my office. She tells me she is going to do discharge phone calls for the rest of her career. She says doing them is easier than telling a mother she does not have a son. This nurse has connected discharge phone calls to her passion for caring for patients, but the lesson is not all hers. I reflect on my leadership, or lack thereof, and am secretly grateful that the CEO made me initiate discharge phone calls.

The college boy graduated; he lives in my community. When I see him, I remember how important it is to be a leader *who leads*. I am grateful for the lesson.

—Julie Kennedy-Oehlert

Key Points in This Chapter

1. Pre- and post-visit phone calls are not a task to check off; they are a critical extension of care for your patients and their families.

2. Pre-visit calls reduce no-shows and tardiness and increase patient satisfaction; for one organization their financial impact was calculated to be $750,000 a year.

3. Post-visit calls also have a tremendous impact. Studer Group finds that its partner organizations that practice Evidence-Based Leadership—including post-discharge phone calls—perform better on HCAHPS than non-partner organizations that don't.

4. These calls are best executed with a foundational script or key words to assure consistency and relevancy.

5. Set goals of attempted calls and patients actually contacted to assure the process is hardwired.

6. Post-visit, discharge phone calls are their own reward and serve as a motivation to provide excellent care. With that noted, it is very important to share the stories heard from patients when they're contacted.

Pillars Affected by Pre- and Post-Visit Calls

Service—Saves lives by reminding patients of appointments and by ensuring they understand post-discharge instructions and are feeling appropriately, improves patient satisfaction results, and are a "wow" to patients.

Quality—Improves understanding of discharge instructions and patient compliance, provides information for continuous quality improvement, and avoids unnecessary readmissions.

Finance—Improves loyalty of patients to promote increased market share, decreases potential for litigation, and impacts reimbursement for avoidable readmissions.

People—Contributes to staff's efficiency, and improves purpose and worthwhile work for those who make the calls.

Growth—Improves word-of-mouth in the community and increases patient volume through improved reputation and evidence of caring!

CHAPTER 10

Hourly Rounding^{SM} on Patients

By Faye Sullivan and Lauren Charles

Earlier in this section you read about nurse leader rounding on patients. Now we'll take it to the staff level with Hourly Rounding^{SM}. This tactic involves your staff rounding on patients every one to two hours and practicing a series of eight specific behaviors—and yes, they'll actually save time.

In fact, they may be able to save 82 hours each week. In a study by Studer Group's research subsidiary, the Alliance for Health Care Research, nurses who rounded hourly on telemetry, surgical, and medical-surgical patients reduced call lights by 4,901 in a four-week period. If an average response to a call light is estimated to take four minutes, nurses saved 326 hours per month or 81.5 hours each week responding to call lights and delivered better clinical outcomes for patients. Hourly Rounding also reduces patient falls and skin breakdowns while improving patient satisfaction—and it drives more nursing care to the bedside, so nurses can be proactive instead of reactive with respect to workflow.

This study—the largest ever conducted on reducing call lights and the impact that hourly rounds has on patient satisfaction and quality of care—was published in September of 2006 in the *American Journal of Nursing*. It catapulted this evidence-based practice onto the national stage. Since then,

Studer Group® has helped hundreds of organizations to successfully implement Hourly Rounding as part of the Patient Care Model.

The study showed evidence that when implemented and hardwired℠, Hourly Rounding will effectively decrease call lights by 37.8 percent; decrease falls by 50 percent; decrease hospital-acquired decubiti by 14 percent; and improve patient satisfaction by an average of 12 mean points! It's rare that a single tactic can make such a difference in patient care!

Figure 10.1

Call Light Reductions
After Implementing Rounds

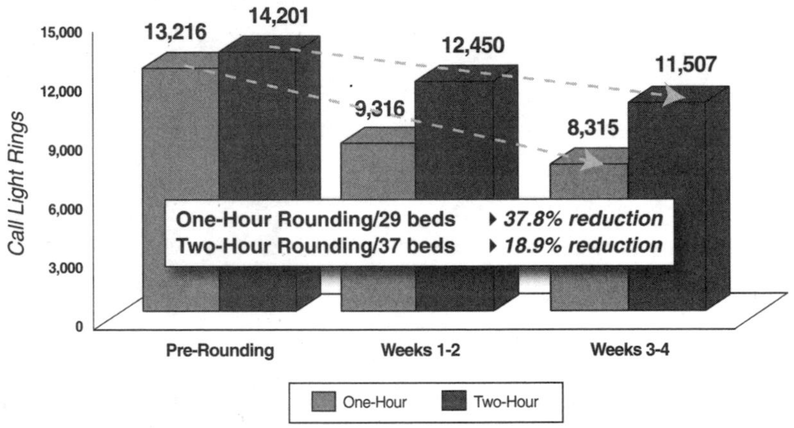

**Reduction for one hour was statistically significant (p=.000)*

Figure 10.2

Quality:
Patient Falls Reduced

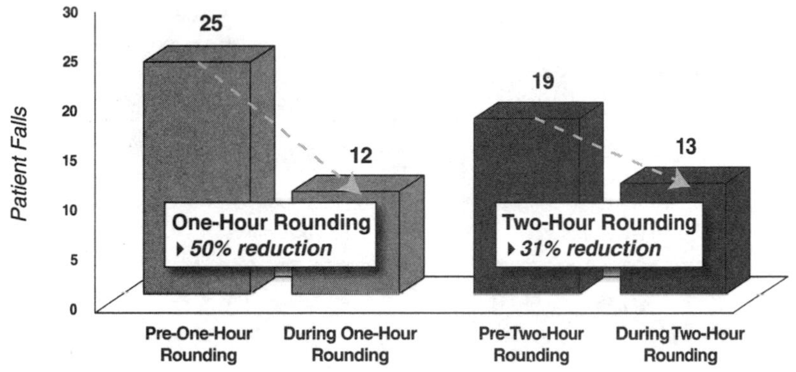

(n=18 units)

Figure 10.3

Quality:
Skin Breakdown Reduced

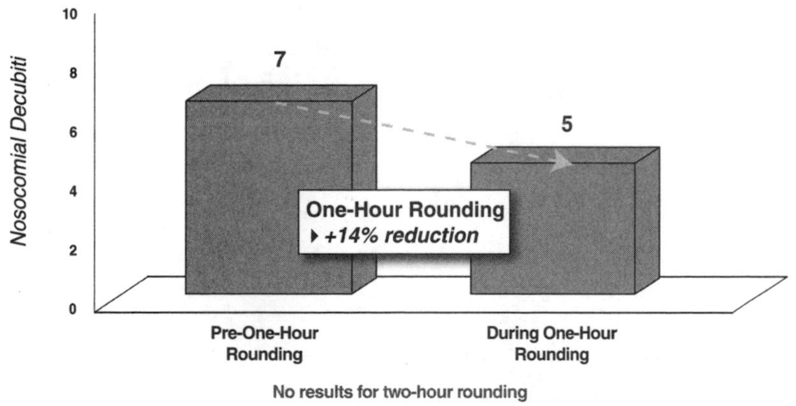

(n=9 units)

Figure 10.4

Service:
Patient Satisfaction Increased

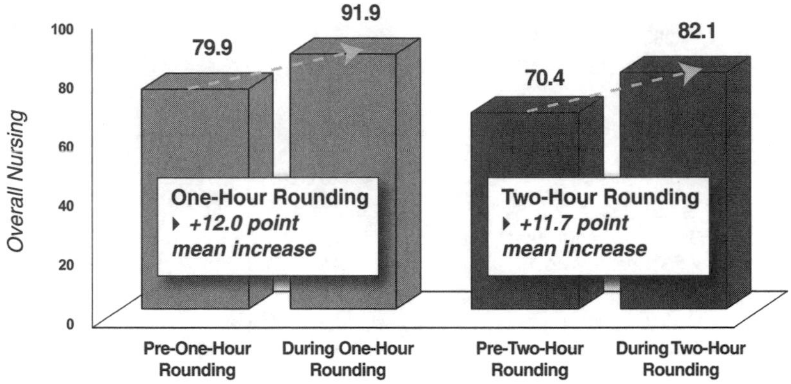

One-Hour: n=18 units *Two-Hour: n=9 units*

Just How Does Hourly Rounding Reduce Call Lights?

When baseline data was collected, researchers learned that the top reasons patients used the call light were: bathroom/bedpan assistance (15 percent); IV/pump alarm (15 percent); pain medication (10 percent); needed a nurse or CNA (9 percent); and position assistance (4 percent), as well as accidental hits of the call light (13 percent) and miscellaneous reasons (13 percent).

By rounding hourly on patients, the units reduced requests:

- bathroom by 40 percent
- pain by 35 percent
- positioning by 29 percent
- IV/pump alarms by 40 percent
- miscellaneous by 39 percent

When you realize that Hourly Rounding is a lot more than just "checking in" every hour, you will see how it leads to the results above. You'll learn about the eight behaviors in the following pages.

But Hourly Rounding isn't just about call lights. In the years since the study was published, many organizations have found that a hardwired system of hourly rounds has been correlated with improvements in other indicators as well—decreases in lost charges, incidental overtime, and medication errors, for example. It has also been correlated with increases in nursing satisfaction.

Implementing Hourly Rounding

Before you get started, it is important to obtain baseline data on falls and hospital-acquired decubiti as well as call light statistics. The first two pieces of clinical information can be acquired from your Quality Improvement Department. For call light stats, have the unit secretary log calls as they come to the desk over a two-week period. Why collect all this baseline data? Because it enables you to demonstrate the gains made by Hourly Rounding after its implementation.

First explain the entire rounding process to the nursing staff, and connect to the "why"—why you're doing it and why it matters. Ask nurses how often they are already in the patient's room and you'll find that for most patients they are there at least every hour. You'll need to reinforce there's a difference between checking on a patient every sixty minutes or so and performing the eight behaviors associated with Hourly Rounding.

It is also the case that staff sometimes overestimate how often they are truly in patients' rooms. When they first hear about hourly rounds they will tell you they are in the room that often anyway. And yet you'll still hear patient complaints about never seeing their nurses. The reality is nurses are in some patients' rooms very frequently, yet they may not see other patients often at all. You can even hear this truth when listening to report. Perhaps you've heard a nurse say during report: "Mr. Johnson is doing well. He has family with him. He is on autopilot." What this tells you is that Mr. Johnson is not only not going to be seen hourly but probably will be checked on only when vitals or meds are due.

Clearly, we as nurse leaders need to emphasize the power of Hourly Rounding. When they truly understand the impact this tactic will have on quality indicators, your high performing nurses will be willing to give it a try. And once they start seeing the benefits, the process is on its way to being hardwired.

As you begin to implement Hourly Rounding, it's imperative to reward and recognize those nurses consistently performing the behaviors. (You can do this when you are doing nurse leader rounding, covered earlier in this section.) Thank them for incorporating this best practice into their daily routines. Ask them, "What are the wins you're seeing as a result of Hourly Rounding? Are there any barriers that I, as the manager, need to address?"

Very quickly you'll see a gap between those who are doing hourly rounds and those who aren't. (You can also verify who is doing them through your nurse leader rounding on patients.) Eventually the nurses not consistently completing the process will need to be addressed via your hospital's disciplinary process.

The eight behaviors of Hourly Rounding are:

1. Use opening key words to reduce anxiety (AIDET[SM]).
2. Perform scheduled tasks.
3. Address the "Three Ps"—pain, potty, position.
4. Assess additional comfort needs.
5. Conduct environmental assessment.
6. Ask, "Is there anything else I can do for you? I have time."
7. Tell each patient when you will be back.
8. Document the process in a rounding log posted in the patient's room.

Each of these behaviors creates a specific desired outcome (as shown in the graphic on the following page). Many times staff and leaders are tempted to "modify" rounds by eliminating certain steps. But in doing so, you're reducing the impact and losing some of the successful outcomes you can achieve. If you're considering cutting out a step, first ask yourself if you're willing to lose the results that it drives. For example, if you don't want to say you'll be back in an hour, can you really afford to write off the efficiency it creates? The answer is clear. Nurses are so very busy that every bit of effectiveness we can achieve with our processes is necessary. You just can't shortchange yourself by refusing to do the essential steps.

Figure 10.5

Eight Behaviors for Hourly Rounds

Hourly Rounding Behavior	Expected Results
Use opening key words	Contributes to efficiency
Accomplish scheduled tasks	Contributes to efficiency
Address Three Ps (pain, potty, position)	Quality indicators – falls, decubitis, pain management
Address additional comfort needs	Improved patient satisfaction on pain, concern and caring
Conduct environmental assessment	Contributes to efficiency, teamwork
Ask, "Is there anything else I can do for you before I go? I have time."	Contributes to efficiency; Improves patient satisfaction on teamwork and communication
Tell each patient when you will be back	Contributes to efficiency
Document the round	Quality and accountability

Building Accountability into the Process

An Hourly Rounding log (see Figure 10.6) for documentation is an excellent accountability tool. Basically, it's a document nurses sign or initial and input minor documentation on after every visit to a patient's room to show that they've completed Hourly Rounding. It's difficult for an organization to get the level of results mentioned earlier without using this strategy.

Bear in mind that during the early phases of implementation, which can last six months or more, you need to continue validating by frequent observation to ensure staff members' initials on the log truly represent all eight behaviors were accomplished. Also, remember to

Rounding Log Brings Reassurance

When a patient's son was upset that his father had a stroke, one manager told us she used the rounding log to reassure the family member that safe care had been delivered. The son, who had thought that "no one was watching," learned from the log that staff had indeed closely observed his father and quickly identified the change in condition.

—Faye Sullivan

use your nurse leader rounding time to check the logs and harvest reasons to reward and recognize employees.

When engaging your staff in the use of the logs, frame the purpose of the rounding log as two-fold: a) It is a visual representation of the promise we make to take excellent care of our patients, and b) It is an accountability system that allows us to recognize high performers and support those who have not yet hardwired the process. Below are several tips to help you:

1. Make certain the logs contain simple checkboxes and limited documentation area. When you overcomplicate the process, it's less likely to be completed.

2. Strategically place the logs in the patient rooms where patients and family members can see them. Tell customers, "The staff is committed to providing safe care by checking hourly to ensure patient needs are being met. The log is the visual representation of our promise."

3. Review logs daily for compliance. A clerical staff person can do this review, leaving the nurse leader's time to be spent on the assessment. When staff see how important the documentation is to the leader, buy-in and compliance become easier.

4. Enlist your charge nurses. Work diligently to get them on board, because staff will go where they lead. Help them understand why it's necessary by telling them about the great results they can achieve. Get them competing for the honor of having the most consecutive shifts with 100 percent compliance!

Figure 10.6

Hourly Rounding Log

Date:_______________ **Room:**_______________

TIME	LOC	POSITION	SAFETY	PAIN	INITIAL
0700					
0800					
0900					
1000					
1100					
1200					
1300					
1400					
1500					
1600					
1700					
1800					
1900					
2000					
2100					
2200					
2300					
0000					
0100					
0200					
0300					
0400					
0500					
0600					

LOC	POSITION	SAFETY GOALS	PAIN
1: Alert 2: Lethargic 3: Confused 4: Comatose	R: Right L: Left S: Supine H: Heel ck	• Bed in low position • Side rails up x 2 • Bed alarm on if needed • Call bell in reach • Pt toileting needs addressed	• Pain controlled • Pain med due

NAME	INITIAL	TITLE

To download a copy of this form, visit www.firestarterpublishing.com/NurseLeaderHandbook.

A Few Barriers to Rounding…and How to Overcome Them

Time. Nurses may initially balk at Hourly Rounding because they see it as adding another time-consuming task to their already busy schedules. Remember, hourly rounds will save them time, but they may not see this upfront. It is the job of the nurse leader to put this in perspective by helping staff connect the dots.

Ask your staff this: When you go to the mailbox to get your mail, do you bring in one piece of mail, open it, then return to the mailbox for the second letter, take it in, open it—and repeat this process until all of your mail is retrieved? Of course not! But isn't that what we are doing when we go to a patient's room with medication, leave, return to the room to respond to a call for pain medication, leave, then return to assist with toileting…? You get the picture—and so will your staff.

Behavior #2 of the eight behaviors, "Perform scheduled tasks," is deliberately included to key staff into the fact that hourly rounds are to be done in association with care they will already be providing to patients. Staff will not be expected to make a separate "rounding" trip to patients' rooms. Instead, while they are in the rooms each hour, checking vital signs, administering meds, or providing other essential care, they will incorporate the other seven behaviors into each patient encounter. This is where the time savings comes in.

When communicating with staff, focus on the facts that:

- This process is a "proactive" one. Answering call lights and taking care of a patient after a fall is "reactive."
- Staff can plan and schedule hourly rounds. As a result, call lights and falls, which can wreak havoc with time, are curtailed.
  - Best Practice: At one organization a brief segment of a song is played every hour to remind staff to round.

Another time barrier is the nurse leader's validation of rounding. Yet while validating skills directly by observation is certainly an investment in precious time, organizations that bite the bullet and get it done will tell you the results achieved far outweigh the time spent.

Tip: We also recommend that nurse leaders engage their Development Department or clinical nurse specialists in educating staff, which can save time in the long run. One organization that did this had an empty room set up where they tested nurses on their clinical competency related to Hourly Rounding. They had nurses round on a "patient," after which each one was evaluated by a clinical instructor and given immediate feedback. Once staff was deemed competent, then it became the nurse leader's responsibility to enforce accountability for the process. (Note: The use of an annual rounding-competency validation will add credibility to this skill, and make it as important as all the other skills validated yearly.)

"Soft" Validation. Sometimes nurse leaders invest time in doing the necessary validation, but use too soft an approach to get the real value. For instance: "Sara, I appreciate being able to shadow you and validate your Hourly Rounding skills. I think you did a great job. The only thing I didn't hear from you was the closing key words. I'll go ahead and check you off, but please be sure to say them next time." It doesn't work! You just left the door open for Sara to continue forgetting to use closing key words. She is much more likely to remember when her nurse leader is firm and instead validates the omission.

Trust Issues. Many nurse leaders will say, "When I verify rounding, staff members feel like I don't trust them. They think I'm checking up on them." Well…that's because you are—but it's the right thing to do. After all, we trust that a physician will do a history and physical on every patient, but we still verify that it's been done. As a nurse leader, you have the ultimate responsibility for the competency of your staff. For critical skills, a "trust but verify" approach is necessary—and Hourly Rounding does qualify.

There is a practice leaders can use to make rounds appreciated by their staff rather than dreaded. Try this: Every time you complete a

The Peace of Mind to Sleep at Home

A daughter of a patient told us her mother was a regular patient in the hospital where hourly rounds were recently implemented. **This was the first admission during which the daughter went home for a night because she was so certain of the care her mother would receive.** She said a staff member was in her mother's room every hour.

—Lauren Charles

set of rounds, go to the nurses' station and PUBLICALLY compliment one staff member for the specific things you observed. "Karen, I rounded on three of your patients this morning. Every person knew your name, and all said you have been in to round on them at least every hour. THANK YOU for taking very good care of our patients." Now, what have you just done? You have sent the message loud and clear that you are looking for "What's right!" and you're willing to acknowledge it openly. Compliments are far more effective at driving consistent behavior than criticism!

Getting Staff Fully Engaged

All nursing staff can be engaged in this process. Many organizations routinely have RNs round on the even hours, with nursing assistants rounding on the odd hours. The rationale behind it is that most medications are given on the even hours, meaning that most likely the RNs are already in the room during those times. This engages nursing assistants in the rounding process and takes advantage of an already established hourly round (the medication visit).

It's critical to reinforce with staff members that hourly rounds are made *in conjunction with*—not *in addition to*—other tasks. For instance, the RN does not pass out medications and then go back to do Hourly Rounding; both actions are done concurrently. Nurses should build established tasks into the Hourly Rounding so they have fewer steps back and forth to the patient's room.

By using key words to close the encounter—"Is there anything else I can do for you before I go? I have time. You can count on one of our team to be back to check on you in about an hour."—a nurse gives a patient the information he or she needs to make the best decision about whether to use a call light. The patient will be able to anticipate when the nurse will return. Once this trust has been established, many patients are less likely to press the call light and also less likely to get up without help. Again, this means more time for the nurse and fewer patient falls.

In areas where the "Three Ps"—pain, potty, and positioning—may not be appropriate when rounding, ask the unit nurses, "Why do most call lights go off on your unit?" Consider also that some departments have their own version of the initials:

- Obstetric Units commonly use PQS: pain, questions, and supplies for baby and mom.

- In the Intensive Care Unit, besides focusing on the "Three Ps," it's recommended that staff concentrate on keeping the family informed as well. Updating the patient's family can decrease their anxiety, improve the perception of care, and reduce the number of interruptions they create while trying to get updates on their loved ones. In the ICU it is not unusual for staff to think the Three Ps don't apply to them "because we are already in the room 24/7 with the patients." However, simply being in the room does not mean staff members are automatically meeting patient and family needs. Many ICUs have adapted the Three Ps to include pain, positioning, alarms, and plan of care (due to the many questions that arise as a result of care by multiple physicians). And because care in an ICU is so highly technical, many are using the hourly rounds as a time to deliberately insert a "human touch"—ensuring that the emotional needs of patients and family are routinely being met.
- In the Emergency Department, Hourly Rounding focuses on pain, plan of care, and duration (PPD). The process can also be carried out in the treatment and waiting rooms. Research conducted in this area has shown significant decreases in leaving without being seen, leaving against medical advice, and patient falls.
- In the Psychiatric Units, the focus has been tweaked to cover plan of care, medications, safety, and food.

Measuring Results

As you begin your implementation of hourly rounds, plan to measure success. We see units measure results in three areas:

- Clinical Quality
- Patient Satisfaction
- Efficiency

You'll also want to plan in advance how you will publicize your results.

Ask yourself:
- Where will we display number of days without a fall? Without nosocomial decubiti?
- What specific questions on our patient satisfaction survey will we watch closely to evaluate our success?

- When will we re-measure the number of call lights to ensure we have achieved the reduction we expect?

Now, we'll briefly touch on how to make this measurement resonate with staff. Let's say that when you started hourly rounds you had 4,200 call lights per month. Two months later, you re-measure and learn that you now have 2,940 call lights per month; in other words, you're avoiding 1,260 call lights per month, a 30 percent reduction.

Now let's make the math work in a meaningful way: 1,260 call lights, at an estimated four minutes per light = 5,040 minutes/month, or 84 hours/month (5,040 divided by 60 minutes). That is 2.8 hours per day (84 hours divided by 30 days in a month). That means you've saved enough time every day for five staff members to have a 30-minute meal break! Using the math to help staff connect to the efficiency they are generating is a powerful message—but only when you break it down to a number that matters to *them*.

No doubt about it: Hourly Rounding gets results. And when staff members start seeing these results in their daily work lives, they'll naturally strive to become even more efficient and effective. When they see that patients are happier and healthier, their enthusiasm will increase even more. Best of all, they become more willing to give other new tactics a chance—and your organization keeps getting better and better.

Key Points in This Chapter

1. Because each of the eight behaviors associated with Hourly Rounding creates a specific desired outcome, it is important that you use every one.

2. Hourly Rounding will improve patient satisfaction along with decreasing falls by 50 percent, decubiti by 14 percent, and call lights by 40 percent.

3. Rounding logs posted within the patients' rooms are a crucial part of the process. They build in the element of accountability and serve as your visual promise to patients and their families that they can trust your care.

4. Measuring and publicizing results is an important leader tool to reinforce the need for continued performance.

Pillars Affected by Hourly Rounding

Service—Improves patient satisfaction by meeting needs on a timely basis; rounding logs demonstrate commitment to providing the best care.

Quality—Impacts three critical areas of quality: falls, skin breakdown, and frequency of call lights.

Finance—Positively affects the bottom line due to improved quality of care, reduced unnecessary days, and the elimination of costs associated with falls and nosocomial decubiti.

People—Contributes to staff's efficiency.

CHAPTER 11

The Bedside Shift Report℠

By Faye Sullivan

Safe handoffs are the responsibility of every nurse. We know it in our hearts and we understand it intellectually. Yet, it's often difficult to make them happen. Why? Perhaps it's because many nurses don't have an evidence-based practice simple enough to ensure that safe handoffs occur with every shift change.

Well, here's the good news. There **IS** a well-defined, proven practice that enables nurses to accomplish safe handoffs: the Bedside Shift Report℠. And you can implement this simple, lifesaving tactic using the information you are about to read.

First, let's talk about the outcomes of bedside reporting. The tactic:

1. Ensures safe handoffs

2. Keeps patients informed about their care

3. Creates trust and reduces patient anxiety by managing up the next care provider

Bedside Shift Report conversations help organizations avoid "dropping the baton" during one of the most critical patient care intervals and provide a standardized change-of-shift procedure for staff to embrace. They involve off-going nurses, oncoming nurses, and patients. Although the details of bedside shift reporting vary from facility to facility, a successful implementation provides a real-time exchange of information that increases patient safety, improves quality of care, increases accountability, and strengthens teamwork.

Here's a well-designed shift report conversation that meets those objectives.

Good morning, Mr. Jones. I am going home now, and Karen is going to be your nurse today. Karen has been with us for three years. I'm leaving you in very good hands.

I'm going to give her the report now, so that she has all the information she needs to take very good care of you today. Please listen, and when I am through, if you have questions, we'll answer them. And, if I've left out anything important for Karen to know, please tell us before we leave.

(Verbally gives report to Karen.)

Mr. Jones, do you have questions? Is there anything more that Karen needs to know in order to provide you with very good care today?

I'm heading home now. Thank you for allowing me to be part of your care team last night.

Read on to learn how to incorporate bedside shift reporting into your organization.

First, Get the Staff Engaged.

Changing habits can be challenging. The first thing you have to do as a nurse leader is make the troops want to follow—that is, to embrace the Bedside Shift Report process.

Find the "WIIFM"—"What's in it for me?"—from your staff's perspective. You might follow the lead of one wise nurse leader who summed it up in a David Letterman-style "Top 10 Reasons for Bedside Reports."

Top 10 Reasons for Bedside Reports

10. Ever had a patient ask with a quiver in her voice, "Who am I getting next?"

9. Ever get into a patient's room and think, *I don't know who she gave her report on??? This guy's really sick!*

8. Ever look at your watch only to think, *Good grief, it's 8:30 and I haven't even laid eyes on every patient yet!*

7. Ever wish someone would help you learn about a tube or drain you've never seen without making you feel incompetent?

6. Ever enter a room to find the IV bag dry and the Foley bag full?

5. Ever think you did not need to hear the details of the domestic quarrel that went on last shift? (When we discuss patients outside their presence, we may often say things that border on gossip and distract us from the medically relevant points.)

4. Ever wish you could find an easy way to keep your patients informed and include them in their health decisions?

3. Ever wish you could get into your shift more easily?

2. Ever wish the off-going nurse would say a few nice things about you to make the transition smoother and help you build trust with your patient?

1. Ever wish we would all practice nursing based on clinical evidence and clearly proven best practices?

It's time to stop thinking of why we CAN'T
and figure out
HOW WE CAN!

Now, you've got your staff's attention. What nurse would *not* want to solve those problems?

Next, role play scenarios with your staff, the most difficult ones they can imagine. Perhaps it's a drug-addicted patient, or one who is terminally ill. Or staff may ask, "What about the patient whose spouse was escorted out by security last night?" In all of these challenging scenarios, you can still give the Bedside Shift Report in a way that accomplishes the goals of safe handoffs, keeps patients informed, and reduces their anxiety. Practicing these scenarios builds your staff's confidence and skill. Let's take the sample script from above and apply it to the patient who has been asking for more narcotics than prescribed.

(Address patient)

Good morning, Mr. Jones. I am going home now, and Karen is going to be your nurse today. Karen has been with us for three years. I'm leaving you in very good hands.

I'm going to give her the report now, so that she has all the information she needs to take very good care of you today. Please listen, and when I am through, if you have questions, we'll answer them. And if I've left out anything important for Karen to know, please tell us before we leave.

(Address nurse)

Karen, you need to understand that Mr. Jones has been very uncomfortable tonight. Managing his pain has been the focus of my care for him. His last pain medication was given at 6 a.m. His next dose can be given at 10 a.m. He asked that I contact Dr. Allen to request an increase in his medication. Dr. Allen and I spoke at 4:30 this morning and he feels we are administering the highest dose we can safely administer right now. We have tried several other things to help Mr. Jones be more comfortable: hourly repositioning, pillows to his back and between his knees, having the TV on to provide distraction.

(Address patient)

Mr. Jones, please rate your pain level now, on a 1-10 scale. Still a 7?

(Address nurse)

Karen, you can see that managing his pain will continue to be the focus of your care today. I know you will do everything you can safely do to help with this.

(Continue report with other clinical information. Then address patient.)

Mr. Jones, do you have questions? Is there anything more that Karen needs to know in order to provide you with very good care today?

I'm heading home now. Thank you for allowing me to be part of your care team last night.

There is plenty of evidence that patients respond well to Bedside Shift Reports. As this graphic clearly shows, when the tactic was implemented in one Florida Emergency Department, patient satisfaction scores for three key survey criteria improved drastically.

Figure 11.1

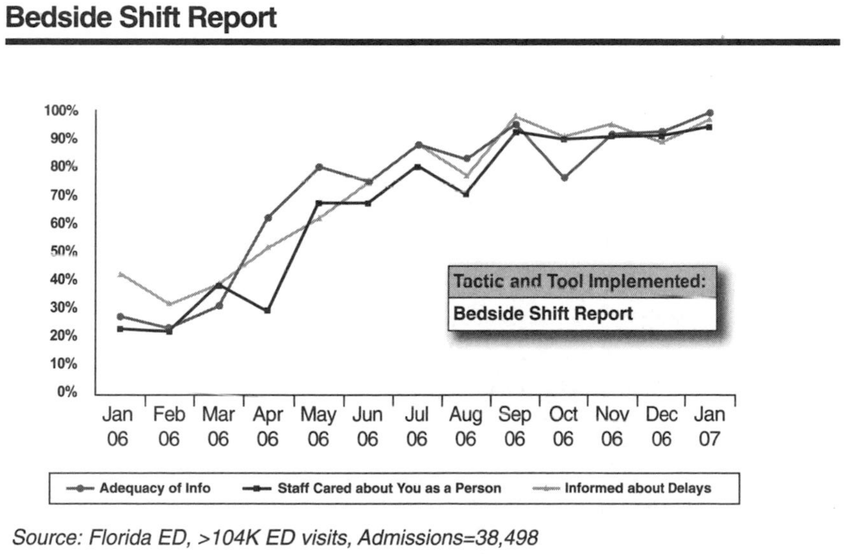

Given this example and an opportunity to problem solve through role play, your staff will devise effective scripts for their own most challenging situations. Keep in mind that if in the judgment of the nurses specific information should not be shared at the bedside, it is okay to save that information to share confidentially. But this is never an excuse to eliminate the Bedside Shift Report altogether.

Guidelines for the Bedside Shift Report

Studer Group® partner Catholic Healthcare West created a Bedside Report Guide containing the following set of detailed instructions:

1. Patient's perspective is valued as being most important—it isn't "about us," our schedule, or comfort zone. At CHW, our priority must be the patients as they are the reason why we are here.

2. If asked questions, you won't have to say, "I haven't seen my patients yet," and therefore you'll be more prepared.

3. The off-going nurse can be "hands-on" in showing the oncoming nurse how to operate special equipment or how special orders are being handled.

4. Introduce the oncoming nurse. Whenever possible, "manage up" him or her.

5. If a new diagnosis (i.e., cancer) or test results occur, give the information the patient is aware of during bedside reporting. You can give additional information to the next shift after the Bedside Report or point to an item on your paper. Do not discuss it in the hallway outside the patient's room, due to confidentiality issues.

6. Discuss with the patient and nursing team the patient's condition as well as appropriate tests and procedures and their purpose. Become familiar with this clinical information in order to properly advise or answer questions for the patient.

7. Check the equipment and supplies in the room—IVs, monitors, etc.

8. What to do if the patient is off the unit or asleep:
   a. Do not wake up the patient, unless he or she has requested to be awake during Bedside Report. This information can be obtained during hourly rounds or as part of the development of the patient's "What's Important to Me Today" items.
   b. Oncoming nurse will observe the patient and quietly check equipment.
   c. Later, the oncoming nurse will review the "Bedside Report" information with the patient/family if they missed it.

d. Off-going nurse will give a verbal report to the oncoming nurse if the patient is off the unit, along with estimated time of patient's return to the unit.

9. If there is a code or crisis at shift change, the oncoming nurse will still go room by room to introduce self and check patients.

10. If visitors are in the room, explain that you are doing bedside reporting and ask the patient if he or she wants them to step out. You should say, "We will be talking about your condition and your progress this past shift. Since we want to maintain your privacy, would you like your visitors to step out for this report?" If there are concerns about the patient being able to answer this question honestly with visitors in the room, ask it when he or she is alone.

11. If the patient is non-compliant, then the off-going nurse should not say "uncooperative" to the oncoming nurse. You could say, "He/she was informed of…but the patient chose to disregard and…." Or, "I have explained that if he/she refuses to use the walker for assistance, the likelihood of a fall and injury increases."

12. Exclude opinions. The Bedside Report is a time for facts. If a nurse is unhappy with the patient (or the physician caring for the patient), the Bedside Report is not the time to vent. Criticism makes the nurse appear less credible.

13. Prior to leaving the room, the off-going nurse thanks the patient for allowing the organization to provide care for him or her.

14. Communicate with your patients before the Bedside Report starts. During your last hourly round you could say,

The SBAR Communication Technique

This technique, whose acronym stands for **S**ituation-**B**ackground-**As**sessment-**R**ecommendation, provides a framework for communication between members of the healthcare team. SBAR is an easy-to-remember and concrete mechanism useful for framing any conversation, including those held in front of the patient. It facilitates an easy, focused way to set expectations and relay important information—essential for developing teamwork and fostering a culture of patient safety.

"We will be doing Bedside Report very soon, so is there anything you need at this time?"

15. Educate the oncoming nursing team if they are float or registry personnel.

16. If the oncoming nurse has a question or needs clarification about a sensitive issue, wait until after the Bedside Report and then ask the off-going nurse. Avoid putting a nurse "on the spot" in front of the patient and/or family.

To download this example, visit www.firestarterpublishing.com/NurseLeaderHandbook.

Figure 11.2

S = situation **B** = background **A** = assessment **R** = recommendation **T**= thank you

S	**"I'm going home now. XX will be your nurse today (tonight). I've worked with XX for a long time and I can tell you I'm leaving you in good hands!" (or some other managing up phrase, i.e., "XX is one of our most experienced nurses; XX is going to take great care of you," etc.)** • State patient name, age • Diagnosis, code status, admit status • Name of primary care MD
B	**"I'm about to give report to XX. Please listen so at the end you can ask any questions or fill in any additional information that XX will need to know to take great care of you today (tonight)."** • Give a brief & pertinent past medical history; explain any co-morbidities or events that led up to this hospitalization or that are having an effect on the patient at this moment in time. <u>Admitted for</u>.......... <u>Pertinent history</u>.......... <u>Pertinent labs/tests</u> (completed or planned for that day and results, if applicable).......... <u>Current therapy</u> (meds, treatments, monitoring, dressings, drains, tubes, oxygen, pulse oximetry, <u>IV sites</u> (PICC, CVC lines, Ports).......... <u>Current VSs</u>.......... <u>Pain</u> (rating, drug, last dose, follow-up assessment, include patient in discussion).......... <u>Other clinical info</u> (PCA/Epidurals—two nurses must check activity level).......... <u>Special needs</u> (precautions, isolations, fall risk, dialysis, fluid restrictions).......... <u>Consults</u> (physician, social worker, case manager, wound care, dialysis, etc.).......... <u>Teaching needs</u> (diabetic, wound care) Ask the patient!.......... <u>Discharge plan and needs</u> (Ask the patient!)..........
A	• Inform the oncoming RN of what you have assessed and/or noted during your shift. • Provide a review of systems (ROS) including: neuron, cardio-pulmonary, GI, GU, peripheral, skin, activity order, diet order, etc. • Mention all tubes, lines, & drains that are associated with each body system assessed. • Include any information or tasks that you have completed in the patient's care. • Mention what the oncoming RN will need to complete or follow-up on. • Include anything that will be coming up for the patient in the near future (procedures, surgery, lab tests, diagnostic studies, etc.). • Be specific about what is going on with the patient now.
R	**"I suggest that you...."**(what needs to be followed up on that shift, patient goals, etc.) • Review the ordered nursing and medical plan of care with the oncoming RN (IV therapy, antibiotic therapy, tube feedings, etc.). • Include relevant medications that have been ordered and any ancillary support services that are working with the patient such as RT, PT, OT, Nutrition Services, Social Services, Discharge Planning, etc. • In giving this portion of the report, include any and all plans for this patient's care (fall precautions, restraint usage, wound care, turning needs, level of acuity, etc.). • Include treatments, consents needing to be signed, pre-op checklists, and any education or psychosocial issues going on with the patient or family unit. • Inform the nurse about the current plan of care for the patient. **"Do you have any questions? Is there anything else XX needs to know about caring for you today (tonight)?"**
T	Thanks—to the patient Prior to leaving the room and in the presence of both nurses, ask the patient the following: "Is your **<u>pain</u>** being well managed? Do you have any **<u>concerns</u>** we need to address? Do you **<u>understand</u>** your plan of care for this hospitalization and your discharge plan?" **<u>Inform</u>** the patient of any diagnostic testing to be completed and what he or she can expect during the upcoming shift. Close with, "We are here to provide you **<u>very good</u>** care! You're in great hands. Thank you for allowing me to care for you today."

To download this example, go to <u>www.firestarterpublishing.com/NurseLeaderHandbook</u>.

Verifying Staff Compliance and Overcoming Resistance

Will you encounter resistance? Of course you will. No change is ever 100 percent smooth. Will you overcome it? Certainly, if you do a good job of validating the efforts of your staff and hardwiring the Bedside Shift Report into your daily operations. Here are some tips for doing just that:

- Create "the vision" by connecting staff to the problems they want solved.
- Dedicate enough time to educate 100 percent of your staff about the *why*, as well as the *what* and *how*.
- Follow through with *personal monitoring of every shift change* yourself, or use a designated leader (perhaps an educator or charge nurse) for 30 days. *Tip: Post a 30-day calendar with the schedule detailing which leader is responsible for ensuring Bedside Shift Report is being done. That way, every staff member knows who will be watching.*
- Publically recognize at least one pair of caregivers who do a very good job of bedside reporting every day for 30 days (or have another leader on your unit to do so). Keep track of who has been recognized in order to help identify high performers who can mentor their colleagues.
- Observe and document competency on every staff member within 30 days.
- Collect stories from your employees about the difference Bedside Report has made for them and share those stories to create momentum.
- Add Bedside Report assessment to your leader rounds on patients by asking patients if nurses are including them in their report at change of shift. Ask if they are using language the patient understands. Ask how the patient likes being included in this process. You can accelerate hardwiring of Bedside Shift Report by using the log in Figure 11.3 to provide feedback to individual staff. It is available for download at www.firestarterpublishing.com/NurseLeaderHandbook.

Figure 11.3

Bedside Handoff Competency Checklist

Date:______________________________

Name:______________________________

Department:______________________________

Evaluator:______________________________

INTRODUCTIONS	OBSERVED	COMMENTS
Knock on door prior to entering—ask permission.		
Foam In		
Manage up—off-going nurse will introduce and manage up, using AIDET format, the oncoming nurse and PCA.		
Use good eye contact.		
EXPLAIN BEDSIDE HANDOFF UPON ADMISSION		
Explain the purpose of bedside handoff (initial visit).		
Use key words "very good" care.		
If visitors are at the bedside, have them leave prior to information exchange to maintain HIPAA regulations.		
SAFETY		
Both nurses check name and allergy bands prior to any care, using key words "for your safety."		
Inform armband checks by all staff prior to any care, tests, or treatments.		
Bring patient into conversation. Encourage to express concerns. Do not talk around patient.		
Check IV sites, solution, & tubing.		
INFORMED		
Update names, date, nursing plan, tests, & treatments on whiteboard. Use laymen's terms.		
Use key words "keep you informed," plan of care, tests & treatments, etc		
Ask, "What questions can I answer?"		
ADDRESS THREE Ps: PAIN...POSITION...POTTY		
How is your pain?		
Are you comfortable?		
Do you need to go to the bathroom?		
ASSESS ENVIRONMENT		
Move items within reach (table, call bell, TV remote, phone, water, and garbage can).		
CLOSING—THANK YOU		
We will round again in about an hour.		
Is there anything else that I can do for you? I have the time.		
Foam Out (If patient has C-Diff, then use soap & water.)		

Goal: 100% Bedside Report is to be given for all patients.
If possible, report is to be written for oncoming shift.

To download a copy of the Bedside Handoff Competency Checklist, please visit www.firestarterpublishing.com/NurseLeaderHandbook.

Figure 11.4

Bedside Report Rounding Feedback—Managers

Date:____________________

To:____________________ **From:**____________________

Room #s:____________________

Activity/Behavioral Items	Comments
Introduced self to patient.	
Explained the goal of the unit (to make sure that the nursing staff helped the patient understand his/her health condition).	
Asked patient if the nurses were introducing next nurse at the end of the shift.	
Asked patient if the nurses were reporting off to one another in the room, with the patient involved.	
Heard key words appropriately.	
Followed up with staff appropriately.	
Has mechanism in place for knowledge of how off-shift rounding is going.	
Rounding is routinely scheduled.	
If watched, observed incorporation of SBAR in report.	

Overall comments:

Staff signature

- Coach, in the moment, any nurse who is not reporting effectively at the bedside.
- When a staff member repeatedly chooses not to give the report as you directed, move from coaching to disciplinary action.

The Many Benefits of Bedside Reporting

Bedside reporting benefits patients, care providers, and organizations in a variety of ways.

First of all, patients see and hear from the team of professionals providing their care. They know who their nurse is on every shift. Plus, they're reassured that oncoming staff is getting all the necessary information to provide excellent care. The report keeps patients well informed and allows them to participate in their care, thereby making them less anxious and more compliant. They're also more satisfied because they know how their care will be attended to and monitored throughout the shift.

The report improves the oncoming shift nurse's understanding of the patient's condition. It also allows the exiting nurse to manage up the oncoming nurse, thus helping to transfer the emotional bank account established during the shift. In addition, since each nurse knows his or her patients' condition at the end of the shift, accountability will increase. Many organizations report a reduction in sentinel events within the two hours on either side of shift change, fewer medication errors, and fewer "near misses" as a result of more thorough and timely assessment by the oncoming nurse.

Figure 11.5

Handoffs and Bedside Report-
Benefits

- Decreases potential for misses and mistakes.
- Increases patient involvement and addresses keeping patients informed.
- Increases trust for patient with managing up.
- Decreases patient waiting at change of shift and feeling forgotten or abandoned.
- Increases accountability for nurses as they report off visually in front of the patient and each other.
- Increases new RN skill level—RNs can see and hear what the experienced RN is doing and why.
- Increases teamwork between shifts.

Bedside reporting is fully appreciated by nursing staff who have worked through the initial discomfort of the tactic and can begin to see the possibilities. Take HCAHPS (a tool now being used to measure patient satisfaction in most organizations with adult inpatients), for instance. One of the questions asked is if the patient received any new medications during his or her hospitalization and if the staff "always" explained the side effects of those new medications. The art of bedside reporting is revealed when the off-going nurse has the conversation with the patient and the oncoming nurse is listening to the recap of their day—rather than the off-going nurse reporting to the oncoming nurse with the patient eavesdropping.

In the case of a patient who's been prescribed a new medication, the Bedside Shift Report might sound something like this:

OGN (off-going nurse): *Mr. Johnson, as you recall Dr. Smith put you on some new medication today for your blood pressure. Can you tell Sherry what that medication is?*

Mr. J: *Oh, yeah. My BP was really high this morning. It was 175 over 100. Dr. Smith was not happy so he's making me take this new medication. Lo-something. I don't remember the name.*

OGN: *Lopressor. He'll get Lopressor 100 mg once a day.*

Mr. J: *That's it. Anyway, I guess I have to take that every day now.*

OCN (oncoming nurse): *Mr. Johnson, do you know the side effects of the new medication we will be watching for?*

Mr. J: *Yes. Lyn went over those with me. She said to watch for dizziness, drowsiness, and lightheadedness. She told me to be careful and not get up on my own.*

OCN: *Exactly. I want you to follow those same instructions while I am here. We want to keep you safe and be sure you don't fall if you were to get up and suddenly experience any of those side effects without warning.*

OGN: *Mr. Johnson, you have been a great student today. Thanks for taking such ownership of your care.*

As you can see, this type of conversation and exchange allows the patient to fully participate in his care plan. It also ensures that he is retaining the things we are teaching. Had he not been able to remember, it would have just been a signal to the OCN that he needs continued reinforcement and she would have made a note to offer that reinforcement throughout her shift. *That*, a real and meaningful exchange between care providers and patients, is the goal of bedside reporting.

Many patients perceive the two to three hours around the shift change to be a time when no one is around. (Sentinel events also occur more often during this time.) Bedside reporting eliminates the feeling that staff is not being attentive.

The following is an actual letter of appreciation written by a patient after her stay at Providence St. Peter Hospital in Olympia, Washington.

A Thank-You from a "Fortunate Cardio Patient"

To Whom It May Concern,

Due to cardiopulmonary issues, I have been hospitalized seven lengthy stays in the past 13 months, at three different hospitals. My greatest care concern, besides the bills and getting better, was the dreaded shift change. With so many different nurse personalities, I was often left wondering if my nurses truly understood my condition, medications, or progress. Were they actually even in communication with my doctor? Then came the fear of starting over again with a new nurse just 12 hours later—or sooner! I often wondered what was being said behind my back, or if there was even time to update my new nurse with an accurate report. The fear of the unknown felt like a weapon formed against me.

To my delight and surprise, Providence St. Peter Hospital changed all that for me two days ago when my night nurse personally introduced me to my day nurse, then proceeded to systematically recall my case, symptoms, and medications with a full Bedside Report. I couldn't believe my ears! My own concerns were actually heard by both nurses and I had the opportunity to interject and clarify. A new confidence in my care grew exponentially in that short 10 minutes! I thought it would be extinguished when the next shift came on but once again I was introduced and then included in the Bedside Report. What an exciting relief.

I now understand this pilot program is being considered a new "Best Practice" on a national level. For once I was the fortunate cardio patient because that was the floor they chose to pilot the new program on! I so appreciate the foresight of Providence St. Peter Hospital to consider adopting this wise "Best Practice" as a goal. I never understood my apprehension of hospital care coordination until I witnessed it being done right! There is an Old Testament scripture (Hosea 4:6) that reads, "...My people will be destroyed by lack of knowledge." Thank you, St. Peter staff, for stepping up to this healthy level of patient care communication. You are now my only hospital!

Very sincerely,
The patient

Key Points in This Chapter

1. Bedside Shift Reports ensure safe handoffs.
2. The process keeps patients informed about their care and allows them to participate in it.
3. It creates trust and reduces patient anxiety by allowing the exiting nurse to manage up the next care provider.
4. Shift reports close the communication loop between incoming and exiting shifts.
5. Patient care is completed from the previous shift, saving everyone time in the long run!

Pillars Impacted by the Bedside Shift Report

Service—Upgrades the level of service due to the communication between shifts and involvement of the patient.

Quality—Provides better quality outcomes because each shift is kept informed of the patient's status, thus reducing the potential for medical errors.

Finance—Impacts financial outcomes through increased awareness of patient status, leading to more timely intervention or discharge planning.

People—Improves teamwork and leads to higher employee satisfaction.

CHAPTER 12

Individualized Patient Care℠

By Pat Treiber and Lauren Charles

As nurse leaders, we're constantly looking for ways to improve both the quality of care we provide and patients' perception of the care they receive. And the latter is not just a quest for higher patient satisfaction scores. The truth is, we recognize that patient anxiety can adversely impact the healing process. With the advent of HCAHPS and the public reporting of hospital care measures, outcomes, and the patient's hospital experience, this issue has never been more important!

In this chapter we'd like to discuss one way to efficiently and effectively improve the quality of care *and* the patient perception of this care. The fourth tactic in the Patient Care Model—Individualized Patient Care℠ (IPC)—can help you do just that.

Individualized Patient Care incorporates the patient's thoughts on **what very good or excellent care means to him or her**. By frequently reviewing performance on what's most important to a patient throughout his or her stay, hospitals can exceed the patient's expectations and ensure better clinical outcomes.

IPC can be utilized in all care areas of the hospital including Inpatient, Outpatient, Ambulatory Surgery, Radiology, and Emergency Departments. By asking patients to tell you what very good or excellent care means to them, you can also avoid or immediately address situations that may create unnecessary anxiety and detract from the healing process.

Ultimately, IPC improves communication between the patient and hospital employees, encourages teamwork and efficiency, and signals to the patient that everyone is working together closely as a team to take care of him or her.

The Value of IPC

The process has been validated by the measurable positive changes the tactic brings about inside organizations that adopt it.

After implementing IPC, one hospital saw a 70 percent jump in patients' rating of "effectiveness of pain management" on its patient satisfaction surveys. Another experienced a 40 percent improvement in patients' "overall rating of care" and a 26 percent increase in "likelihood to recommend."

IPC leads to reduced patient anxiety and improved patient perception of care. It also improves the "likelihood to recommend" on the part of patients and family members.

Shown on the following page are several examples of IPC's proven value.

Figure 12.1

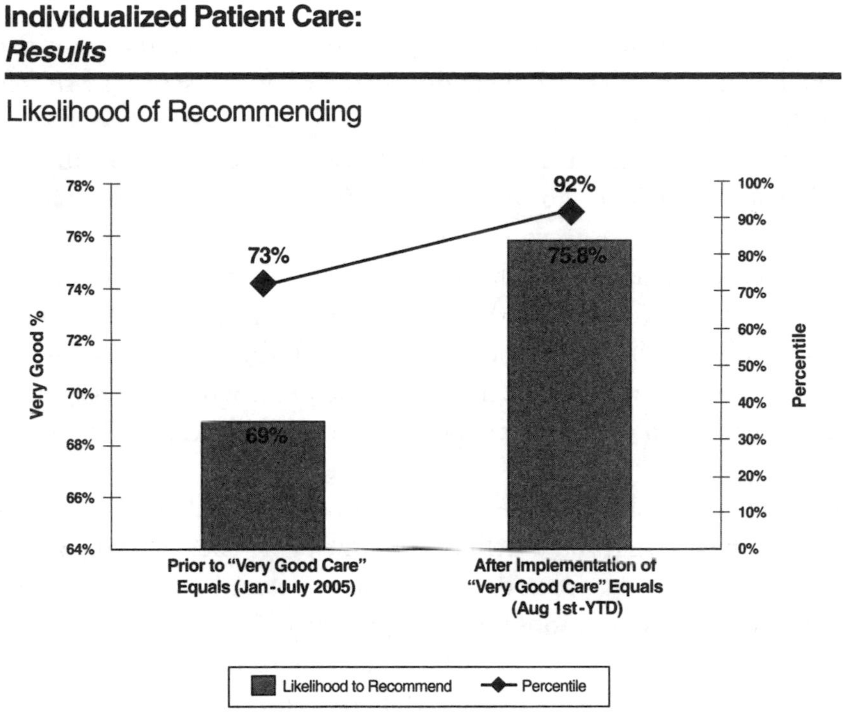

Figure 12.2

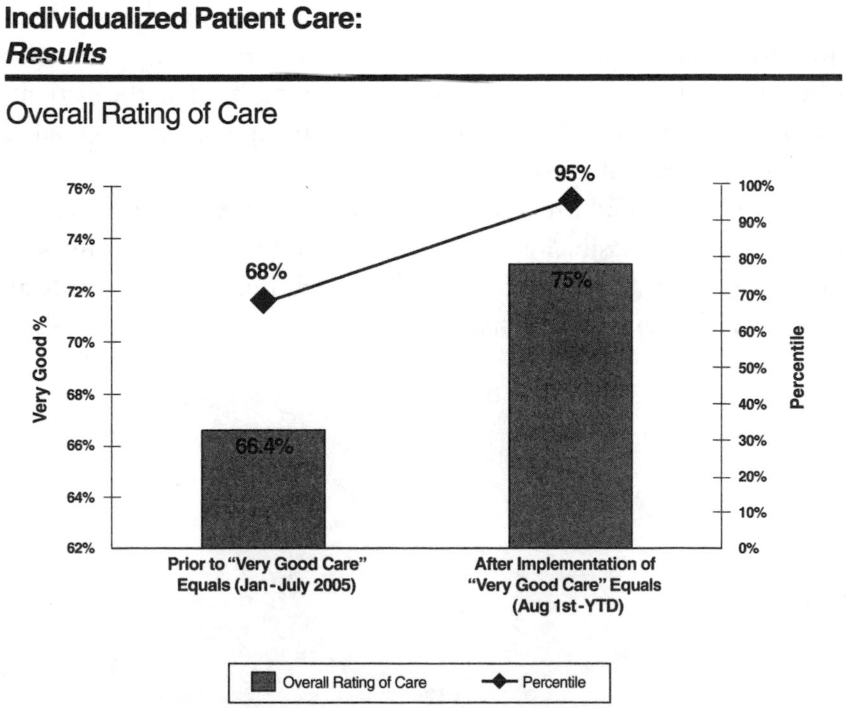

Getting Started: How to Implement Individualized Patient Care

Essentially, IPC involves the staff asking patients to identify and prioritize what will be most important to them during their hospital stay. It's a simple process that yields a big payoff.

Here's how it works. At the time of admission, the nurse asks the patient, "What does *very good* or *excellent* care (use the words of the patient satisfaction vendor) mean to you?"

(Bear in mind that staff might feel awkward asking, "What does very good care look like to you?" As their leader, you can help by role playing with employees to help them get comfortable with the process.)

Once the patient answers the question, the nurse writes the responses on the whiteboard in the patient's room where all healthcare workers can easily read them.

The nurse then asks, "Where are you on the pain scale of 1-10?" followed by, "Where would you LIKE to be on the pain scale?" (Asking about the desired pain level may provide a teaching opportunity for the nursing staff to set realistic expectations with the patient.) The patient's responses are also posted on the board, along with the time of the next pain medication administration. Thus all who enter the room—from physician to transporter to housekeeper to family—see the board and can focus on what is most important to the patient.

At shift change, nursing staff reviews this information at the bedside (Bedside Shift Report℠) with the next caretaker and follows up on what is most important to the patient. During nurse leader rounding, the whiteboard becomes a key part of the conversation to verify that the patient's expectations for care and pain management are being met; it also enables timely service recovery, if needed.

In the Outpatient and Emergency Departments where white or greaseboards may not be accessible, we recommend using cards to identify what is most important to the patient. After they're completed, these cards are then placed on the front of the chart.

Figure 12.3

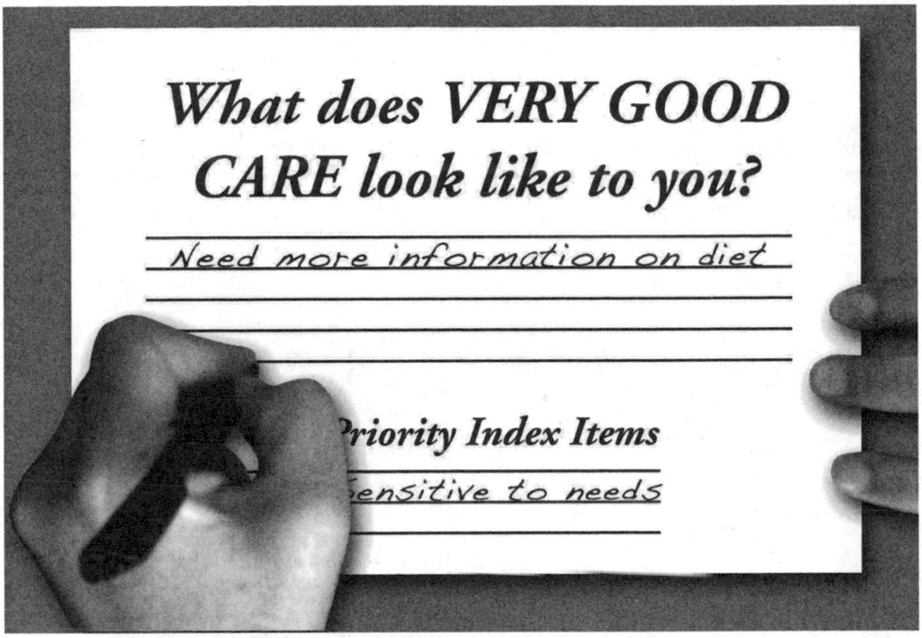

Figure 12.4

How to Implement Individualized Patient Care

Action	How it works
1. Use key words.	Upon admission, the nurse says to the patient: "Our goal is to provide very good care. *(Use appropriate language from your patient satisfaction survey.)* What three things can we do to make sure your care is very good?" If the patient doesn't know, dig deeper using items from the survey. Say: "How important is your pain management? Keeping you informed? Ensuring your call lights are answered?"
2. Note items on the whiteboard.	There should be a whiteboard in every patient's room. Also write the patient's pain goal and the next time medication is due.
3. Ask during daily rounds.	The nurse manager should ask, "How well are we doing (with each of identified needs)?" and connect these to survey questions.
4. Ask at shift change.	Nursing staff should repeat as above.
5. Ask at discharge.	Both nursing staff and case managers should ask, "How well have we done at (identified needs)?"
6. Review the survey tool.	At discharge, the case manager should review the survey tool. Say, "We survey our patients. It is one way we learn how we are doing and is a way to recognize staff. Will you please do me a favor and complete and return this when it arrives in the mail? Thank you. This is so important to us." (Note: If the patient is not happy, use service recovery!)
7. Make discharge phone calls.	During the call, ask how well the hospital did at meeting the needs identified by the patient.

It may also be a good idea to verify that IPC is getting done by including the item on your rounding log:

Figure 12.5

Individualized Patient Care Patient Rounding Log

Rounding on Patients

Unit__________ Manager__________ Date__________

Patient Name (Introduce and Acknowledge)	What are your three priorities for very good care?	How are we doing meeting your three priorities?	Who can I reward and recognize?	What physicians can I recognize for giving very good care?	Is there anything else I can do for you?	Thank the patient	Action/ follow up
1.							
2.							
3.							
4.							
5.							
6.							
7.							
8.							
9.							
10.							

To download a copy of this rounding log, please visit www.firestarterpublishing.com/NurseLeaderHandbook.

Getting the Staff on Board

One best practice that enables you to engage staff in the effectiveness of IPC is the use of daily shift "huddles" mentioned in Section 1 of this book. Remember, these are about five- to ten-minute, stand-up meetings used to connect to the *why* of IPC through the use of stories. While some nurses might at first be reluctant to share their stories, they will quickly jump in as their peers begin to participate.

Tip: As the nurse leader, you can round on patients prior to the huddles to collect positive stories to tell at the start of the meeting. It's also a good opportunity to compliment staff members who've been recognized by patients for their use of IPC.

What's great about these huddles is that as nurses start sharing what is going well and how patients are positively responding, staff members are motivated to do it more—a true connection to purpose!

A Couple of Great Stories That Illustrate the Impact of IPC

From a nurse manager in Lake City, Florida: I asked a post-partum patient what very good care meant to her. Her response was: "Please teach me to hold my baby safely." I had not realized that the patient had a problem with her right arm and her biggest fear was dropping the baby. That knowledge allowed us to provide not only good patient care, but also peace of mind.

From an orthopedic surgeon in Springfield, Vermont: I do about 300 knees every year. For the longest time I had the mindset that "a knee is a knee." Once we implemented IPC, I started noticing there was something on the whiteboards and that it was different from patient to patient. Knees have become people to me now!

From a director of nursing in Charlotte, North Carolina: A nine-year-old girl who had a spinal injury with a tracheotomy was admitted to our hospital. A few months ago, we would not have asked her to tell us what excellent care meant to her, as we knew it would be difficult for her to speak and us to understand. Generally "trach" patients prefer not to speak.

But ask we did, and she said (very clearly): "Don't just look in on me—talk to me." We put this on the board. As it turned out she was there for 14 days. Can you imagine what a lonely experience that would have been for her if we hadn't asked and written her words on the board? Think how many staff members would have looked in, smiled, and gone on their way. The child had a wonderful stay because we were not "uncomfortable" asking our patients what excellent care meant to them. I will never care for a patient again without asking that question.

The huddle also enables clarification of any questions regarding the process to ensure standardized execution. For instance, nurse leaders can ask staff:

- What is going well with IPC?
- What do you need to be more successful?
- Tell me what you are hearing when you ask the patient what excellent/very good care means to him or her?
- What have the patients said about the whiteboards?

Of course, staff members won't always embrace IPC right away. As the nurse leader, you will most likely hear statements such as, "This is just one more thing you are asking me to do!" Connecting staff members back to the "why" will help. So will explaining to them that, in the end, IPC will save them time because they'll be focusing on what's most important to the patient.

Remember, as nurses we sometimes feel we know what's best for patients, or even what's most important to them. IPC can serve as a gentle reminder that, in fact, we don't. This process lets you align priorities based on the customer's actual input. And when you listen what the patient really wants and needs, it's hard to go wrong.

Meaningful Care: A "Whole Team" Effort

Finding out what really matters to patients—and making it happen—is the heart of IPC. And it isn't only a job for nurses. Every staff member can provide deeply meaningful Individualized Patient Care. The following story illustrates this truth beautifully:

Helen Kowalow, a housekeeper at Meno Ya Win Health Centre, was working her normal shift the week of May 11. As she was cleaning a patient's room during her rounds, she could tell that he was in great discomfort and obviously very sick. She had gotten to know the gentleman after weeks of cleaning his room and through the general conversations that she has with all of the patients in her area. She asked the man if there was anything she could do for him, such as getting a minister. The man explained that there was one thing she could do for him that would mean a great deal: He wanted to see some spiritual native leaders to help him along with his journey. He had never received his "Native Name" and he was a bit distressed about it as he felt his time was coming to an end.

At first, Helen was unsure how she could help the man, but she felt compelled to do something. So after her shift she made phone calls to many of her friends in the native community. The next day spiritual leaders showed up with their drums, tobacco, and other native spiritual instruments. They performed a wonderful full native ceremony for the man. During the ceremony the spiritual leaders asked the man if he visualized anything at all during the drumming. He replied that he had envisioned a bear. The spiritual leaders then bestowed on him his "Native Name" of "Great Spirit Bear." The man was noticeably moved and very happy with what had transpired. Now he could continue his journey, he explained.

Days later, the man passed away with family and friends at his side. Among them was our housekeeper Helen Kowalow.

Helen was so moved by what had happened that she now volunteers at our long-term care facility on her days off. The Meno Ya Win Hospital also recognized her efforts with the first of its "Patient Service" Awards, making her an example to all employees of what the hospital is looking for when it comes to patient care and doing the right thing first.

Helen was the first recipient of one of my I-Impact thank-you cards two years ago. She and her family thanked me for the gesture and explained that the small thank-you card was a very important recognition and that it had brought the family to tears. Helen understood her actions did not go unnoticed.

Helen Kowalow is a perfect example of how an ARAMARK housekeeper is not just a cleaner, but is integral and connected to all in our hospital providing excellent patient care.

Al Kernohan
Manager Dietary, Environmental,
and Laundry Services
ARAMARK HEALTHCARE
MENO YA WIN HEALTH CENTRE

Key Points in This Chapter

1. IPC helps *all* your staff members as well as all members of the care team focus and customize their efforts to meet each patient's particular needs.

2. The IPC process yields better patient satisfaction scores in the areas of effective pain management, overall perception of care, and likelihood to recommend organization to others.

3. Asking where the patient would like to be on the pain scale provides an excellent teaching moment in pain management.

4. It is important to connect the dots about the purpose of IPC by communicating patient stories daily with each shift. This is the *why* behind the *what* that increases engagement of all staff in the process.

Pillars Affected by Individualized Patient Care

Service—Improves patients' perception of care due to staff's focus on what's important to them.

Quality—Enhances the quality of care by making staff aware of issues with pain. Posting patient information on the whiteboards also reduces the potential for errors.

Finance—Makes it more likely that, because they're more satisfied, patients will choose your hospital in the future.

People—Increases employee satisfaction through additional opportunities for employee reward and recognition.

Growth—Positively impacts the patients' likelihood to recommend, thus driving volume.

CHAPTER 13

Key Words at Key Times (AIDET℠)

By Tonya Fuller and Terry Rose

What are Key Words at Key Times? Basically, they are carefully chosen words healthcare professionals use to "connect the dots" and help patients, families, and visitors better understand what we are doing—and most importantly, *why*.

Most patients are distracted and frightened and sometimes they're in pain. We may think we have conveyed a particular message, but in reality what we thought we were communicating may not have been heard. That's why key words need to be simple. They help the patient understand his or her care better, and they align the behavior of the staff to the needs of the patient.

When we talk about key words, we are really talking about building a mutually beneficial relationship with our patients.

Examples of Key Words

Below are a few examples of key words used by nurses and other staff members:

- "I am closing the curtain for your privacy."
- "I want to make sure you are very satisfied with the cleanliness of your room. Have I missed anything?"
- "Do you have any questions before I leave?"
- "We are very committed to managing your pain. I have been specially trained in pain management."
- "Your doctor wants to see how you are doing. I need to draw some blood now so that the results will be available for when she will be looking in on you."
- "Dr. Jones is one of the best physicians at this hospital. He is highly trained and has been practicing for more than 20 years. Most patients love him."

How do these words help patients? Well, consider what communication could potentially be missed if these words were absent. Take the first example, for instance. If you silently close the curtain in front of a patient, he may make any number of wrong assumptions—that he's annoying you, that you're doing something you don't want him to see, or that something scary is about to happen to him and you need to shield the eyes of others.

In general, patients are apprehensive about what will happen to them, they don't understand staff's "language," and they struggle to reach a comfort level. Key Words at Key Times help the patient feel more comfortable about his care. They make him feel more engaged so he will be more likely to ask questions.

Key words also help to build a stronger relationship between the nurse and doctor. Why? Because by saying nice things about the doctor to the patient, the nurse confirms the patient's physician choice and reduces his anxiety—which means he'll be in a much better state for the visit. Plus, feeling like he knows a little about the doctor will further increase his comfort level and his willingness to interact with her.

When and How Often Do We Use Key Words?

Key words should be used for any behavior you want staff to do consistently. Let's say nurses know that pain management is mentioned on the priority index and is a focus for them. Building in key words that ask how pain is being managed forces the behavior of checking on patients' pain levels. (Then, in nurse leader rounds, the prioritized behavior is verified again when the leader uses her own key words: "Has your pain been managed?")

Studer Group recommends that key words be chosen based on patient priorities. You can review your patient satisfaction survey priority index to determine areas that need improvement and build key words around these. (Remember to focus on only one item at a time, and once that improves move to the next—this will give you the best chance for success.)

Let your team be part of the process by helping to choose three to four sets of key words that support patient care. Staff will be more likely to use the words if they are part of determining what to focus on and if they understand the impact.

AIDET: A Framework for Key Word Success

We have found AIDET℠—also called the Five Fundamentals of Service—to be a good system for applying key words. AIDET is an acronym for a communication framework that utilizes just five very important key words: Acknowledge, Introduce, Duration, Explanation, and Thank You.

When you as a nurse leader educate, support, and coach staff on how to incorporate AIDET into daily practices, the results are amazing. Evidence shows it greatly improves patients' perception of the care your staff is providing, drives quality outcomes, and builds customer loyalty. But first, the key words themselves:

> **A** stands for **Acknowledge** the patient. Use the person's last name if possible. "Hello, Mrs. Jones."
> **I** stands for **Introduce**. Introduce yourself, your skill set, your professional certification, and your training. "My name is Tonya and I will be your nurse today. I am trained as a registered nurse—I'm an RN—and have been in this profession for 10 years now. In a little while, Mary, a phlebotomist, will be in to draw your blood. She is very good at what she does."
> **D** stands for **Duration**. "It will only take Mary a few minutes to get a blood sample, and your physician will have the results later today."
> **E** stands for **Explanation**. "The physician wants to check your blood in order to confirm his diagnosis. When Mary arrives, the

first thing she will do is look at your wrist band to verify who you are—this is for your safety and is a part of the excellent care we provide here."

T is for **Thank You**. "Thank you for choosing our hospital, Mrs. Jones."

What Do Key Words and AIDET Accomplish?

As we mentioned earlier, Key Words at Key Times create better patient experiences. They help patients feel more relaxed and confident about their care, they help nurses, physicians, and other staff members do a better job, and they improve outcomes. Therefore, it's not surprising that organizations adopting key words and/or AIDET have better patient satisfaction scores.

Figure 13.1

Key Words at Key Times–AIDET℠
Outcome-Medical Imaging

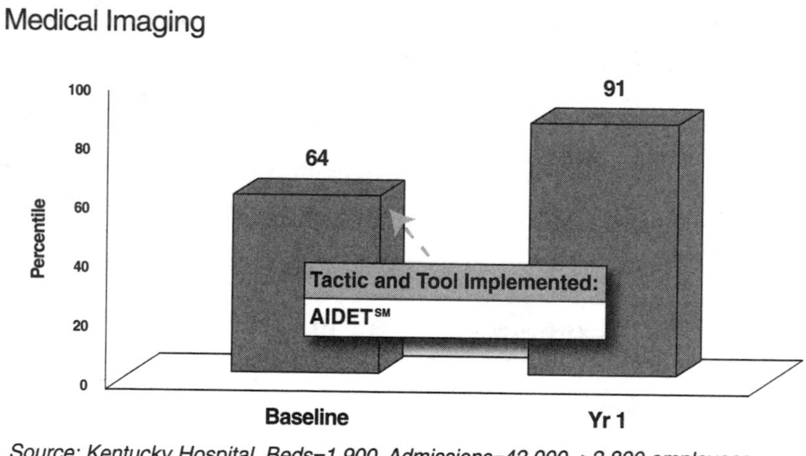

Source: Kentucky Hospital, Beds=1,900, Admissions=42,000, >2,800 employees

As you can see, when the Medical Imaging Department at one Kentucky hospital introduced AIDET, it moved from the 64th to the 91st percentile in patient satisfaction in just one year!

This tactic helps your staff be perceived as a high-performing team. It assists with delivering the kind of service that raises the bar on "likelihood to recommend." Also, patients and family members are less likely to complain because they've been kept informed at every point of their experience. For example, one hospital in Arizona decreased complaints by 50 percent over three quarters of the year when AIDET was implemented!

No doubt key words and AIDET benefit hospitals financially in many other hard-to-measure ways. They reduce errors and improve compliance, which leads to less litigation. They improve employee satisfaction, which decreases costly turnover and attracts the best new talent in the field (winners always want to work with other winners). And they increase physician satisfaction—sometimes dramatically! All of these factors create a positive impact on an organization's bottom line.

Figure 13.2

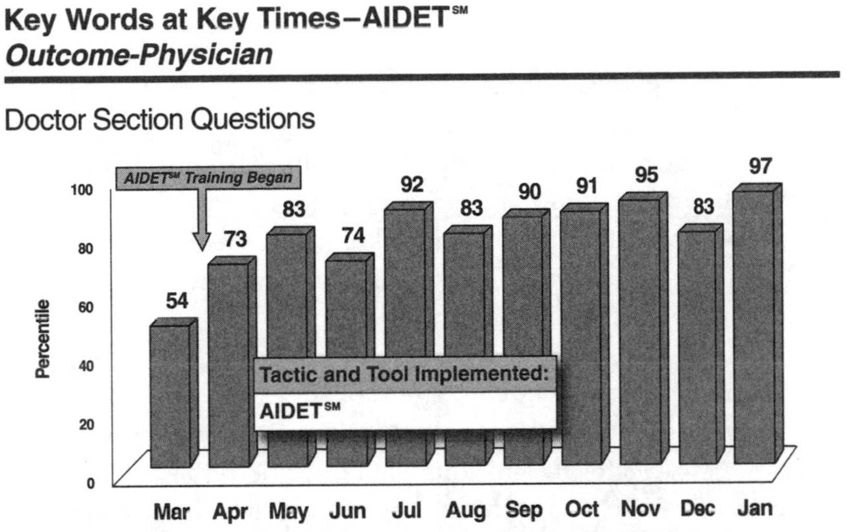

Source: Florida Hospital ED, 80,000/yr volume - Level I Trauma Center, >3,700 employees

Get Staff Engaged by Helping Them Connect the Dots

First things first: You've got to communicate to employees the impact the use of key words/AIDET will have on patients. It's helpful to have listened to some conversations and to share examples of when key words or portions of the AIDET acronym have been used. As you talk with your team, explain what the process is, what you need from staff, and what success will look like. But, most importantly, connect the dots between why you are asking the staff to do this and what can be gained. Share an example that shows the impact key words can have on patients and their families.

Start making the connection by explaining that AIDET is a process deeply rooted in quality. Evidence shows its use decreases patient and family anxiety. When they are less anxious, they hear caretakers better and are more compliant. Patients are also able to grasp crucial points about their plan of care or discharge instructions that otherwise might have been missed; this results in improved quality outcomes.

In addition, explain that the use of AIDET improves patients' and families' perception of care. They feel they're being kept better informed; things are explained clearly; and staff is showing more courtesy, respect, and compassion.

Below is an exercise that is very helpful when engaging staff to utilize key words/AIDET.

"Need to Have" vs. "Nice to Have":

This is a simple exercise that you can do at a staff meeting. Ask the staff to think of themselves as the patient coming in for a procedure so they put themselves in that frame of mind. Then, go through each step of AIDET and ask staff: "As a patient, is this a need to have or a nice to have?" It would go something like this:

> "If you are the patient coming in for surgery today, is the staff caring for you acknowledging you by name a need to have or a nice to have?" Most staff will agree this would be a need to have as it is a patient safety issue, and even patients coming for routine activities want to know that you know who they are.
>
> Now ask, "If you are a patient, is the staff introducing themselves to you and telling you something about their skill set or expertise a need to have or a nice to have?" Again, they will usually agree that this is very important as many patients are not automatically trusting of our qualifications and they want assurance they are in safe, competent hands.
>
> Continue the process with asking about duration. "Do patients need to know about time frames or is it simply nice to know?" If they are being honest, they will say it is a need.
>
> Next ask about explanations. Of course, they will agree it is a need.

Lastly ask them about thank-yous. Okay, you can give in on this one, but staff members will have to admit that saying "thank you" is the polite thing to do.

At the end of this exercise, you have essentially gotten the staff to agree that 80 percent of AIDET encompasses the NEEDS of the patient, and therefore it is our professional responsibility to meet those needs.

Once they have come to that conclusion, you are no longer discussing how comfortable they are with doing it; you've moved on to, "How do we make sure it happens?" After all, nurses weren't comfortable the first time they started an IV or inserted a Foley catheter, but their discomfort couldn't stop them from doing the procedure. The patient's needs took precedence. It is no different with AIDET. And just as with IVs, the more you do it the more comfortable it becomes.

Remember and remind your staff that key words and AIDET are a dynamic process of communication. It is not a script or something that you deliver once and then you're done. Rather, it changes organically during the course of your experience with the patient as her needs change. You might be four hours into the shift and the patient now needs an IV started. Does she need a new AIDET? Sure she does. She needs you to acknowledge her, to tell her you are good at this, to tell her how long this will take and to explain what you are going to do. She may not need as much of an introduction, but it should be modified to the expertise based on that procedure.

Employees might ask you: "What about patients? Do I have to introduce myself with those I care for over and over again?" Explain that it's okay to say, "Mrs. Smith, I am so honored to care for you again. Remember, my name is Terry and I was your nurse (or personal care assistant or certified nursing assistant) the last time you were here." However, they should use the full AIDET upon entering the patient's room and seeing that a family member has arrived who does not know the staff.

AIDET will need to be done over and over again during the course of care. Treating AIDET as a process of communication and not as a memorized script will allow it to be more meaningful in terms of meeting the patient's needs.

Best Practices for Implementation

There are several best practices you can adopt when implementing AIDET:

- Introduce to the organization through senior and middle management first. They can practice (role model) AIDET in department meetings, Leadership Development Institutes, employee forums, leader rounding, orientation sessions, and wherever they routinely introduce themselves. Having senior and middle management practice the tactic first helps staff members see its value.
- Use and communicate a timeline for implementation. Successful units roll out AIDET to employees within one to three months, depending on the size of the individual departments. Create a presentation or use a flip chart in training sessions to explain the meaning of each letter of AIDET, and to explain the valuable purpose it serves. Include physicians who are working closely with your individual unit.
- Develop and share AIDET key words. During training, split staff up into small groups and have each employee develop a personal AIDET to share with the group. Then divide staff into teams of two people to role play AIDET behaviors in everyday patient experiences. After that, each team presents to the group overall, with staff rating the performances on a scale of one to five, five being the best.
- Start with one letter at a time. Some nurse leaders prefer this because it allows effective focus on the patient satisfaction survey. For instance, if explanation of test and treatment is an area of opportunity on a particular nurse unit, focusing on the "E" in AIDET will drive timely results.
- Spend extra time on the "I" in AIDET. The introduction will be the most difficult for employees to hardwire. It's not the introduction itself; rather the challenge comes when staff members feel it seems like bragging when they talk about their skills, certifications or training, and how long they've been on staff. Connect the dots for employees as to why managing up their skill set is important: Evidence shows that when patients learn about a nurse's skills or years of experience, their anxiety is decreased.
- Deal with AIDET stragglers. There are always at least a few employees who are hesitant to adopt new behaviors or different

ways of doing business. Our advice regarding them? *Support, coach, support.* Observe them closely, and when you do see them practicing AIDET, be sure to immediately reward and recognize. Provide coaching on areas for improvement. Communicate very specific follow-up actions required, and let them know you will revisit to see their progress. When you see improvement, reward and recognize again. However, if you see no progress, then it's time for the low performer conversation.

Once you are confident that 90 percent of staff is competent with executing AIDET, leadership can include the process in orientation so new employees can see it being demonstrated. On your unit, choose those who excel at it to mentor new staff.

It's important to clearly communicate your expectations for the practice of AIDET. Emphasize that it's not a program or "flavor of the month" with a beginning and an end. Rather, it's the way staff will always do business in the future because it's what's right for your customers. And remember: You must be the change you wish to see on your unit. Role model AIDET at all times—your staff watches and listens to everything you do!

Finally, schedule time to review your team's key words/AIDET to update them and adjust them based on new priorities. You may have initially focused on the management of pain and thus improved patients' perception of this. At some point you'll need to look at the latest priority index to focus on another item to improve.

Six Ways to Hardwire Key Words/AIDET

A (Acknowledge)
I (Introduce)
D (Duration)
E (Explanation)
T (Thank You)

Once training has taken place, the next step is hardwiring the use of key words/AIDET on a daily basis. As with any new process, you must trust but validate. There are numerous ways this can be accomplished.

1. Rounding on Employees and Observing Them in Action

In rounding conversations verify compliance by asking employees to share an example of how they used AIDET in the past month:

- *Give me an example of how you delivered a difficult "E" this month.*
- *Give me an example of how you took the "I" to the next level* (introduced self and skill set, managed up experience and training).
- *What's the hardest part of AIDET for you?* Then role play and work through the barriers with that employee.

In some instances rounding conversations may not be enough. You may want to accompany the nurse on patient rounds to observe and coach.

Reward and recognize for any positive use of AIDET. Don't wait until your staff has perfected the process to provide praise. For example, you might see someone doing the Acknowledgment and Introduction well, but failing to communicate the Duration. Praise what's being done right, then provide positive coaching on the gap. Finally, identify trends across the unit/department and share these with staff to reduce variance and enhance outcomes.

During the first year of implementation, utilize the AIDET competency assessment (Figure 13.3) biannually to observe and check off each employee. It measures *consistent proficiency* in using the process when communicating with patients, visitors, physicians, and peers. (You may download this tool at www.firestarterpublishing.com/NurseLeaderHandbook.)

Figure 13.3

AIDET Competency Assessment

Name: ________________ **Job Title:** ________________ **Department:** ________________

Competency: Using the AIDET Communication Technique

Instructions: Complete the self-assessment portion of this document using the key. Record completion of each performance criteria. The evaluator's signature validates the completion of each skill. Return to the department manager for your file. Assessment Key: 1- Needs improvement 2- Can perform independently 3- Independent/can teach Method of Evaluation: S- Simulation DO- Evaluator Direct Observation If competency is assessed on multiple dates (other than the date noted with the signature), place the date in the evaluator's assessment column.	Competency Statement: All staff will display consistent proficiency in using AIDET when communicating with patients, visitors, physicians, peers, managers, volunteers, internal and external customers. Policies to Review and Learning Resources: AIDET handout Observes peers

Performance Criteria	Self-Asessment Place an X in box 1, 2, or 3 (see legend)			Evaluator's Assessment (see legend)					
				1		2		3	
	1	2	3	S	DO	S	DO	S	DO
Identifies the purpose of using the AIDET principle.									
Utilizes the AIDET principle to communicate with others, with a focus on patients and their families.									
ACKNOWLEDGE: the customer • Smiles, makes eye contact, greets them and calls them by name in a pleasant manner									
INTRODUCE: self • States name and role at HOSPITAL NAME • Highlights skill and expertise of self and other healthcare team members									
DURATION: • Gives the customer a time expectation • Keeps the customer informed as to the amount of time a procedure or process will take • Includes letting them know if there is a wait time, gives time expectation for that wait									
EXPLANATION: • Keeps customer informed by explaining all processes and procedures • Communicates clear expectations of what will be occurring									
THANK: the customer • Thanks the customer for their time • Expresses appreciation to the customer for their cooperation and communication • Asks if there is anything else he/she can do for the customer before ending the interaction									
Ensures non-verbal communication conveys the AIDET principle: • Makes eye contact • Respects the patient's personal space (as possible) • Listens to what the patient is saying, allows for silences, does not interrupt with his/her own thoughts • Ensures body language is relaxed, open and non-threatening • Displays calm manner									

Employee signature **Date**

☐ **Competency Met** ________________ **Evaluator's signature** **Date**

Employee signature **Date**

☐ **Improvement Plan Completed** ________________ **Evaluator's signature** **Date**

Employee signature **Date**

2. Rounding on Patients

In your rounds as the nurse leader, ask patients or family members questions to validate staff's usage of key words/AIDET.

- *Our goal is to have all staff members introduce themselves and keep you informed. Did they introduce themselves to you?*
- *Did the staff share the plan of care with you and keep you informed?*
- *Our goal is to ensure we explain your plan of care and answer your questions. Did staff explain your procedure* (or discharge instructions, or why you were waiting and how long it would take, and so forth)? *Did staff members answer all of your questions?*

3. Reviewing Patient Satisfaction Survey Results

Review the results of specific questions on the survey. This information will tell you the parts of AIDET that staff are not adhering to consistently.

- Courtesy and friendliness of staff—This perception is impacted by A, I, and T
- Kept informed of delays—Perception impacted by D and E
- Promptness in response to call—Perception impacted by D and E
- Wait time/explanation of tests and treatments—Perception impacted by D and E

Then, using your survey data, create a "tactics" dashboard to track progress and communicate incremental wins to staff. Remind them that the information in this tool represents the "voice of the patient." Below is an example of a dashboard you might use.

Figure 13.4

AIDET Dashboard

Baseline= ______________________ Goal= ______________________

Week or Month	n size	Nurses' courtesy (A, I, T)	N Nurses informative re: treatments (D, E)	Explanation of tests/ treatments (D, E)	Informed about delays (D, E)	Courtesy of the EVS staff (A, I, T)

4. Reading Patient Satisfaction Survey Comments
Review comments for evidence of AIDET and coach on negative remarks made by patients. (These are opportunities for improvement!)

- Staff/physicians named in comments—Coach on A and I
- Kept informed/explanation—Coach on D and E
- Courteous, kind, helpful—Coach on A, I, T

5. Tying AIDET to the Standards of Behavior
When AIDET is tied to the Standards, staff understand that the use of

key words is non-negotiable. It's part of the performance code that every employee is expected to adhere to when approaching a patient or providing a service. In addition, as an important part of the Standards, AIDET becomes incorporated into each person's performance review.

6. Communicating "Wins"

When you receive positive letters from patients or families, highlight the key words that relate to AIDET. Then pass the correspondence around in your daily huddles and post it on your communication board. Following is an actual letter a patient wrote.

The Nicest People I've Ever Met

To whom it may concern:

I wanted to pass on a compliment to you and the staff. On Wednesday, March 18, my mother-in-law (I call her "Mom") was scheduled for an unexpected computer tomography (CT) scan. When we arrived at outpatient services, we were greeted by Missy, who was friendly and pleasant, and introduced herself in a way we have never experienced before. As we sat in the waiting room, one of the workers from Radiology came out to ask us if we had everything we needed and to tell us how much longer it would be.

When Mom was called back for her CT scan, staff escorted her to the room. Afterwards, an employee promptly returned her to me, saying she would be back in a few minutes after checking to make sure the films were of good quality. While we were sitting there, Mom said, "While I was in the CT scanner, everyone introduced themselves to me and told me how long they had worked here—one person has worked here 40 years! I know they did this because they thought I was nervous and wanted me to know they were qualified so I wouldn't be scared. I have never met such nice people."

Then one of Radiology's personnel came out and said she had talked with the doctor's office, the scan was negative, and Mom was cleared to go home. She expressed her thanks to Mom for choosing that hospital and said it was a pleasure to provide excellent care to her. My mother-in-law just thought this was the greatest thing since sliced bread!

As we were walking out, Mom said, "I really like this hospital; these are the nicest people I've ever met." Everyone we came in contact with truly made a difference in the way my mother-in-law was treated and how she interpreted that hospital visit.

Tips for Using Key Words

While the words used are very important, the actions accompanying them are just as significant. Positive body language, maintaining eye contact, smiling, and giving the patient your full attention are necessary. Your attitude and the nature of your voice when saying the key words are critical! People pick up on insincerity very quickly.

When talking with patients, families, and visitors, refrain from using the following negatives: *can't... but...not our policy...we're short staffed...I can't believe they kept you waiting so long.*

Use phrases such as: "Thank you so much for telling me," "I apologize for the inconvenience," "I promise I'll do my best to resolve the situation as soon as possible," "I can help you better if...."

Studies have shown that effective communication turns complaints into compliments. The power of a few words at the right time...equals Key Words at Key Times!

Overcoming Staff Reluctance

It is not uncommon for nurse leaders to get pushback from their teams on the use of key words. Staff may feel you are "scripting" them because you don't trust how they interact with patients. Often this concern can be overcome by connecting the usage to the purpose. Explain to staff that patients and family members want to know what's going on and why certain procedures, processes, or actions take place. This is only human. But knowing how busy staff members are, they hesitate to "interrupt" them with questions. They may also fear they won't understand what they're hearing or will look foolish.

Remind staff that AIDET is a *communication* tool used to keep patients informed at every step of their healthcare experience in a very consistent way. You are reassuring them that the best possible care is being delivered. This, in turn, creates the "wow" factor that fosters loyalty!

AIDET also ensures that patients hear the words and see the actions that mean the most to them. It puts their emotional experience at the heart of the healing process. When staff members use key words properly, they won't come across as mechanical or phony and they won't sound like robots. The nurse leader can help employees erase reluctance to use key words via role playing exercises, positive reinforcement, and reminders of what AIDET accomplishes: It helps them be the very best caretakers.

Mr. White's "Concern"

Have you ever had one of those days in your healthcare life where before you know it, it's three p.m. and you can't remember if you've eaten or taken a restroom break? Let me take you to that day. A staff member came to inform me that the husband of one of our patients wanted to see me. Now, was I thinking on the way to Mr. White's room about the praise I know is coming my way? Not really! But I was pleasantly surprised.

I introduced myself to Mr. White, shook his hand, and asked him to be seated. I listened as he shared a story about the staff. His wife was recovering from anesthesia after a colonoscopy, a test she must have frequently. It was their first time in our hospital. I learned quickly it would not be their last! In fact, Mr. White told me that if the doctor changed hospitals going forward, he would change doctors.

Mr. White's glowing praise referenced many key words: "Every staff member introduced themselves. I know how long each of them has worked here. While they prepped my wife for her procedure, I learned how many intravenous lines Gina has started in her career. I heard how many colonoscopy procedures Russell and Karen have helped Dr. Smith with. I did not want for anything, nor did my wife. Every staff member asked me before they left the room, 'Is there anything I can get you? I have the time.'"

I told Mr. White how much I appreciated his sharing with me the names of the employees who had gone above and beyond. But he did have one concern. "Terry, I am a workplace engineer by trade. While I appreciated the attention we had today, you may want to find other things for your staff members to do. They seemed to have too much time on their hands."

I thanked him for his suggestion and left the room. Then I high-fived the staff as I shared Mr. White's praise and his "concern."

—Terry Rose

You will have employees who are quick to adopt the process because they see the importance and understand the "why" behind AIDET. Latch on to their coattails, so to speak. Praise, praise, and praise them again in public for the good work they're doing. But don't expect that every employee on your unit will adopt and practice AIDET consistently overnight. In fact, it might take several months or longer to achieve. The key to positive movement forward is continued communication, as well as reward and recognition for behaviors practiced well. When you observe the process being used by employees, commend them. Share patient comments and stories from rounding that demonstrate AIDET utilization, and reward the staff members responsible.

Ensure that your leadership team members (charge nurses, unit supervisors, etc.) are firmly in your camp and serve as role models. When they also connect employees to the reason why they must use AIDET with every patient...every interaction...every day, then the reluctance barrier is easier to breach.

Calming Words: Reducing Anxiety Leads to Better Patient Outcomes

In 1990 I was diagnosed with Graves' disease. A goiter as big as a man's fist had grown in my neck. After several rounds of iodine therapy, it was decided it had to be taken out, and I entered a Tennessee hospital for total thyroid removal.

The surgery went off without a hitch. My physician, Dr. J, took very good care of me. I emphasize the words "very good" because each time he spoke to me and my family, he assured us I was in very good hands. Dr. J was pleased with the outcome of the procedure, and we anticipated a speedy recovery.

Several hours had passed when the unthinkable happened: A hematoma formed in my neck, obstructing the airway. My mother called the nurse, who, upon entering my room, assessed the situation. Then in a calming, direct, controlled, and reassuring voice said, "Don't worry, Tonya, you're in very good hands. We've already called your physician and he is on his way. Breathe in through your nose and out through your mouth." As she placed the oxygen mask on my face, Dr. J entered the room, removed the bandages from my neck, and ordered the staff to prepare for surgery right away. While they rolled me down the hallway, my life literally flashed before my eyes. My husband had not made it back to the hospital—I felt frightened and alone.

When I entered the surgery suite, the first voice I heard was Dr. J's. I wasn't able to respond, but I trusted I was in very good hands and he would do all he could to take care of me. Why? Because he, as well as the nursing staff, told me they would. Not only did they use key words to decrease my anxiety during one of the scariest times in my life, during my recovery they executed what they said they would do, every day, every time.

Key words provided better clinical outcomes for me and my family. We listened and complied with staff's instructions. My anxiety decreased due to consistent communication and updates. The nurses talked to me using key words: They introduced themselves, communicated the number of years they had been in nursing, and explained what was happening and what would happen next. Consequently, I felt safe, respected, and I felt my privacy was not jeopardized. I felt valued.

My husband later told me that when he entered the area where I was recovering, Dr. J held up his hands, smiled, and said, "She is doing well. The surgery was a success and she's sleeping. We took very good care of your wife." My husband said he took a deep breath and felt a sense of relief because he too trusted that Tennessee hospital physician and staff. Dr. J has often referred to me as the best patient he's ever had. I refer to him, now and forever, as the best physician I've ever had.

—Tonya Fuller

Key Words at Key Times Can Transform Your Culture

Essentially, the use of key words puts the patient's emotional well-being at the heart of the healing process. We all know that the healthcare environment creates anxiety in most people. With the consistent use of AIDET, patients feel that their caregivers understand and are responsive to their needs. It also helps to take away a lot of the fear factor.

When AIDET is hardwired, you can expect to see improved perception of care by patients and their families. You can even drive "unit loyalty." We've seen patients request a certain unit upon a return visit or ask for a specific care team based on their prior experience.

When your staff "narrates" the care given—all the while showing courtesy, respect, and kindness—you gain loyal customers. And that allegiance leads to improved growth, market share, and revenue. The return on investment when effective implementation of AIDET is hardwired across the organization is huge. Bottom line: Creating an AIDET culture of execution is priceless!

Key Points in This Chapter

1. Key Words at Key Times/AIDET is a communication framework that improves patients' perception of their care; it helps reduce their anxiety, thus improving outcomes; it builds customer loyalty; and it ensures your staff is delivering the same consistent messages of concern and appreciation.

2. The tools to hardwire and validate AIDET usage include the following: rounding on staff and patients; satisfaction survey results and comments; tying AIDET to your Standards of Performance; reward and recognition; and communicating the "wins" to staff.

3. You can overcome reluctance to using key words through connecting the usage to the purpose, role playing exercises, and positive reinforcement when employees demonstrate the behaviors.

Pillars Affected by AIDET

Service—Using the key words reduces patients' anxiety and helps them be more compliant, thus boosting physician and patient satisfaction.

Quality—Clinical outcomes improve (nosocomial infections decrease), resulting in better quality rankings and a reputation in the community for excellence.

People—Reward and recognition opportunities increase, resulting in enhanced employee satisfaction and engagement, reduced turnover, and fewer vacancies.

Growth—Higher volumes are generated. When patients are treated with respect, kept informed, and are confident in staff's ability, they choose your hospital every time. Word of mouth is often underestimated!

CHAPTER 14

Service Recovery

By Liz Jazwiec

What is service recovery? Put simply, it's the art of fixing things that have gone wrong. There are two reasons why it's important for you as the nurse leader of a division, department, or shift to understand the components of service recovery. One, you'll be in the position of having to "fix things" more than you could ever imagine. Two, this knowledge will allow you to demonstrate and teach the right recovery process to staff, thus empowering them to take responsibility for it.

If you're looking for a more official definition, try this: Service recovery is a formalized approach to effective complaint management and resolution. It means you train all staff to be alert to service recovery opportunities and empower them to respond appropriately. Service recovery is about salvaging the customer relationship by regaining trust and building loyalty. It can be as simple as apologizing or as complicated as providing meal tickets or a small gift.

According to *Making It Right* by Paul Alexander Clark and Mary P. Malone (HCPro, 2005), each act of service recovery has three steps: recognizing that something went wrong, apologizing, and taking action/making amends.

Many organizations already have service recovery plans in place. The strategies range from filling out an incident report to setting forth criteria for handling complaints. However, unless coached on how to do service recovery, employees are far more comfortable passing the problem off on their leader, or worse yet, calling in a patient or service advocate. This is where many organizations drop the ball.

The good news is that it's not that hard to teach nurses and other staff members to handle complaints themselves. This should be an important part of your service recovery plan.

And here's the even better news: Doing service recovery right leaves you with an often more loyal customer and also provides some real return on investment.

Service Recovery Yields Measurable Results.

Overall, the process of effectively service recovering customers is a good, fundamental business practice that turns a negative experience into a positive statement about the organization. It curbs bad public relations—and make no mistake, dissatisfied patients and family members tell others about the incident!

> The Technical Assistance Research Program Corporation of Washington, DC, which publishes statistics on customer complaints, concluded that for every complaint a company receives, 26 other customers are dissatisfied but don't take the time to tell us. Each of those 27 people will tell 16 others and about 10 percent will tell more than 20 other potential customers. Can you afford that much negative publicity?

There is considerable evidence that implementing a good service recovery program more than pays for itself. The following graphics illustrate:

Figure 14.1

Hospital Service Recovery Program Return on Investment Adds up to $266,000!

Estimated National Average Payment for 31 Elective Surgeries		Operating Profit Margin (low estimate)		Profit per Patient
$14,308	X	4%	=	$572.32

Potential Patients Lost Through Bad Word of Mouth (Based on 100 people receiving deficient service)		Profit per Patient		Total Potential Return on Investment with Service Recovery Program
465	X	$572.32	=	$266,129

Sources: CMS - Top 31 Elective Inpatient Hospital DRGs at http://www.cms.hhs.gov/HealthCareConInit/02_Hospital.asp#TopOfPage;
American Hospital Association - Trends in Hospital Financing 2008 (for estimated Operating Profit Margin);
The TQM Magazine - Impact of deficient healthcare service quality, 2006 Vol 18, Issue 6, Pages 563-571
http://www.emeraldinsight.com/Insight/viewContentItem.do;jsessionid=0F61444BD51587A1EDAC3776FC86C965?contentType=Article&hdAction=lnkhtml&contentId=1576242

Figure 14.2

Estimate Service Recovery Program Return on Investment at Your Hospital

Estimated National Average Payment for 31 Elective Surgeries		Insert Your Operating Profit Margin		Profit per Patient
$14,308	X	%	=	#VALUE!

Potential Patients Lost Through Bad Word of Mouth (Based on 100 people receiving deficient service)		Profit per Patient		Total Potential Return on Investment with Service Recovery Program
465	X	#VALUE	=	#VALUE!

Sources: CMS - Top 31 Elective Inpatient Hospital DRGs at http://www.cms.hhs.gov/HealthCareConInit/02_Hospital.asp#TopOfPage;
American Hospital Association - Trends in Hospital Financing 2008 (for estimated Operating Profit Margin);
The TQM Magazine - Impact of deficient healthcare service quality, 2006 Vol 18, Issue 6, Pages 563-571
http://www.emeraldinsight.com/Insight/viewContentItem.do;jsessionid=0F61444BD51587A1EDAC3776FC86C965?contentType=Article&hdAction=lnkhtml&contentId=1576242

Studies also show that your "response to concerns/complaints" is highly correlated to a customer's likelihood of recommending the organization to a friend. Further, research demonstrates that a "recovered" patient is actually more satisfied with the healthcare experience overall than one who did not experience any problems!

And service recovery programs pay off in harder-to-measure, but no less valid, ways as well. Your staff will feel a sense of empowerment when able to make service recovery decisions, leading to more satisfaction with the job. Plus, identifying and resolving complaints becomes their springboard for performance improvement.

The Power of Acknowledging Inconvenience

There are ways to teach and implement service recovery so it becomes second nature for your team. But the first step is not the process *per se*—rather, it's the act of acknowledging inconvenience. I find that organizations spend a lot of time and money on educating teams on the recovery method, but they don't address this critical, initial action. It's like teaching someone to run before they can walk!

Many nurses assume that people are intolerant of inconvenience, but this isn't so. Rather, human beings are intolerant of ***being ignored***—or the perception that we're being ignored. (You and I both know that to the perceiver, perception *is* reality—regardless of the actual intent of the person doing the ignoring!)

I travel a lot and I know that sometimes things can go wrong. Still, when a flight is delayed by an hour, I want someone to acknowledge it, to say they are sorry for the inconvenience, and thank me for my patience. Otherwise, my perception is that no one cares. Similarly, when a patient or family member is inconvenienced, unless it's recognized as such, they feel a distinct lack of personal regard.

Here's an example I always use when training staff on *Service Recovery 101: Acknowledging Inconvenience*. Let's say you are tapping your toes as you stand in line a long time at a grocery store, waiting to check out. The place is packed. When you finally make it to the counter, the employee is crabby; she obviously hasn't had a break from working hard, and she starts giving you "attitude." She never looks up, starts shoving stuff down the conveyer belt, slams down your gallon of milk, manhandles your eggs, and squeezes your bread.

How does this make you feel? If you're like me, you are seriously tempted to put on your most menacing face, lean across the counter, and say, "Listen, honey, I've been standing in this line for 20 minutes. KNOCK IT OFF." But of course you don't actually do that, although you might wish you could.

Okay, now imagine if when you get up to the counter, the girl says to you, "Oh, my gosh, I'm sorry you had to stand in line so long. I don't know why everybody's in the store today—it's not like we're giving things away! All of a sudden, people just flooded the place. I'm sorry you had to wait."

What do you say to her? "That's okay, hon'." Maybe you even look for a way to help her: "Here, let me get that heavy laundry soap in the bottom of the basket."

Why are you being so reasonable? Because the inconvenience was acknowledged and you weren't ignored. Deep down inside, you know the cashier didn't make the schedule or control the flow of the grocery store. You realize she's been working hard and not slacking off to flirt with the bag boy or gossip with the cashier on the other lane. But it's her simple words of apology that help you deal with it.

As the nurse leader, you need to make sure your teams understand the importance of acknowledging inconvenience. Inevitably, things go wrong every day at work—surgeries get delayed, tests have to be repeated, and things get lost. Most patients understand that; what they can't accept is you not addressing the situation or apologizing.

It Really *Is* Okay to Say, "I'm Sorry."

Implementing and hardwiring the behavior of saying "I'm sorry" isn't always an easy thing to do. While it's absolutely crucial for an effective service recovery model, many nurses are resistant. Why? Because most were told early in their careers they should never utter those two words.

When I started my first job, I heard this myself during new nurse orientation. I can still remember the risk manager warning us: "Don't ever say you're sorry because the hospital can get sued." That is ridiculous! And I think the failure to acknowledge that something went wrong probably led to more legal action.

The other reason why people in general don't like to say they're sorry is because they don't like to accept blame. You'll hear your nurses say things like, "Why should I say I am sorry? I'm not the one who lost the lab tests." Or, "Say I'm sorry when it's not my fault that Admitting never called us back?"

The best way to engage staff is to connect them to the purpose: Tell them they say they're sorry to <u>express regret</u>, not to <u>accept blame</u>—and when they do that, patients respond favorably. Remember the grocery store scenario? The first cashier ignored you; she actually wanted you to feel sorry for her because she had to work so hard. The second cashier got it right. As soon as she said she was sorry, you recognized it wasn't her fault. Her expression of regret left her blameless.

It really works! Human beings are not intolerant of inconvenience; they are intolerant of being ignored. Emphasize to your team that if a simple "I'm sorry" can soothe those angry feelings and make the customer happy again, why should they object? It can only help their organization, which clearly has a positive impact on them as individuals. And if you really need to drive the point of the story home, ask your nurses, "Which cashier do you think goes home in a better mood?"

Acknowledging inconvenience and saying you're sorry makes the entire service recovery process more successful. When these two steps are the prelude, patients and family members are far more receptive to dealing logically with the situation.

Immerse Your Team in Your Service Recovery Policies.

It's important to make sure that your entire team is familiar with your hospital's service recovery policy/process. Give them copies of the policy for review and role play scenarios to make sure they are comfortable with utilizing the policy.

On the following page is an example of a service recovery process. For additional examples go to www.firestarterpublishing.com/NurseLeaderHandbook.

Figure 14.3

Service Recovery Opportunity Process

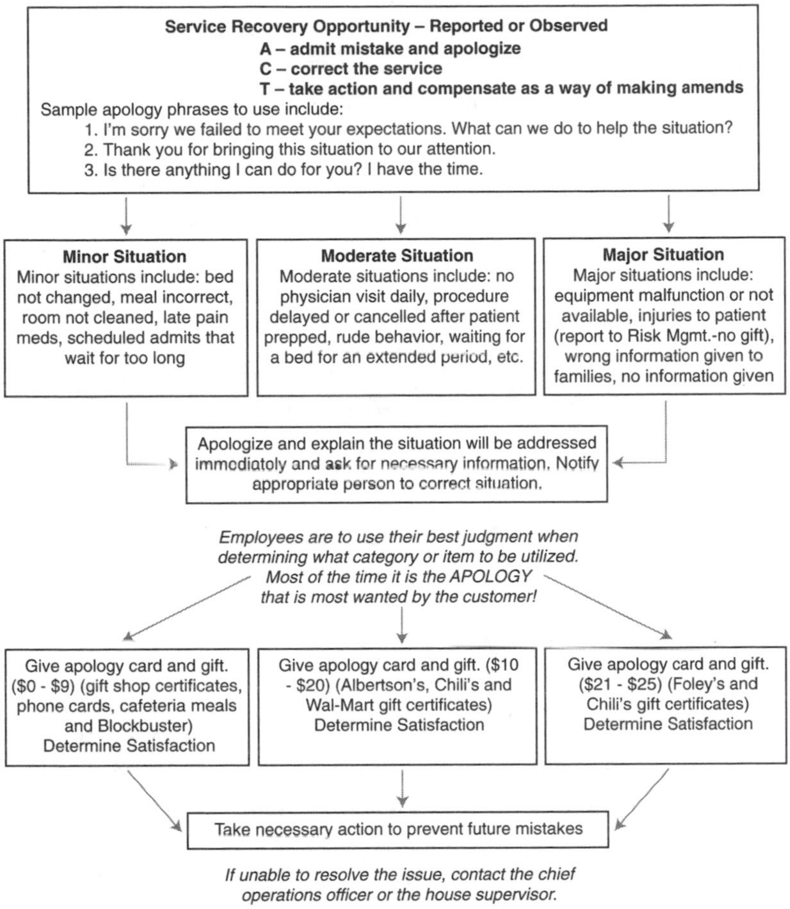

During your role play and eventually the actual practice of service recovery, utilize key words to ensure the patient is hearing the same message. What you say to patients and families during service recovery (along with your body language) makes all the difference. These well-chosen words ensure that staff have the right words on hand to help defuse customer frustration when something goes wrong. Come up with service recovery key words for the inevitable occasions in which frustration may occur.

Let's say, for instance, that a staff member must field complaints about the quality of your hospital's food. You can teach staff members key words such as these excerpted from *"I'm Sorry to Hear That…": Real-Life Responses to Patients' 101 Most Common Complains About Health Care* (Fire Starter Publishing, 2008):

I'm sorry to hear you're not enjoying your meal. I'll check your nutrition orders and ask the dietician to visit you. She may be able to suggest some alternatives. Shall I make you a cup of hot tea right now?

I'm sorry. Good nutrition is important to your recovery. We have some snacks on the unit. Is there something I can get you? I could make you some fresh toast or a sandwich.

Even though some special diets are very strict, our Food & Nutrition team strives to provide tasty food. I'm going to ask your nutritionist if there are spices we can use to add flavor to your meals. What do you use at home?

Remind your staff that the majority of customers who seem difficult are *not* choosing to be difficult. They are frustrated or angry, and sometimes for good reason. Our job is to become so skilled at service recovery that the customer or patient who started out saying he or she would never come back becomes one who says he or she would never go anywhere else.

The CARE Approach

CARE is one tool that allows us to accomplish the seemingly impossible mission of gaining the loyalty of a disgruntled patient or customer. Its name is an acronym for the actions to take when confronted with such an individual:

CARE

C for **connect.** Introduce yourself; make eye contact; say, "What is the problem and how can I help make it better for you?"; allow the patient to vent.

A for **apologize. No excuses!** Confirm that whatever happened is not up to your usual standard of customer care. Be careful not to stray into excuses or laying blame. If the customer has come to you, own the problem. Even if the situation is unavoidable or you feel the customer is unreasonable, you can say you're sorry that the customer is unhappy.

R for **repair.** What would it take to make the customer happy? If you don't know the answer to this question, ask. Sometimes the customer just wants acknowledgment. Ask, "What can I do to make it better for you?" Some situations are not in our power to change, but at least you can apologize and, if possible, offer information (not an excuse!) that will help the patient understand the rationale behind what occurred. Other times you may be able to do something to repair the situation—perhaps re-assigning a nurse or altering a care plan. Unless there's a compelling reason not to take a corrective action, it's best to strive to meet the patient's wishes.

E for **exceed.** Don't just meet but instead exceed customers' expectations. It costs more than five times more to recover a customer than it does to get one initially; the economics of service recovery tell us that exceeding expectations is an effort that is well worth the investment.

Some examples of exceeding expectations include:
- Patient is lost and frustrated: physically take the customer to his or her destination.
- Patient is kept waiting in Radiology and missed lunch: offer an apology and a cafeteria pass.
- Customer has to spend excessive time getting an account straightened out: an immediate verbal apology and a follow-up written note from the Billing Department.

Practice with your staff what to do in those rare instances when there is a customer who cannot be satisfied. If a customer is still not approachable after you have tried the **CARE** process, try to deflect his anger by listening and remaining calm. The customer may not be in full control of his own emotions. It will sometimes help to continue to express empathy, such as, "I would feel that way too."

It is important to let a customer vent, but it is also important to define acceptable behavior, such as, "I want to help, but I cannot do anything until I understand how I can help you." Ask him to sit down, or come to a quiet place to talk about how you can help him. Always, if you feel the customer is a threat to others, notify Security and try to get the customer to move into a nonpublic space.

> Often, if we take the time to get to the bottom of a problem, it is an issue that we can resolve. But if we refuse to take the time now, we lose the opportunity forever. The first step may be our attitude and realizing "difficult" customers are in fact an opportunity for service recovery and improved relationships.

Three Tips for Hardwiring Service Recovery

1. **Know your organization's process and policy.** Also, know where you can access it quickly to answer any questions.
2. **Create a service recovery notebook.** Put together a notebook clearly identified as "Service Recovery." Add clear vinyl zipped pockets. In the pockets include:
   - A set of hospital-logo-enhanced cards that each contain a printed message like: "We are sorry we did not meet your expectations. In recognition of the inconvenience we have caused you, please accept this token of our appreciation. We look forward to serving you again in the future."
   - Envelopes for the cards, imprinted with the hospital's logo
   - Service Recovery Tracking Chart (see the following pages for more information)
   - Hospital gift shop vouchers
   - Cafeteria vouchers
   - Local grocery store vouchers

You might also create a Service Recovery First Aid Box. Just label a box with an "unhappy" face and fill it with items from the list above. The benefit of the box is that it can also hold larger gifts like inexpensive books or lap blankets, visors, or mugs complete with the hospital logo.

The idea, of course, is to have this notebook and/or box fully stocked and in a convenient location so staff members can find it when they need it.

3. **Use a Service Recovery Tracking Chart.** This allows your organization to track and trend service recovery. These forms can be completed to include:

- Patient/family member's name
- Employee's name
- Department
- Date
- The gift certificate or item given to the recipient
- Reason service recovery is necessary
- Instructions to forward the form to the Measurement or Service Recovery team

Figure 14.4

Service Recovery Tracking Chart

Date	Room/ Dept	Problem Code	Problem			Employee	Item #	Item Description	Amount* If Appropriate
			Minor	Moderate	Major				

Item #	Legend
1	Dog
2	Coffee Cert
3	Movie Tkt
4	Phone Card
5	Mod. Plant
6	Lrg. Plant
7	Dinner G.C.
8	Meal Tkt
9	Gift Shop
10	Med. Bear

Code	Description
1	**Meals**
1a	Late/missed
1b	Incorrect
1c	Other
2	**Time**
2a	Wait to get into ER/Urg. Care
2b	Wait in ER Dept.
2c	Wait for room/dir. admit
2d	Wait for procedure
2e	Trauma displaced
2f	Equip. delay
2g	Discharge delay
2h	Other
3	**R.N./CNA/TECH**
3a	Long response time
3b	Rude
3c	Long wait for meds
3d	Didn't communicate
3e	Didn't listen
3f	Rough/injury
3g	Discharge problem
3h	IV stick
3i	Staff reward
3j	Other

Code	Description
4	**Transport**
4a	Rough
4b	Bumped/dumped
4c	Other
5	**Physicians**
5a	Didn't visit
5b	Rushed
5c	Didn't communicate
5d	Unable to reach for meds
5e	Rough
5f	Discourteous to pt.
5g	Discourteous to pt. family
5h	Did not schedule/cancelled test
5i	Discharge problems
5j	Other
6	**EVS**
6a	Room not ready/clean
6b	Bed equip. not working
6c	TV not working
6d	Phone not working
6e	Other equip. not working
6f	Other

Code	Description
7	**Miscellaneous**
7a	Family need
7b	Fear of hospital/procedure
7c	HIV test due to stick
7d	General frustration
7e	Lost belongings
7f	No interpreter
7g	Need "comfort"
7h	Held NPO and not changed
7i	Adjacent code blue
7j	Other

Figure 14.5

Service Recovery Resource Log

Date:____________________ **Patient Name:**__________________________

Unit & Room Number of Patient:________________________________

Name & Title of Staff Member:________________________________

Reason for Item Given (Detailed):______________________________

____

____

____

____

Resource Item Used:

APOLOGY CARDS ARE TO BE USED FOR ALL ISSUES

(Please check additional item(s) used)

Minor **Moderate** **Major**

Not Sure What to Do? Seek Guidance from a Leader.

As the nurse leader, when you're in a situation where you truly don't know the best thing to do and need guidance, tell the patient and/or the family you're very sorry they're experiencing the problem. Assure them that you'll make it a priority to follow up on the issue—then make sure you do that, resolving the situation as quickly as you can.

If you are going to a superior for guidance, such as the vice president (VP) of nursing, I suggest you already have one or two ideas in place prior to the conversation. For example, "Betty, we have a patient who was scheduled for a test today and her son took off work to be with her. But due to a problem with the equipment, we had to reschedule it for tomorrow. I think it would be nice to offer him a couple of service recovery options, but I'm not sure what to do. Maybe we could give him a cash reimbursement for gas, travel, and lunch. I was thinking perhaps $100. If we can't do that, maybe we could tell him we'll get a volunteer to sit with his mother tomorrow so he doesn't have to take another day off from work. The volunteer will have an in-house cell phone he can call directly."

Now, if the VP is not okay with either of those options, perhaps she can suggest something else. But at least you went to her with solutions, and not just a problem. I can tell you from my experience that most of the time, your leader will be fine with your suggestions and offer only slight modifications. Plus, the more you do service recovery, the better you will become with potential resolutions.

Remember, it's not until you have mastered service recovery yourself that you'll be able to educate, drive, and lead your team. The nurse leader needs to set the example, and every time you do so, use the situations as opportunities to teach your staff. This is a great chance to do one-on-one mentoring. Let the nurse involved know what you did and why; suggest that the nurse might be able to do something similar using your hospital guidelines regarding service recovery.

> Once your team becomes confident in handling the disappointments and inconveniences that arise every day, they'll get better and better at identifying and resolving issues before patients even bring them up. Imagine working on a unit where the patients and visitors hardly complain at all, because the staff is so proactive at service recovery! I have to believe that not only would it be a great thing for the patients, but that the staff would benefit as well.

Great Service Recovery Leads to Customer Loyalty.

Service recovery can have remarkable results. It can actually let you transform an unhappy customer into a deeply satisfied one—and often, one that returns to your organization again and again.

The Marriott Corporation did a study on guest complaints. Interestingly, it learned that people whose grievances were recognized and addressed immediately actually expressed better satisfaction with their stay than guests who never had a complaint at all!

Think about your own experiences. When someone does a good job at service recovery, it's very impressive and you remember it for a long time. For instance, 15 years ago when attending a conference in Tampa, Florida, I stayed at the Hyatt Hotel near the airport. Instead of eating lunch with the attendees, I thought it would be nice to eat outside. (It was February, and since I lived in Chicago, the idea of eating outside was pretty appealing.) The bar was open, but the restaurant wasn't; nevertheless, the hotel served a light menu on the patio. The bartender was the only server, and when he came to my table, I ordered an iced tea and crab cakes.

When he served my lunch, he also brought silverware wrapped up in a napkin. He walked away and when I opened the napkin, I found the fork was caked with old, dried-on food; there wasn't even a spoon in the packet, just a knife. So I waited for him to return, but he was very busy. It took him probably 10-15 minutes to come back. In fact, I think he thought I might be done eating. He seemed surprised to see that I hadn't touched my lunch. When I showed him the fork, he apologized and brought me a clean one.

Upon finishing my meal, I asked him for the check. He said there wouldn't be one because of the mix-up with the fork. I was stunned! I wasn't even upset and yet he addressed the issue without hesitation. That was a long time ago—but whenever I'm in Tampa, I stay at that same hotel because of a bartender who waived a $20 bill for crab cakes and iced tea. He knew the importance of service recovery!

Don't you want your organization to have customers with that kind of loyalty?

Key Points in This Chapter

1. Human beings are not intolerant of inconvenience; they are intolerant of being ignored.

2. Say you are sorry to express regret, not accept blame.

3. People are most loyal when you *immediately* address their issues yourself.

4. If you fix a problem or complaint while the person is still with you, the individual is actually more satisfied with the healthcare experience than if they never had a problem at all.

5. The more you are involved in service recovery, the better you get at it.

Pillars Affected by Service Recovery

Service—When staff apologize and resolve incidents immediately, the patient's perception is one of very good service.

Finance—Improves loyalty of patients, thus driving increased market share; decreases potential for litigation.

People—Staff members are empowered to make important decisions, thus improving job satisfaction.

Growth—Improved word of mouth in the community increases patient volume.

SECTION 3: KNOWLEDGE FUNDAMENTALS

Introduction

By Lyn Ketelsen

If you were hired into your management position after a few years of being a staff nurse, raise your hand. I'm imagining lots of hands in the air. That's typically the way most nurse leaders get their first opportunity. In fact, it's what happened to me. After only a year of being a charge nurse on the second shift, part-time no less, my nurse manager said to me, "Lyn, would you be interested in working the day shift?"

Now, I had often told her I had no desire to work days. I didn't like the additional stress of all those "suits" being around. (Okay, that was just an excuse because we never really saw them anyway. The truth was I just didn't want to get up that early.) I replied, "Deb, you know I don't like working days." Then she said, "I don't mean as a staff nurse. I'm leaving and I think you should apply for my position."

I was surprised. I didn't possess the usual management pedigree and lacked some required education, so I really questioned her judgment. Nonetheless, I was intrigued enough to apply, and after an extensive interview I was chosen over nine other candidates. I was told it was clear I had "innate" management skills. I also had to go back to school and build my resume. But in the meantime, I applied the skills gained from other areas of leadership (I'd owned my own business) to running my department.

Thus far in the book, we have concentrated on the skills you need to manage people and the processes to implement for success. Next we'll focus on the fundamental skill sets a strong nurse leader must possess to effectively manage the *business* of a nursing unit, such as finance and quality.

Gone are the days when simply being a good clinician was enough to be an effective nurse leader. Today, first-rate clinical skills gain you respect, but business acumen is what you need to keep the job and be successful.

As a leader in today's healthcare environment, you're in charge of more than just your team. You're accountable for every aspect of operations: staffing, scheduling, workforce competency, financial performance, growth strategies, and the quality of the care and service being provided to patients and their loved ones. In other words, you must think like you are the chief executive officer of your area!

The chapters in this section will help you build the necessary skills to be an excellent leader and to help your team provide the kind of patient- and family-centered care that organizations and customers alike have come to expect.

CHAPTER 15

Goal Management

By Bonnie Forsh and Stephanie Baker

Goal management is the foundation for accountability and achieving outcomes. Without goals to provide direction, managerial actions can be futile. Once we've established clear goals—by which we mean objective, measurable, and weighted targets aligned with the organization's overall strategy—the ability to manage becomes objective instead of subjective. And that means performance can be evaluated on results versus effort.

Why Goal Management Matters

One of the biggest reasons for goal management is, quite simply, that it makes life easier for nurse leaders. One of the biggest frustrations these key players experience is the feeling of being overwhelmed. In many cases this is due to a lack of focus on the true priorities. An objective, measurable, and weighted set of goals helps define where to put the most energy.

In addition, goal alignment leads to consistently better outcomes under all organizational initiatives (pillars) and less of the silo effect. As leaders become knowledgeable of the organization's goals and work to ensure both vertical and horizontal goal alignment, they develop a real sense of ownership for "the big picture." As a result, collaboration between departments becomes the norm, not the exception.

The old saying "What gets measured gets done" is so true. Tracking to a specific goal outcome improves teamwork and processes. The graph below demonstrates how patient care is also impacted positively.

Figure 15.1

Impact of Organizational Goals Hardwired into Leader Evaluation on Patient Perception of Care

Leader Evaluation

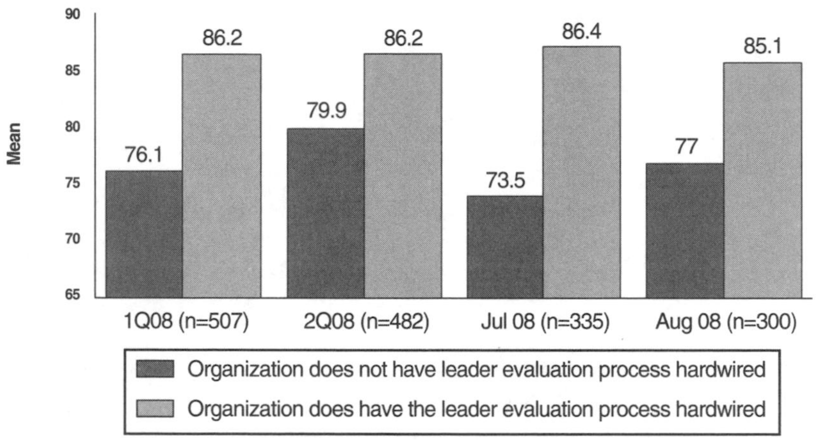

Source: Studer Group® October 2008 Measurement Spreadsheet; Organizations that hardwire the leader evaluation process show patient perception of care ratings that are significantly higher than those that do not. Patient perception of care mean score average includes all partner selected vendors including Arbor, Avatar, Gallup, HCAHPS, Healthstream, Jackson, NRC, PRC Picker, Press Ganey, RPM, and Statisquest.

How Goals Cascade Downward

As a nurse leader, you want to be sure you're contributing to the organization's success as defined by its overarching strategic goals. Typically leaders develop goals for each year using a strategic framework that's broken down into basic categories the organization must concentrate on for success. Most often these categories are Service, Quality, Finance, People, and Growth—commonly referred to as "pillars."

Senior management typically identifies specific measurable goals under each of the pillars, thus further defining the direction of the organization and what takes precedence (as exemplified in the graphic below). Understanding these goals will help you as a nurse leader align your focus to that of the organization. It will also help you showcase your results so they align with your organization's goals.

Figure 15.2

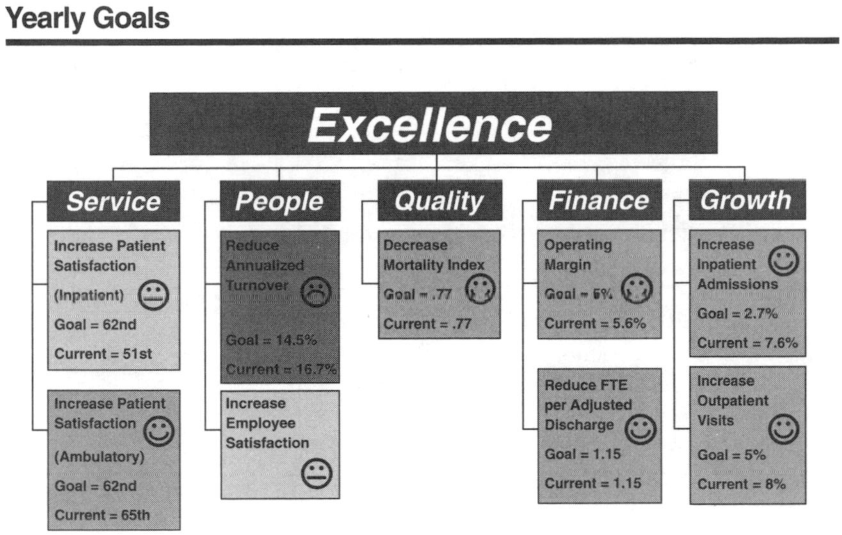

As you think about your department or area goals, you'll cascade the organization's goals down to your area when appropriate. For example, if the CEO sets a goal under the "Quality" pillar to get Core Measures to 90 percent or higher, then every leader below him would work toward sub-goals that would be carried out via tactics completed by the people underneath them.

On the following page is a table that illustrates how goals cascade from the CEO level down to unit nurse manager and Emergency Department manager levels:

	Quality	Service	People	Finance	Growth
CEO Goals	Core Measures at 90% or higher	Patient Satisfaction for all lines of service	Organization-wide Turnover, Employee Satisfaction	Operating Margin	IP Admissions, ED Volume
CNO Goals	Core Measures rollup at 90% or higher; e.g., decrease infections for entire hospital or reduction of falls	Patient Satisfaction for all lines of service	Turnover in Nursing Areas, Employee Satisfaction in Nursing Areas	Nursing Variance to Budget	IP Admissions, ED Volume (if the ED is the CNO's area of responsibility)
Director of Nursing Goals	Core Measures rollup at 90% or higher; e.g., decrease infections for entire hospital or reduction of falls	IP Satisfaction	Turnover in IP Nursing Areas, Employee Satisfaction in IP Nursing Areas	Nursing Variance to Budget	IP Admissions
Unit Nurse Manager Goals	Reduce falls, reduce hospital-acquired infections	Increase Patient Satisfaction on unit	Turnover on Unit, Employee Satisfaction on Unit	Variance to Budget for Unit	IP Admissions
ED Manager Goals	Reduce left without treatment	Increase Patient Satisfaction in ED, door-to-doctor time	Turnover in ED, Employee Satisfaction in ED	Variance to Budget for Unit	ED Admissions

*Ensure heavy weights on the areas that need the most improvement/focus for leaders.

These are sample goals. The table is meant to demonstrate how the goals are modified as they cascade down from a broader goal to a more area-specific goal. As you read further, you'll learn more about differentiating between a goal and a tactic, weighting goals, and making goals measurable.

Goals Vs. Tactics

As you work to set your goals, it's important to understand the difference between a goal and a tactic. A *goal* is defined as a desired outcome that can be objectively measured, whereas a *tactic* is a tool or process used to accomplish the outcome. However, determining the difference between the two can sometimes be a matter of perspective.

Let's look at an example. Suppose one of your goals as the nurse leader is to be on time with staff members' evaluations. This goal is *actually a tactic* to reduce employee turnover. Completing evaluations in a timely manner brings about employee engagement—which in turn means staff is less likely to leave the organization. With this in mind, you might redefine the goal to read, "Reduce employee turnover from 13 to 10 percent by year's end." Thus, you have an objective, measurable goal, along with the tactic of timely evaluations to focus on during the months ahead. Figure 15.3 walks you through the process of determining the difference between a goal and a tactic.

Figure 15.3

Goal Decision Matrix

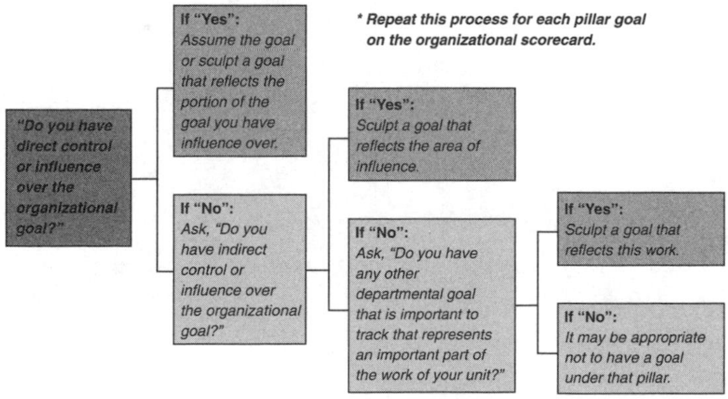

Once supervisor goals are drafted, they're cascaded to frontline managers who then create individual unit/department goals. Supervisor and frontline leaders work together to ensure both sets of goals are aligned and supportive of the organization's overall goals.

This teamwork process fosters clarity in carving out the goals, as well as ownership by the frontline manager who is directly (or indirectly) responsible for meeting those targets. Supervisors review the final goals and determine metrics for tracking the measurable outcomes.

Four Ways to Hardwire the Goal Management Process

1. **Goal Cascading**

   Deployed properly, the cascade process can ensure alignment among the goals of the organization, leadership, and frontline managers. Cascading includes the validation of *vertical alignment* (working to ensure the goals cascade down the leader's division appropriately) and *horizontal alignment* (determining which leaders across other departments or divisions may need to ensure successful achievement of a particular goal).

   Let's consider vertical alignment first. Perhaps a quality goal belonging to a chief nursing officer (CNO) is reduction of the hospital's overall infection rate by 30 percent. Achieving this goal might be weighted at 20 percent of her overall evaluation—in other words, one of her higher priorities.

   How might she cascade it to her ICU nurse leader? You can see in the example on the following page that she made 75 percent of that leader's evaluation dependent upon reaching quality goals, including reduction of central line infections and ventilator-associated pneumonia. In doing so, the CNO made a very clear statement to the ICU manager where the priorities needed to be. And with such an intense level of focus, the officer has a much greater likelihood of meeting her own objective.

   This is the power of objective, measurable, and weighted goals! The weight can be leveraged to provide focus and set priorities.

Figure 15.4

ICU Manager Leader Evaluation Sample
(75% weight on Quality)

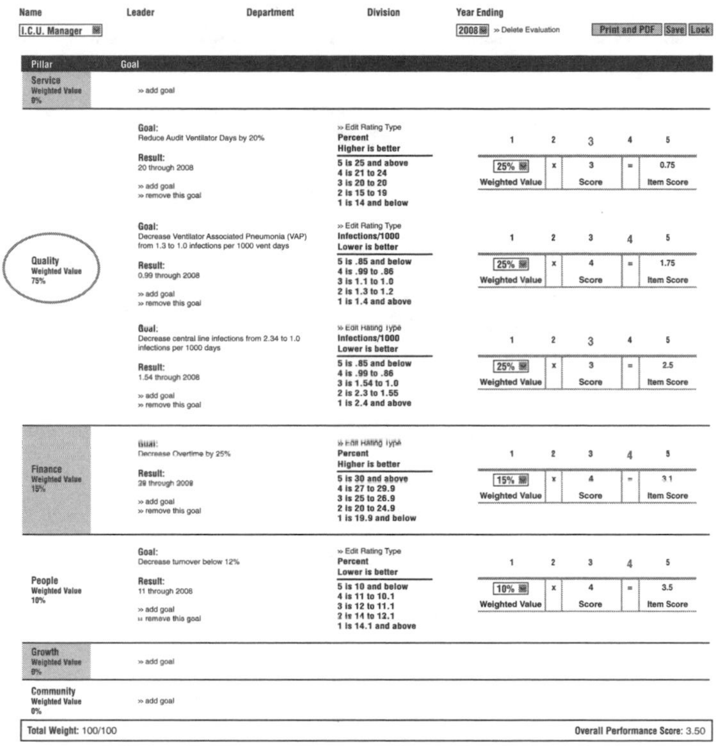

An example of horizontal alignment would be as follows: An Emergency Department (ED) manager has a goal of reducing treatment turnaround times by 15 percent. That leader will also need the Laboratory and Radiology managers to reduce their turnaround times by 15 percent. Therefore, he would check to see if those two managers had listed this goal on their evaluations as well, thus ensuring the necessary side-to-side alignment.

2. Regular Results Reporting

Another tool to maximize goal management is the monthly/quarterly results report. (Studer Group offers a template called the Monthly Report Card—shown on the following page—but you can easily create your own version.) You enter results for all goals on a monthly (or quarterly) basis, thus providing "real-time" information on performance. This lets you make necessary course corrections so you don't have to wait for feedback at your annual evaluation.

Figure 15.5

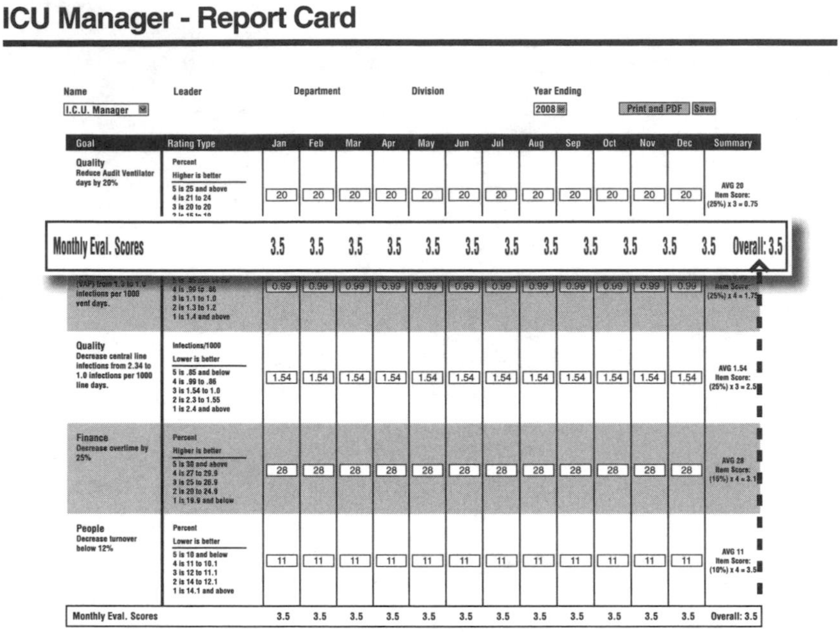

3. **90-Day Plan**

The 90-Day Plan gives you a way to capture specific action items to achieve goals. As you're creating your plan, it may help to talk with other managers and staff to determine the most effective tactics to work with other departments to maximize results. We recommend no more than two to three measurable tactics for each goal in the 90-Day Plan. This will allow you to focus clearly on the processes and behaviors that need to be hardwired[SM] for successful outcomes.

4. **Supervisory Meeting Model**

The supervisory meeting model is perhaps one of the most effective tools for hardwiring goal management, and is an essential practice for achieving and sustaining long-term results. It dictates a monthly one-on-one meeting between a manager and his or her supervisor to review goals being pursued, results achieved as documented in the monthly report card, and the tactics from the 90-Day Plan in current use.

What makes the supervisory meeting model so effective? It fosters regular and open dialogue between managers and their leaders, ensures a clear representation of current results, and creates urgency to make any necessary course corrections. In fact, this tool is so effective that we have devoted a whole chapter to it in Section 4.

Getting Staff Members on Board

Your staff members want to do a good job. They come to work with a passion and want to serve in a place where good quality care is provided. Having specific, measurable goals in place shows staff where the department is doing well and what improvements are needed. Once goals are developed, it's important for you as the leader to share them in a way that people can understand. It's also critical to discuss how achieving the department's goals will contribute to the organization's overall success.

As you build your 90-Day Plan, staff should be actively involved. Since employees are closest to the daily work, they may know better than anyone else what processes and systems need to be improved to achieve outcomes. Including them also assures their buy-in from the beginning and accelerates the change process.

It's important to post your goals, 90-Day Plan, and monthly results on the department communication board. The transparency fosters ownership of, and accountability for, the outcomes. It also creates friendly competition between shifts, promotes teamwork, and supports patient-focused care. The end result is consistency in behaviors and processes, which in turn allows the organization to achieve long-term sustainability.

Will there be pushback? Sure, a certain amount. Some staff may be naysayers: "There's no way we can meet that goal." Or, "We tried that before and it didn't work." But remember, knowledge is power. The more employees know about your goals, the less resistance they will have to embracing them. Effective goal management is about creating a critical mass to deploy evidence-based tactics and behaviors. Those who consistently push back should be dealt with in an appropriate manner.

Finally, put a process in place to share the results frequently and reward and recognize employees! This not only helps staff connect to purpose and passion, but inspires the repetition of behaviors that deliver results. Remember, you are there "to make healthcare a better place for patients to receive care, employees to work, and physicians to practice medicine."

Key Points in This Chapter

1. Make sure you, the leader, have in-depth knowledge of the organization's overall goals.

2. One tool to help you with goal management is the cascading process: Cascade your goals down from your leader's goals, thus ensuring vertical alignment; for horizontal alignment, work directly with key stakeholders who share the same or similar goals. Other tools include regular results reporting, 90-Day Plans, and the supervisory meeting model (the last one is covered in Section 4 of this book).

3. Involve your direct reports in developing goals that are then posted on bulletin boards and made a part of 90-Day Plans.

4. Share results in a timely and transparent manner; frequently reward and recognize positive outcomes. The idea is to drive consistency in behaviors and processes, thus achieving long-term sustainability.

Pillars Affected by Goal Management

Service—Consistency of service goals from top to bottom helps ensure the targets are met.

Quality—The weight of quality goals can be leveraged in leader evaluations to provide focus and to set priorities.

Finance—The organization is best sustained through effective financial goal management.

People—Staff members are more engaged due to involvement in planning unit/department goals and being rewarded for behaviors that bring about the desired outcomes.

Growth—Measurable outcomes foster actions resulting in organizational growth.

CHAPTER 16

Understanding Financial Impact (From ROI to Revenue Creation)

By Brian Robinson, Linda Deering, and Davy Crockett

As a nurse leader, you are always concerned with the clinical care your patients receive. Therefore, the equipment and behaviors that will impact the care of your patients are always at the forefront of your mind. Just as you quantify the impact of clinical care, it is to your advantage and to the advantage of your patients to understand its financial aspect.

No doubt about it: Finances are a critical element of patient care. There are salaries that need to be paid, investments that need to be made, and supplies that need to be purchased—and, ultimately, there is a balancing act to ensure the organization is providing the best possible patient care while keeping finances in order so that it will still be around in the future. If you understand this balancing act, you'll be able to position your needs in a format that all at the organization understand, and you'll be far more likely to get the outcomes you desire.

By using economic linkage (framing your need or goal in terms of ROI), you can ensure that your voice is heard at all levels of the organization—from senior leaders on down.

Great Nurse Leaders Are Multilingual.

No, we're not talking about the ability to speak English, Spanish, French, and Mandarin! In this context, being multilingual means being able to communicate with everyone—from the senior leaders who control the purse strings to the nurses who must carry out the goals you set to the patients and families you serve.

Most nurse leaders are quite proficient at switching from "patient language" to "staff language" to "doctor language" at will. It's just as important to be able to speak the language of CFOs and other senior leaders. Remember, communication isn't just about saying what you want to say—it's about ensuring that those you're speaking to hear and understand your message.

It's probably safe to say that the toughest language for nurse leaders to learn is that of senior leaders. To communicate with them, it's important to understand how all the little pieces fit together along with a linkage to clinical outcomes to show the sustainability of a new program, a new piece of equipment, or a new hire. If, for example, you wanted to bring a physician in house, to showcase clinical, you can discuss the ways this will improve care metrics; to showcase financial, you can highlight decrease in lost charges, decrease in overtime, and volume growth by extending hours to meet physician need.

Compare and contrast the following scenarios:

1. Nurse Leader One: The nurse leader walks up to her boss and says, "I need X, Y, and Z in order to provide good care for my patients." The boss will most likely look like a deer in headlights.

2. Nurse Leader Two: The nurse leader presents all sides of the enhancement—not just clinical—and explains how it will improve the bottom line of the organization. She also holds herself accountable for ensuring the results.

Clearly the nurse leader in the second scenario is more likely to be taken seriously by the senior leader, and her request is more likely to be met! You can see why it's so important to build a compelling case for the change you want implemented.

There is plenty of research out there you can present to support your case. Consider the following example, which shows how doing the right thing for your patient also yields positive financial impact.

Decreasing Ventilator Infections: A Clinical and Financial Victory!

In 2004 at Advocate Good Samaritan Hospital in Downers Grove, IL, the ICU manager asked for the department's help in reducing ventilator infections. The manager wanted to do this by implementing Hourly Rounding℠ and daily multidisciplinary rounding on ventilator patients. While it's true that nurses already spend a lot of time in the rooms with ICU patients, Hourly Rounding was used to remind them to focus on specific key behaviors. Each hour the nurses repositioned the patients, evaluated the need for suctioning those on ventilators, and made sure heads were elevated. The nurse leader was able to share great outcomes with the senior leaders.

As of the publishing of this book, the hospital has gone about 15 months without an instance of ventilator-associated pneumonia. Also, during the past six years, central line infections have decreased and ventilator days have decreased. Multidisciplinary rounding with respiratory therapy, nutrition, pharmacy, and physical medicine improved the communication between teams taking care of ventilated patients and improved efficiency of care.

Figure 16.1

ICU Ventilator-Associated Pneumonia

Per 1,000 Ventilator Days

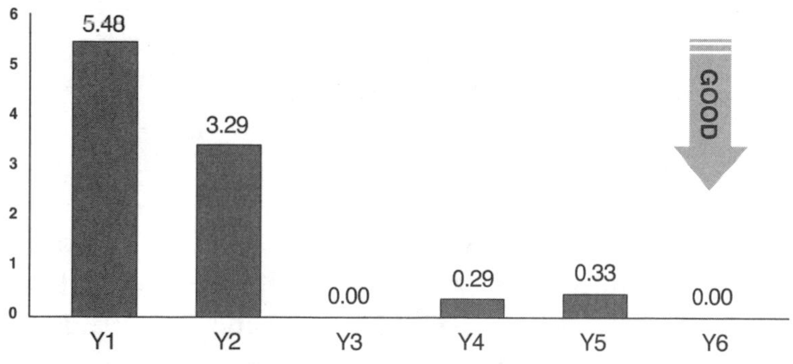

Source: Advocate Good Samaritan Hospital, Downers Grove, Illinois; Beds = 320; Admissions = 18,300; 2004-2008

In Year 1, Good Samaritan had 18 cases of ventilator-associated pneumonia (VAP) for a rate of 5.48. It estimated the cost of each VAP at about $45,000. So, in Year 1 it had $810,000 in extra costs due to VAPs. In the past four years, the organization has had two VAPs. That means it has considerably reduced its costs during this period—in fact, Good Samaritan reports a net cost reduction of $3,150,000. Incidentally, many of these patients were DRG Medicare.

Plus, capacity increased because there wasn't a backlog of patients stuck in ICU—and that in turn meant throughput increased. In the end, Good Samaritan's rounding tactics allowed the organization to save more lives.

Figure 16.2

ICU Central Line Blood Stream Infections

Per 1,000 Device Days

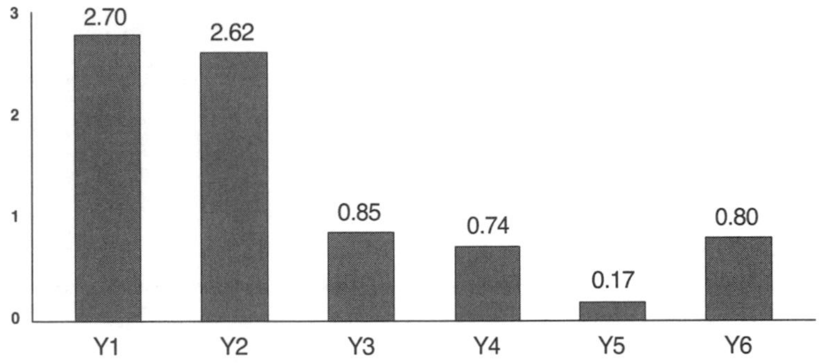

Source: Advocate Good Samaritan Hospital, Downers Grove, Illinois; Beds = 320; Admissions = 18,300; 2004-2008

As the nurse leader, knowing how to look at this issue from several different points of view will help you effectively get buy-in and showcase impact. Implementing these changes (Hourly Rounding to reduce ventilator infections) was the right thing to do for the patient, but it also had a tremendous positive financial impact for the organization.

Now, let's say you're a nurse leader who has set an annual goal of reducing ventilator days inside your own ICU. You can cite the above case study as compelling evidence that achieving your goal will benefit the organization both clinically *and* financially.

Being able to discuss the benefits of reducing ventilator days in both clinical and financial terms shows the C-suite that you "get" the realities they deal with every day. It earns you a seat at the table. And the respect you receive allows you to be a better advocate for your patients and staff.

Speaking the Staff's Language

So let's say that you've used the Good Samaritan ICU case study as support for your annual goal in conversations with senior leaders. And let's say they've signed off on it. Now, how do you sell your new goal or tactic to staff members? We all know that nurses as a group don't necessarily value the same things senior leaders value. Therefore, when you're trying to get them to make a change in order to meet a goal, you need to think: *What's in it for them? What's their stake in the game? And how can I find their "sweet spot" and tell the story in a way that inspires them to act?*

If you're asking staff members to implement a new tactic in order to decrease the patient's days in ICU, you'll have to face the reality that they might not be motivated to do so. In fact, they might actually prefer keeping the patient in ICU longer in order to keep a watchful eye on them. Sure, they'll help you with your goal, but you need to approach them in a different way.

When you were discussing this goal with the senior leaders, you may have emphasized patient volume. That made sense because "volume" means "revenue" to the C-suite. But to nurses, "volume" may mean "extra work."

When you're talking to staff members about ventilator days, you'll want to emphasize what they care most about: the well-being of the patient. You'll point out to them that fewer days on the ventilator means fewer infections. It means less suffering. It means healthier patients who get to go home sooner to be with their families.

Yes, you'll tell them the "why" behind what you're asking them to do. You'll help them connect the dots between the hospital's financial well-being and the well-being of their patients. But mostly you'll want to connect them back to their passion and their sense of purpose—because that's what truly motivates nurses.

Now, let's take a look at why it's so important for everyone in healthcare to have a good understanding of financial realities.

Healthcare Faces Tough Economic Times.

In healthcare today there is a lot of discussion about cost. What most people typically mean by *cost* is their *personal* cost—what the government, the insurance companies, or the patients themselves are willing to pay. They're actually talking about reimbursement.

For instance, when the government says it's going to lower the cost of Medicare, it's actually referring to what Medicare is willing to reimburse the healthcare provider for its services. This has nothing to do with the cost a hospital has for that care.

Real costs (i.e., hospital costs) are up and climbing—and reimbursement is not keeping pace. In fact, it's going down. In many cases, the typical net revenue for hospitals is only 25-35 percent of charges, after they deal with bad debt, charity cases, government discounts (Medicare, Medicaid, Champus, and so forth), and managed care discounts. In addition to the constant pressure from the government attempting to slow the growth in Medicare expenditures, insurance companies also seek to pay less and less. It's typical for an insurance company to say, in effect, "If you want a contract that allows our members (covered lives) to come to your hospital, then give us a bigger discount."

This reality has had a detrimental effect on healthcare organizations and patients alike. The industry is forced to resort to "cost shifting," which means having other groups pay for those who either don't pay or don't pay enough. (It's similar to how retailers must build the impact of shoplifters into the cost of their goods.) These rising charges lead people to label hospitals as "greedy"—when many of them are actually struggling to stay afloat.

In fact, a huge percentage of hospitals—possibly more than 25 percent—currently operate at a loss.

Obviously, in order to continue to be successful (and sometimes even to survive), healthcare organizations must be really good at managing their costs. And that's where you, the nurse leader, come in. When you understand the impact of certain expenditures, you can make decisions that help your organization stay financially healthy.

Nurse Leaders *Can* Impact the Organization's Bottom Line.

There are several areas in which nurse leaders can have a positive impact on their organization's finances. They are:

- Day-to-Day Expenditures
- Cost Avoidance
- Capital Investments
- Net Revenue Creation

Let's discuss each one separately.

Day-to-Day Expenditures

The two biggest day-to-day expenditures are 1) employees and their benefits and 2) supplies (this category includes utilities, maintenance contracts on items like radiology machines, and even lightbulbs).

Nursing is the biggest department in any hospital. Some 40 to 70 percent of the organization's expenses are wage and benefits costs. Thus, it makes sense for nurse leaders to focus heavily on staff issues: good selection processes, excellent training, scheduling the right number of staff members, and performance management to ensure productivity.

In addition, the nurse leader must properly schedule the staff to match the demand of service. This is accomplished through planning (forecasting) staffing needs based on historical data of patient volume. Certain regulatory standards—for example, care of patients by licensed registered nurses—also dictate minimum staffing requirements. It cannot be emphasized too much that in a human-resource-rich industry like healthcare, it is critical to match staffing needs to the actual needs of the patient! At the same time, the nurse leader must balance that match with financial expectations (salaries) and realities (revenue).

Productivity is a critical issue that can be impacted daily. Some organizations have started implementing daily productivity monitoring. This means leaders must show daily progress toward a target of 100 percent productivity by payroll's end—or they must meet with the executive team to explain what they'll do differently the next payroll period. Being held accountable in these ways forces nurse leaders to learn the nuances of scheduling and staffing. (See Chapter 17 for more detail on productivity.)

Just as nurse leaders should take care not to "waste" payroll hours, they should also be mindful of supplies. It's all too easy to think, *Well, it's just a box of exam gloves—so what if it's a couple of bucks more expensive than the competition?* Well, that "couple of bucks" multiplied hundreds of times over the course of the year can translate to a good amount of money. Likewise, don't automatically put a pile of linens in every room if there's a chance they won't be needed. Linen service is expensive. Practice good stewardship.

Remember, people and supplies are the most controllable expenses. Pennies are easier to find than dollars, and pennies really do add up.

Cost Avoidance

Cost avoidance is a pretty broad topic. It can include anything from creating systems to ensure that people aren't wasting supplies like linens or surgical sutures to implementing tools and tactics that boost productivity.

One example of how a nurse leader can decrease expenses is by reducing turnover. This can be accomplished through consistent rounding on employees to make personal connections, assess problems, and determine which tools and equipment are needed. The outcome, improved nurse retention, can save money in several ways: the dollars associated with staff vacancies, orientation costs, overtime, and agency usage. (Incidentally, it's best to avoid the use of outside agency nurses if at all possible.)

Improving clinical outcomes and staving off safety issues is a natural form of cost avoidance. According to one article—"Preserve Independence with Fall Prevention Strategies," Nurse.com, January 30, 2007—one patient fall can cost a hospital about $22,000 in care. Hourly Rounding by nursing staff decreases the incidence of falls, thus improving clinical outcomes and avoiding unnecessary costs.

In addition, better management of tests—which leads to fewer test repeats—can result in cost avoidance.

Capital Investments

Capital investments are generally thought of as investments in new pieces of equipment, buildings, and property. As a nurse leader, you may not be directly involved in influencing major purchases (like adding a new wing onto the hospital), but at some point you may find yourself advocating for a new piece of equipment. And quite often you may be involved in requesting salary increases or asking that more staff be hired (these are capital investments as well).

The most important point to remember is this: justify, justify, justify. Before you ever go to an executive team with your request, it is critical that you do your homework. You must approach your request in terms of ROI and back it up with data.

Let's say you're a home health leader and your technician in the field is making below market salary. If you don't come up with a pay increase, you will lose her, which means you'll have to turn patients away. So before you ask for the increase, figure out what the organization will gain in return: decreased turnover, increased patient volume, increased revenue.

In many organizations you'll have to put these requests in writing and go through a formal process. You may even have to convince a council of peers. And in some cases you may have to come back to the table a few months later and prove that you've achieved your projected results. If you say that the additional FTE will increase patient and employee satisfaction, be prepared to deliver that outcome. Would you be prepared to return the FTE if you don't achieve the outcome as promised? That's the kind of thought process that needs to go into the ROI message and justification.

Net Revenue Creation

It's true that nurse leaders are more likely to have an impact in the arena of cost avoidance than revenue generation. However, it's certainly *possible* to directly affect the creation of (measurable) net revenue.

For instance, you might implement a tactic that impacts the number of patients who leave the Emergency Department without being seen. Obviously, fewer left without being seen (LWBS) translates to more volume… which translates to more money for the hospital.

However, there is another very important way nurse leaders can contribute to net revenue: They consistently provide great service and deliver the best possible clinical outcomes. This may not be as easy to measure as the LWBS example, but it is surely no less significant.

Let's say a nurse leader decides he is going to eliminate or decrease the number of nosocomial infections in the ICU. This will have a dramatic impact on consistency of care and will shorten length of stay (LOS). This then impacts throughput, which impacts ER and OR volume.

Essentially, he has improved the outcome for patients, which leads to dramatic impact on all the pillars:

Service—patients are happy
Quality—fewer infections
Finance—lower cost of care, more throughput
People—more engaged and aware of impact they have
Growth—more throughput, greater physician satisfaction
Community—greater sense of peace due to all these factors combined

The Twelve Commandments for Finance-Savvy Nurse Leaders

By Linda Deering

- When you don't understand part of the financial "big picture," get educated. Read up on the subject or talk to someone in finance. It's your job to understand how the money works.
- *Always, always, always* present the ROI before you ask for something. Put it in writing, even if it's not required. This will force you to focus on whether you really need it or whether you can make do without.
- If you can't deliver on it, don't promise it. You'll lose credibility—and once it's lost, it's hard to build back up.
- Think of the needs of the entire organization, not just your own. Understand that when your department gets a "yes," someone else will get a "no."
- Don't make excuses and don't get defensive. Explaining why the goal didn't get met is a waste of time; repeating history doesn't propel you forward. Communicate only what you're going to do to change the outcome.
- Before you bring in an agency, ask yourself why it's necessary. What's not being well managed within your own team? Needing outside agency staff is often the outcome of ineffective leadership or planning.
- Declare war on waste. Before you open a new pack of supplies, make sure it's absolutely needed. And before you schedule an extra nurse, make sure he's absolutely needed.
- Constantly seek to improve your work processes, your productivity, and your outcomes.
- Empower people and encourage autonomy.
- Keep your staff connected to what things cost. Teach them to think like owners, not renters.
- When talking to staff, always frame patient volume in positive terms. Never say, "What a horrible day!" when census is high. Having lots of patients is good for the organization!
- Accept the realities of payer mix. Organizations serving less affluent populations will never have the same resources and amenities as those serving more affluent ones. Bloom where you're planted or find a new job.

So, as you see, nurse leaders *can* have a major impact on the organization's financial health. Indeed, it is your responsibility to do so.

Everyone associated with a healthcare organization—from the CEO to the leaders to the staff to the patients to the community—wants it to thrive. And understanding finances allows you to measure the "vital signs" of that organization and prescribe appropriate, cost-effective remedies that yield a positive return on investment.

Can you imagine a scenario in which the CFO goes to bat for a new program or capital expenditure suggested by a nurse leader? Yes, it can happen. The nurse leader just needs to have a working knowledge of the basic components of financial management so she can build a compelling case—and, ultimately, better serve her patients, staff, and the organization as a whole.

For a listing of helpful financial terms and definitions, go to www.firestarterpublishing.com/NurseLeaderHandbook.

Key Points in This Chapter

1. Finances are a critical element of patient care. Nurse leaders must understand the financial impact of their decisions in order to do their jobs well.

2. Great nurse leaders must be able to speak the language of the C-suite to advocate for process changes and expenditures that will better serve patients. They must also be able to inspire staff members to carry out goals. And often, what motivates senior leaders and what motivates staff are entirely different things!

3. Nurse leaders can affect an organization's financial bottom line in several areas: day-to-day expenditures, cost avoidance, capital investments, and net revenue creation.

Pillars Affected by A Good Understanding of Financial Impact

Service—When nurse leaders understand finances, they can persuade senior leaders to invest in improvements that benefit patients.

Quality—Nurse leaders can use their influence to effect changes that improve patient safety (going to all latex-free gloves to better secure the safety of patients allergic to latex).

Finance—When nurse leaders are connected to financial realities, they are able to make smart ROI decisions, contain costs, and even generate revenue.

People—Financially savvy nurse leaders teach staff how to think like owners and make smarter decisions. This creates an engaged, cost-conscious culture that attracts and nurtures good people.

Growth—Better outcomes and more satisfied patients lead to higher volume.

Community—A financially healthy organization is good for everyone in the market area.

CHAPTER 17

Productivity Management

By Bob Murphy

I find it ironic that I'm writing the chapter on productivity. While I have certainly learned a great deal about how productivity affects patient care generally and nursing specifically, I did not start my nursing leadership career as someone knowledgeable about this subject. In fact, I was unconsciously incompetent—which means I did not know what I didn't know. I thought I was a pretty good leader, but in actuality, I'd had very little training on some very important basics.

Here's how my eyes were opened.

During the month of December, I was promoted to nurse manager of a busy Emergency Department (ED) that handled approximately 50,000 patients a year. I had a good staff who took great care of those patients every day, and my hospital was doing okay financially, so there were some things I didn't have to worry about.

My first lesson in unconscious incompetence happened in July the following year when the patient care services budget director and I were beginning to prepare our fiscal year budget for the following October. We were discussing my statistics, revenue, number of employees (referred to as FTEs), and expenses. When we got to the FTE part, I began to get a little anxious. My number didn't match Debra's number—in fact, it was significantly higher. I really needed those employees. *How could I possibly cut so many positions and still take good care of patients?* I wondered.

The more I tried to explain what we did in the Emergency Department, the more frustrated Debra became. We could not see eye-to-eye. Finally I asked if she would be willing to spend some time shadowing me in the ED to see what "we really do down there." I was hoping to get her on my side. She agreed, and we moved on to revenue calculations.

After a few minutes of discussing revenue, Debra looked off into space and smiled. She then asked, "Hey, Bob, do you know what an FTE is?" I said, "Of course, it's a full-time employee." Debra then explained to me that an FTE was actually a full-time *equivalent*. It refers to a mathematical equation where one FTE is actually 2,080 hours per year for a full-time person.

As it turns out, I was counting heads. She was counting full-time equivalent hours. When I saw 75 FTEs, I was thinking 75 people. She was thinking 2,080 hours per year x 75 to calculate the total hours needed.

I was shocked. I'd had no idea! No one had ever mentioned the definition of FTE in nursing school. No one had ever talked about it in the seven months since I'd been promoted to manager. Boy, did I feel like a fool.

Then I wondered, *How could I have been running this department with 75 FTEs for seven months and not know this basic thing?* I could not possibly be hitting budget. How come no one else noticed?

A Crash Course in Productivity

I tell this story often while speaking to organizations about leadership development. And the amazing thing is that about every other time, someone comes up to me to thank me for giving the definition because that person didn't know what an FTE was either. While it makes me feel good I can help others, it also concerns me that leaders are still not taught this basic skill at times. Let's change that now.

Here are a few things I would like to accomplish with this chapter:

1. Take some of the mystery out of productivity in nursing.

2. Help you be more confident in your discussions with financial leaders.

3. Help you learn the right questions to ask.

So, why should this issue be so important to you? Well, more and more, nurse leaders are being held accountable for staff's productivity. Even hospitals that didn't focus on it in the past are doing so now.

First, Let's Define Our Terms.

Simply put, productivity on a nursing unit is utilized to determine the efficiency of the care being given. There are many systems organizations use to track and report productivity, but it's usually a calculation involving how many patients were cared for by how many staff in what time period (usually expressed in hours). Some standard productivity terms used by organizations are listed below:

Worked hours per patient day (WHPPD): This refers to the number of budgeted hours within a 24-hour period that your staff is expected to provide direct patient care. For budgeting purposes, this might be expressed as something like 7.22 WHPPD: meaning in a 24-hour period, the expectation is that a little over seven hours of direct patient care will be delivered by an RN, LPN, or nursing assistant. In many cases, the WHPPD varies based on the type of unit you oversee. For example, the worked hours on a medical unit are usually lower than those in an Intensive Care Unit (ICU). This is only logical because ICU patients are typically much sicker, requiring more direct patient care. It's not unusual to see an ICU's WHPPD to be 12.0 to 16.0, or higher.

WHPPD is used in determining overall productivity—defined as the *ratio* of expected labor to actual labor used. For instance, you expected (or budgeted) 9.0 WHPPD on the unit, but staff actually used 10.0 to deliver direct patient care. To get your ratio, you would divide nine by ten, which tells you the unit is operating at 90 percent productivity. Ideally, 100 plus or minus 5 percent is the target used in most productivity processes. The higher the productivity, generally speaking, the more favorable the situation. However, extended periods of very high productivity can impact quality and increase risk. Extended periods of low productivity, on the other hand, have a direct impact on labor expense and overall financial viability of the organization.

In most cases, there will be national standards for productivity targets within the various nursing specialties. Contact your professional associations for established targets from which you can benchmark. The worked hours per patient day excludes nurse leaders, clinical nurse specialists, and secretarial support, as none of these positions provides direct patient care.

The WHPPD is not only used for budgeting purposes, but is also reported to provide *actual* performance towards the budgeted goal.

Paid hours per patient day (PHPPD): This refers to the number of budgeted hours attributed to *all positions* in a unit, including those scheduled as well as employees not in direct patient care. It also incorporates the hours associated with, and charged for, vacation and sick days. Again, PHPPD is used for budgeting purposes as well as current productivity monitoring. Paid hours are typically higher than worked hours—but too much of a gap between the two is indicative of an area carrying a lot of overhead.

Full-time equivalents or FTEs: A full-time employee who works 40 hours per week for a full year will work 2,080 hours. Any increment of that will be expressed as a decimal depending on the number of hours worked. A nurse who works 1,040 hours equals .5 FTE; one who works 520 hours is a .25 FTE.

Positions in nursing are typically posted by allocating a portion of an FTE, which defines if the position is full- or part-time. A 1.0 position is full-time. A position posted for .6 FTE is part-time; the individual would be required to work 1,248 (2,080 x .6) hours per year or 24 hours per week.

Employees per occupied bed: To get this statistic, divide your number of FTEs by the average daily census.

FTE per adjusted occupied bed: An FTE's total paid hours in one year's time (2,080 hours x 365 days) is divided by the adjusted occupied bed.

> **Adjusted occupied bed** = Total patient days divided by days in the period x (times) gross patient charges divided by the total gross inpatient charges.

Patient days: This is the sum of all admitted patients in the hospital at the time of the midnight census (it usually excludes newborns). Patient days is typically the number used to calculate things like medication error rates (usually expressed as the number of errors per 1,000 patient days) or productivity measures as described above.

Total patient days: This figure reflects the number of patient days for a specified time period (e.g., week, month, year, etc.).

Acuity: Many systems take into account how sick the patient is, i.e., the acuity. Additional hours of care are allocated for sicker patients. Acuity systems are more often used in day-to-day staffing decisions than in budgeting or forecasting strategic plans for staffing.

Skill mix: This refers to the compliment of RNs versus LPNs, nursing assistants, or other provider levels scheduled on your unit.

Budget: Your productivity budget or plan may be fixed or variable. Variable assumes that as your department cares for more patients, you are allocated more hours of care.

Average daily census: The beds in service x the occupancy rate. Or you may divide the number of inpatients at the time of midnight census by the number of calendar days.

Why Nurse Leaders Need to Speak the Language

I have found that organizations use different definitions for many of these terms. As a nurse leader, your job is to find out how each one is defined at your hospital. Also, you have to understand the reports that come out describing what's budgeted for your area, and how you are currently performing against that budgeted number. Why do you need to know all of this? Well, as you talk to your chief financial officer or chief nursing officer, these are the terms that will be used in the conversation.

In today's healthcare environment, managing productivity is a continual balancing act between meeting the care needs of those you serve and maintaining fiscal responsibility. You need to be hands-on in your approach to this activity—and make no mistake, it will be an ongoing, day by day, shift by shift, and sometimes even hour by hour, endeavor. You must be able to make good decisions at a moment's notice without losing sight of the unit's strategic, overall objectives of meeting budget. This means managing overtime carefully and ensuring an adequate skill mix to provide quality care.

The Cost of Non-Productive Time

I wanted to share a great win my organization had using the exercise from Studer Group's senior leader toolkit around time spent on unproductive things. I decided to use it at our hospital's first leadership development session.

At the individual tables, leaders calculated their non-productive time and then each table came up with a total, which was given to me during the break. I added these up for a grand total of hours per week and year for the group (there were 160 leaders in the room, 3,121 hrs/week, **162,292 hrs/year**).

The chief financial officer gave me an average salary for the group and we quickly calculated it for a year. The total came to **$3,652,000/year**! The group was shocked. We talked about the significance of potential gains in efficiency. Buy-in of the group was very clear from that point forward, and what had been learned was shared with staff.

—A productivity-minded leader

Five Tips for Effective Productivity Management

There are several strategies available to assist you with productivity management. Here are a few to consider:

1. Be sure your staff and charge nurses also understand the terms associated with productivity and the need to continually manage to this concept. When you are not on the unit, they will be responsible for making the shift-to-shift and mid-shift adjustments that will have dramatic impact on the unit's performance. For instance, the charge nurse may have to call in a nurse mid-shift in anticipation of an admission, but the patient doesn't come up from the Emergency Department until three hours later. That's unneeded time that will count against your productivity. It doesn't mean that nurse wasn't busy working; rather, it means what she was doing probably could have been absorbed by other employees. When your charge nurses understand the impact of their decisions on the overall

functioning of the unit and organization, they make better decisions and demonstrate their ownership.

2. Don't forget to communicate your current performance and productivity goals to nursing supervisors. As another resource for making staffing decisions, they can support you by adhering to your objectives.

3. Encourage staff to think in terms of blocks of time shorter than eight hours. For instance, you might need an extra nurse when the patients all come back from the operating room, but that may not be until after noon. So you don't need the additional nurse at 7 a.m., but rather could bring someone in for a four-hour block late in the morning or at 12:00 p.m.

4. Look carefully at skill mix in the staffing decisions. Perhaps you're short a nurse, but based on the patients' needs, a certified nursing assistant would be just as helpful. While the substitution doesn't impact the total hours, it does affect the dollars associated with those hours. As long as you aren't compromising safety and quality, consider choosing an option that will help manage labor costs.

5. Beware of the quick fix. With the nursing shortage looming large, it's tempting to use agency staff as a way to fill gaps. This can be quite addictive and a hard habit to break. But the financial costs are phenomenal; the quality and safety risks increase; and current employees' satisfaction decreases because they usually don't like working with temporary staff. While certain circumstances dictate use of agency people, it should be a last resort and as rare as possible. Many organizations have found effective ways of minimizing and even eliminating this practice through effective management systems designed to retain current staff.

Remember, people are the largest expense of any hospital. Obviously, their cost needs to be managed for the financial health of the organization.

But this is not meant to imply that holding employee costs down is the be-all, end-all of productivity management. Ensuring that the right mix of staff members is working in a particular area at a particular time benefits the organization on many levels: clinical outcome quality, safety, patient well-being and satisfaction, and employee work/life blend, just to name a few.

Here's the bottom line for nurse leaders: Factor productivity into your daily decision-making, and, over time, you'll have a tremendous positive impact on the health of the organization.

Key Points in This Chapter

1. Nurse leaders should work with financial leaders to analyze labor productivity based on data gathered from payroll, patient accounting, time and attendance, and budgets.

2. Nurse leaders should understand current trend data for patient days and equivalent observation days, target and actual hours worked, overtime and agency hours, and any variances.

3. Smart productivity management works holistically. Not only does it help contain costs, it helps an organization achieve better clinical outcomes and results in happier patients and employees.

Pillars Affected by Productivity

Service—Good productivity management helps eliminate the need for agency nurses who might not be familiar with your organization's standards of performance.

Quality—Unless productivity is managed well, the use of temporary nurses can impact quality and safety due to their unfamiliarity with your tools and processes.

Finance—Productivity means you manage staff's time and skill mix to achieve the unit's financial goals.

CHAPTER 18

Measurement

By Terry Rose and Tonya Fuller

Historically, nurse leaders have been excellent data gatherers. And in years past, the process stopped there—we rarely thought about what to do with the information we'd compiled. Nobody ever asked for the measurement data. We seldom discussed it. We just had it. It was piled high in our offices; periodically someone would ask for something and we would go digging through the stacks.

True, we set goals, but many times those goals were not linked to the data we were so busy collecting. Nor were we objectively assessed based on our performance of any of these measures.

My, the changes we've seen since transparency arrived in healthcare! Today we measure direct outcomes and many processes to ensure we are continually improving the care we provide. We measure "to align leadership and employee behaviors, processes, and systems."

While this chapter will focus primarily on measurement as it relates to the use of patient satisfaction data, the conceptual framework of thoroughly understanding your measurement tool and data and the analysis of that information to drive results applies to all types of measurement in which nurse leaders are involved. Some common examples of data and measurement for nurse leaders are:

- Financial measures: Budget, productivity, LOS
- Quality measures: Core measures, hand hygiene, medication errors
- People measures: Employee and physician satisfaction

In each of these examples, the nurse leader must be intimately familiar with how the information is collected and reported. In many cases it will become part of the process of effective analysis and thus impact the strategies that need to be applied to move the result.

Today it's incumbent upon you, the nurse leader, to know your measurement results—backward, forward, and inside out. Not a data expert? Need help in understanding your survey results? Need to know what *that* number means? Most organizations have a resource you can access—typically, it's the expert related to any particular measure. For instance, for financial measures it might be the CFO. For the quality measures we outlined above, the expert would likely be the quality director. For people measures it's probably the human resources director. For patient satisfaction it is the person who has been designated the "super user" or "hospital representative" for the survey vendor. Seek out the expert in your organization to help you with measurement across your strategic framework.

Your first step in understanding what it's all about is learning the terminology.

How to Think About the Data

Mean score, percentile rank, top decile/quartile, and *top box percent* are terms associated with various patient satisfaction surveys. What do they all mean and what significance do they have for you?

- **Mean score:** Computed by adding all the results in the database and then dividing that sum by the total number of results (N).
- **The raw score:** Determined by various methods and can be different for various tools. This is when you need to be very knowledgeable about the tool so you understand what method is being used to produce it. One example would be a Likert scale but there are others.
- **Percentile rank:** Tells you how you perform relative to others in the database you're benchmarking against. For example, a percentile rank of 50 indicates you scored higher than 50 percent of the others in your peer group.
- **Top decile** and **top quartile:** Terms used to describe the "top" of a metric you are benchmarking against. Top decile means you scored in the top 10 percent of hospitals in your peer group. Top quartile indicates you scored in the top 25 percent of your peer group.
- **Top box percent:** Term used to denote the percentage of the "best" answer available on a particular survey.
- **Correlation coefficient:** Used to indicate the relationship of two random variables, including strength and direction. It varies from -1 to 1. It is used in measurement tools to assist with prioritization and analysis.

As you may remember from Chapter 15 (Goal Management), not all questions are weighted equally. For instance, a mean result of 88 for an Emergency Department (ED) may not rank at the same percentile as an 88 mean result for an outpatient unit (OP). The relationship is *dependent on the average result of all the participants in a given database.*

As a leader, have you ever combined data points within a given metric to make the results look better? For example, 40 percent of patients said you provided them with "good" care and 50 percent said you provided them with "very good" care. If you add the two metrics together, then you can say that 90 percent of patients are satisfied with the care provided to them.

We suggest you think about this in a different way. Do you really want to combine a "better" metric with a "best" metric? All that tells the world is that staff is doing "okay" under your leadership!

Instead of trying to manipulate percentages, set a goal of delivering world-class care on your unit and performing at the top. Ask your data guru what term is used to describe the top of the particular metric you are benchmarking against. Is it top decile (top 10 percent) or top quartile (top 25 percent)—and aim accordingly!

The lesson here: Know the key documentation points in order to achieve excellence. Share with employees how many patients, how many hours, how many dollars it will take to reach the unit's goal. You will find the staff eager to hit a defined target!

HCAHPS

The term "top box percent" has taken on increasing importance due to the Hospital Consumer Assessment of Healthcare Providers and Systems (HCAHPS) survey reporting process. Designed so that consumers can compare hospitals objectively, the survey produces data about patients' perspectives of care. It serves to drive accountability in healthcare by increasing the transparency of the quality of care provided.

Figure 18.1

What Will CMS Report?

Composite	Scale	Top Box
During this hospital stay, how often did nurses listen carefully to you?	Always Usually Sometimes Never	Always
Did you get information in writing about what symptoms or health problems to look for after you left the hospital?	Yes No	Yes
Using any number from 0-10, where 0 is the worst possible and 10 is the best possible, how would you rate this hospital?	0 = worst hospital 10 = best hospital	9+10
Would you recommend this hospital to your friends and family?	Definitely Yes Probably Yes Probably No Definitely No	Definitely Yes

Survey results are published for consumers on the Centers for Medicare & Medicaid Services (CMS) website *Hospital Compare*. CMS has chosen to publicly report *only the top box percent*. For example, patients are asked to rate their likelihood to recommend a particular hospital. They have choices ranging from "definitely no" to "definitely yes." But only the percentage of "definitely yes" answers (top box) from patients is published. In the following table, you will see numbers between 73 and 79 expressed as a percentage. That means that between 73 and 79 percent of the responses were "definitely yes" to that question.

Here are a couple of examples pulled from *Hospital Compare* and modified to hide the identity of the organizations:

Figure 18.2

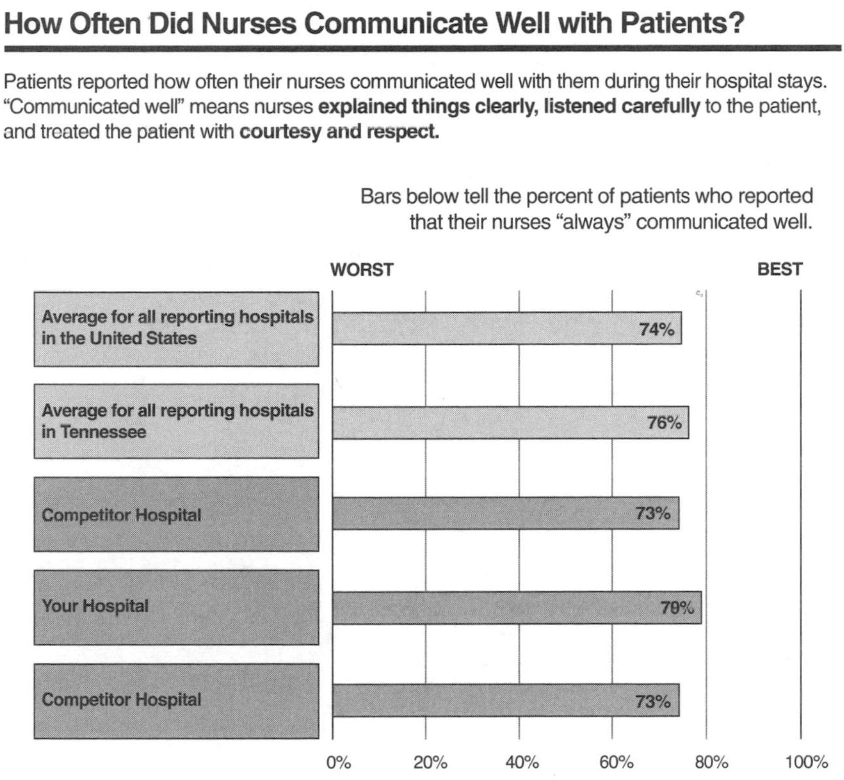
How Often Did Nurses Communicate Well with Patients?
Patients reported how often their nurses communicated well with them during their hospital stays. "Communicated well" means nurses explained things clearly, listened carefully to the patient, and treated the patient with courtesy and respect.
Bars below tell the percent of patients who reported that their nurses "always" communicated well.
WORST
BEST
Average for all reporting hospitals in the United States
74%
Average for all reporting hospitals in Tennessee
76%
Competitor Hospital
73%
Your Hospital
79%
Competitor Hospital
73%
0%
20%
40%
60%
80%
100%

Figure 18.3

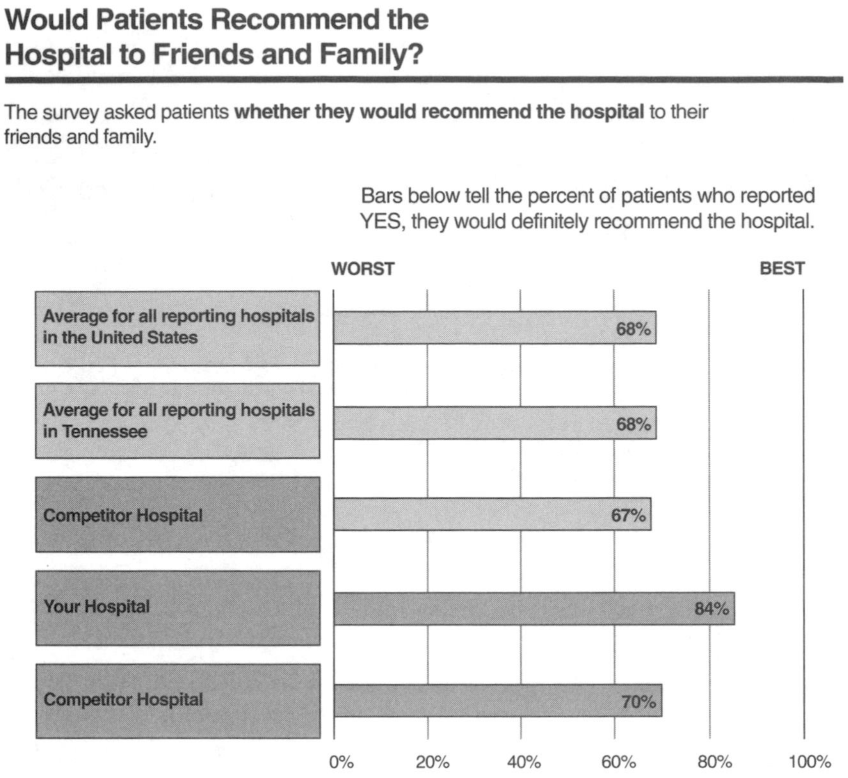
Would Patients Recommend the Hospital to Friends and Family?
The survey asked patients whether they would recommend the hospital to their friends and family.
Bars below tell the percent of patients who reported YES, they would definitely recommend the hospital.
WORST
BEST
Average for all reporting hospitals in the United States
68%
Average for all reporting hospitals in Tennessee
68%
Competitor Hospital
67%
Your Hospital
84%
Competitor Hospital
70%
0%
20%
40%
60%
80%
100%

The Frequency Table

While you are in discussion with the appropriate measurement expert or the vendor that supports the measurement tool for the item you are focused on, it is also good to know how to find and use the frequency table—or frequency analysis, as it may be called. (In regard to patient satisfaction, this document may come from the vendor; however, some organizations build it internally.)

This frequency table data provides you with information on how answers were distributed relative to available answers for a particular question. For instance, the question may contain responses on a numeric scale of 1-5, and the frequency table will show you how many of the responses were a 1 versus a 2 versus a 3 and so on. Knowing this information is also useful in guiding your analysis.

One of the most important philosophies in driving results is to not fall into the trap of working on the lowest results. In fact, more often you will move the overall result faster by focusing on moving someone who rated you a 4 on a 5-point scale to a 5 than trying to move someone who is very dissatisfied. The person who gave you the 4 already thinks you are pretty good. What is the one thing we could have done to wow these 4s and turn them into 5s?

Focusing on the 4s will allow you to drive overall results much faster. Again this applies to any survey process, whether you are referring to patient, employee, or physician satisfaction. It is also the case in many quality improvement opportunities as well.

Figure 18.4

4 vs. 5
Sample Distribution of Patient Satisfaction Score

	1s	2s	3s	4s	5s
99th Percentile Hospital	1%	1%	5%	19%	74%
66th Percentile Hospital	1%	2%	8%	35%	53%

Many times, the issues that are keeping our lowest performing areas from improving are bigger than just that one measure. They will require more focused leadership attention to repair those issues. Departments that are performing in the middle of the curve are better positioned to have the resources to move results. Start with them.

Figure 18.5

Sample Survey Questions

Sample Survey Questions	Very Poor/ Very Dissatisfied	Poor/ Somewhat Dissatisfied	Fair/ Satisfied	Good/ Very Good/ Very Satisfied	Very Good/ Excellent/ Completely Satisfied
Overall satisfaction or overall quality of care	0.0%	0.9%	2.9%	21.0%	75.3%
Friendliness/courtesy/respect of the nurses	0.5%	1.2%	5.4%	22.6%	70.3%
Promptness in responding to call	0.7%	3.0%	5.8%	23.3%	67.2%
Nurses' understanding and caring	1.2%	1.6%	7.5%	25.1%	64.6%
Nurses' explanation of tests/treatments	0.5%	1.0%	3.8%	21.4%	73.3%

Making Patient Satisfaction Data Work for You

Does this scenario sound familiar? You get the patient satisfaction survey results and you hang the report on the bulletin board for the staff to see. Unfortunately, the results are down again. As a matter of fact, if you look at that trend line of the graph, it looks more like the EKG of a patient with V-tach. You, as the nurse leader, are increasingly frustrated because you have talked until you're blue in the face about how important it is to improve these scores. You've done everything. You've told them that any of these patients could be your mother. You've reminded them that all these patients are someone's loved ones. You've threatened them. You've begged them to be nicer. What else can you do?

In other words, you've had it. You come to that staff meeting ready to do battle. You throw out the question: ***What happened to the patient satisfaction scores? They look terrible. What did you do?*** The staff sit silently and then someone always starts throwing darts at the dartboard by saying, "Well, we were really short staffed." Or, "That was the week that Sarah was going through her divorce." Or, "The census was really high." Or, "That was flu season." You get the picture.

What these staff members are really saying is, "We don't know." And it's true. Staff get as frustrated as leaders do. They will say (or at least think): "I don't know what makes those results go up and down. I don't do anything differently. Sometimes they come back good and sometimes they come back bad. It's a crap shoot."

It's really important to help yourself and your staff begin to understand there is a cause and effect relationship to patient satisfaction results...and it will appear in the data when they begin to understand it a bit better.

It will help to start this conversation by asking them a few rather strategic questions:

1. Do you think there is variability in the way one person on our unit practices versus another? For example: Do you think the order in which everybody does their assessments is the same? Is the way we each deliver medications the same? Is the way we admit a patient the same? Do we all say the same words? The answer is usually *yes...there is a difference.* As a matter of fact, you may hear the second shift complain about the day shift because "they never get their stuff done."

2. Is there variability in the behaviors that staff members demonstrate with each other and with patients? They will usually agree there is.

3. Do you think the patients notice this variability? (The answer is YES!)

Once you have staff members at this point, then you can show them the patient satisfaction results and help them see that they can expect variability in the results only because there is variability in the processes and behaviors. To change the results, we have to change the processes and behaviors.

Now the question is where to start...and you use your knowledge of data analysis and correlations to guide you to that answer.

Consider this fact: The more ways you can look at patient satisfaction survey data, the more effective processes you can put into place to drive quality improvement. Have you even seen the scores for your unit sliced and diced by age, gender, first-time admittance, impact of day, evening, and night shifts? We call this type of score breakdown a "filter." Just by using a qualifying question or piece of information, we can look at data through a different lens.

Simply by asking what filters are available to you for your unit, you can discover a wealth of valuable information. For instance, we had an Emergency Department (ED) leader share frustration over her staff's failure to check on patients regularly. As a result, the patients' perception of care was low because they weren't kept informed of delays. (How well patients are kept informed of delays is a common question on patient satisfaction tools and is usually highly correlated to improvements in overall satisfaction.)

The leader had tried and tried to change behaviors. After much time spent on education, hands-on observation, and coaching, the survey scores still didn't budge. But then she "filtered" the data to look at patient satisfaction scores by shift. It became clear the gap existed with the day shift—the night shift "got it." With this information, the ED leader knew where to concentrate on training.

Data Changes Attitudes

At one very large ED in an inner city, the discussion with nursing leadership during a coaching visit centered on their reluctance to make post-discharge phone calls. *With over 200 visits a day, how is the team supposed to find any time for the calls?* they wanted to know. *And even if they could, how would this make any impact on the patients' perception of quality of care?*

When the nurse director showed them survey results for the patients' perception of care when they received a call (99th percentile), versus when they did not receive a call (10th percentile), the discussion changed. It went from "Can we?" to "*How* can we?" Data can provide you with a powerful "connect to purpose."

Why was the nurse leader so focused on that one question? Because it centers on a "hot button" issue that tends to color patients' overall view of the service provided. All vendors who administer healthcare patient satisfaction surveys provide us with key indicators that "correlate" most closely to the patients' perception of their entire care experience. You may hear terms applied to key survey questions such as "priority index," or "key driver," or "correlation coefficients" or just simply "correlation." All terms simply mean that a relationship exists between how patients feel about a particular question and their overall perception of care.

Thus, how patients score you on just one question, such as how well they're kept informed of delays, will have a strong relationship on how they feel about their overall satisfaction. When in front of ED patients like the ones we're discussing, if they perceive they *have* been kept informed of delays, then based on correlation information we can expect to see a positive improvement in their overall perception of care.

Our point? If the survey vendor provides you with correlation information, use it to your advantage. You may choose to focus on improving the top two or three "correlation" questions for your unit quarterly by educating staff on key tactics such as AIDET and rounding on patients. When you do, we promise you will see a positive impact on the patients' perception of the overall care they received.

Read your patient survey comments lately? You should. They can provide you with ways to harvest more wins for staff or physician recognition. The comments may provide you with key words, such as, "The staff kept me informed when there was a delay," or, "Everyone introduced themselves when they came in my room." Comments will also provide you value in validating consistent practice of staff behaviors that bring about the best results.

Using Measurement Data to Engage and Motivate Staff

As we've established, the real purpose of gathering data is to identify areas where the organization needs improvement. But that's just the beginning. We also need to get staff members connected to these "problem areas" and inspire them to make necessary changes.

When you're striving to make process improvements, consistency is key. Measurement can provide you with proof of whether a practice is consistent or not. It helps you as a nurse leader validate that your plan is working and provides the information needed to make adjustments mid-course. We often hear the concern voiced from leaders about "validity" of weekly patient satisfaction survey data. Don't worry about validity. Statistical trends will become evident over time. Use the information instead to reinforce the positive behavior that produced results that week.

> In many cases the data function much like a thermometer in the clinical world. Let's say you take a patient's temperature and find out the patient has a fever. The thermometer doesn't tell you what's wrong, and it isn't going to tell you how to fix it. The reality is you are going to have to do more assessment and more tests to get that answer. These measures in most cases function the same way. They indicate if you have a problem, but to determine exactly what the problem is and how to fix it, you will likely have to do more study.

In one case, on a nursing unit, we were working on trying to improve the patients' perception of pain management. The nurse leader had asked the staff to implement two very prescriptive tactics. One was to update the whiteboard to reflect the time the patient could have the next dose of pain medication, and the second one was to be sure that PRN pain medications were offered at the scheduled interval rather than having the patient request the medication.

The nurse leader then started watching her monthly survey results and didn't see any movement. She became quite frustrated. However, with a little education about the survey tool, she drilled down and re-sorted her results by the date the patient was discharged rather than the order in which the survey was received. Also, she looked at the results of this one question on pain weekly instead of monthly.

These simple changes allowed her to see that the results on the question about pain management had in fact moved up significantly since they had implemented this practice. These results would have been hidden had she not learned this analysis skill. She now posts the results on the pain question weekly so the staff get good feedback on how they are progressing. If the results dip, it serves as a reminder to refocus or to do some further assessment.

Besides formal weekly or quarterly surveys, measurement information might also come from rounding on patients, families, employees, and physicians. It is important to capture information or comments patients provide during rounding. Perhaps you discovered while rounding that Karen has been keeping patients informed and treats them with kindness. Pay attention to this finding; there may be a way to standardize what Karen is doing and get other nurses to emulate her.

How do you drive process improvement using measurement? First, reward and recognize the positive behavior identified from data points. Second, tabulate trends. Third, communicate, communicate, communicate, communicate, communicate, communicate, communicate, and communicate. Yes, we said *communicate* eight times! It takes this level of consistency to cascade important information throughout the unit to all your staff members, and they need to be kept informed of your measurement progress.

What are the most effective ways to communicate data to employees? Following are some best practices we have gathered over the years to help you.

Communication Boards: 80 mph Reports

How often do we measure? We measure and communicate the results often enough to change behavior. That means we measure more often than we previously had (perhaps weekly instead of monthly, like the nurse leader in the pain management example) in order to identify behaviors or trends that might be affecting results. This way we can respond immediately rather than waiting long enough for the results to be statistically relevant.

A department communication board is an excellent tool to keep the staff informed of its progress as a team. The information posted should include:

- Patient satisfaction survey results
- Employee satisfaction survey results
- Monthly budget
- Quality metrics such as fall prevention data, hand washing compliance, pain management, or discharge instruction data
- Department goals

We call this data "80 mph reports," a reference to the rate at which staff is busy working. (They always seem to be running at a proverbial 100 mph pace.) Therefore when we post material that employees need to be familiar with and see regularly, we format it in easy-to-read trend lines and bar graphs. This allows staff to zip past the bulletin board, glance at it, see if the indicators are up or down, and conceivably know what should be done differently that day to help. If you post the information in numerals, staff will have to stop, read each number, and calculate whether the trend is up or down. This stalls productivity.

Huddles

As you communicate with staff, you should always connect back to purpose and worthwhile work. This is why "huddles"—sometimes referred to as stand-up meetings—are so important to daily operations. And they're also a great time to focus on how measurement reflects the patient experience. The most successful huddles encompass transparency practices such as the reporting of current measurement results, what's working well (as determined by leader rounding outcomes), and identified barriers to high performance. The nurse leader also communicates simple action steps to improve patients' perception of care. Finally, huddles provide an opportunity to reward and recognize desired behaviors that have improved how patients feel about the care they received.

Education Sessions for Support Staff

Allied health and support services are rarely considered when nurse leaders begin training and educating the staff on measurement and the use of key words. Yet employees of ancillary departments—housekeeping and food service, for instance—also make a great impact on the patient's perception of care. Representatives of these departments should be invited to educational sessions to gain an understanding of their role in ensuring the best patient experience possible. As the nurse leader, meet with the managers of support departments to discuss your patient experience strategies. It's a smart move and rewarding in the end.

Reports: Green, Yellow, and Red Are Beautiful Colors

A great way to keep staff informed of progress on data from formal surveys is by distributing a report using the colors from a stoplight. Green means you've achieved the desired goal. Yellow tells staff you're near the goal. (Most organizations use yellow to mean that progress is being made, with the goal being within 10 percent.) Red signifies you're at less than 90 percent of goal. The value of this report is that it provides leaders and staff with a quick look at progress. Here is an example:

Figure 18.6

Questions	Sept 08 % Rank	Oct 08 % Rank	Nov 08 % Rank	Dec 08 % Rank
Std overall	19	3	33	50
Std arrival	42	18	40	54
Waiting time before noticed arrival	31	12	28	43
Helpfulness of first person	42	4	47	32
Comfort of waiting area	51	30	64	50
Waiting time to treatment area	58	44	53	65
Waiting time to see doctor	50	11	37	71

Embracing BEST PRACTICES within Your Organization

As healthcare providers we often look outside of our organizations for best practices. We scour the internet, buy "how to" books, and even go as far as researching a competitor hospital to learn best practices. But the truth is, best practices are right there within the walls of your hospital. They can be discovered through leadership development training and director or nurse leader meetings.

For example, let's say you discover that the patient's perception of how quickly staff respond to the call light on your unit is less than optimal. You then remember that a nurse leader colleague of yours, Jim, was recently recognized at a leadership meeting because his unit is a high performer in responding to patient call lights. How quickly would you schedule some time with Jim to better understand how his team performs with this to get great results? Remember, the solution may be just a climb of the stairs or an elevator ride away.

Your fellow colleagues are doing great things and getting positive sustainable results. Find them and benchmark internally.

Here is a story that shows how one Florida hospital transferred several best practices:

Measurement data showed that 5 out of 7 inpatient units were failing at pain management. Two nurse leaders, Veronica and Sabrina, were struggling to improve their respective outcomes in this area.

Veronica did a very nice job of educating and training her staff on the proper execution of the eight behaviors of Hourly Rounding℠. She placed special emphasis on pain. Every nurse and patient care assistant communicated hourly to the patient, "It is our goal to ensure your pain is well managed during your time with us. How well are we doing with managing your pain?"

However, Veronica discovered through rounding documentation that her staff was *still* having a hard time ensuring their patients' pain needs were well managed! She also learned that when a patient responded that pain was not being dealt with, it was due to medication needed outside his or her prescribed frequency. What made it worse was the patient had to remain in discomfort while the nurse waited for a physician to call back with an additional pain order.

So Veronica and her team decided to educate physicians on the current measurement data reflecting poor pain managements. They also reminded the physicians how instrumental they were in helping improve these outcomes. The physicians agreed to become more involved in taking ownership and partnering with the nurses. This meant not leaving the floor without writing PRN pain orders. If for some reason a doctor failed to do this, the nurses did not hesitate to stop him or her from leaving the unit. This practice and engagement by physicians led to improved results.

In the same Florida hospital, a call was made to Sabrina by her direct leader, who had similar concerns about pain management. The leader asked Sabrina if she was aware of what her colleague Veronica had done to improve the patients' perception of pain.

It turned out Sabrina was not—and she was only too glad to hear about what had been accomplished and adopted the same practices on her unit. Like Veronica, she educated physicians on how important it was to manage the pain; after all, when patients were experiencing it, they would not have an excellent experience regardless of any other service delivery efforts.

The nurse leaders also implemented a pain protocol program to include physician input and action steps. Overall, it was a combination of using the measurement data to effect process improvement, along with physician education, that produced sustainable results on Veronica's and Sabrina's units. Hourly Rounding, leader patient rounding, and documentation also helped.

Measurement Pays Off in Many Ways.

In conclusion, measurement supports the alignment of desired behaviors. It holds staff accountable for results, shows where progress is being made, and helps determine when improvements are needed. Employees motivated by measurement data are better able to connect the importance of their behaviors with the patient's healthcare experience. They also come to understand it's the patient's perception that drives the survey results.

Nurse leaders can use measurement data to their advantage when they learn all the ways it can be looked at—that is, become familiar with how it can be "filtered." This helps them put the most effective processes into place to drive quality improvements. Survey outcomes also provide leaders with more opportunities to recognize and reward staff.

Remember, measurement results cannot be over-communicated. They are valuable only when everyone, from top to bottom, knows the current status of patient satisfaction. So measure and communicate relentlessly—the payoff will be tremendous!

Key Points in This Chapter

1. In today's healthcare environment, where results are driving more and more of our strategic priorities, nurse leaders *have* to understand what measurement is all about. The first step is learning the tool and a strong working knowledge of the data.

2. Nurse leaders should know and understand which questions with respect to their areas are the most influential for patients' perception of care. Enlist the help of a measurement expert to define the basics and interpret the nuances of the measurement system your organization uses. Learn how to make the data work for you.

3. Engage staff in the measurement process through education (connect the dots for them concerning key words to use), communication, and the transfer of internal best practices. Help employees see the relationship between the actions they take and patient satisfaction scores.

4. Always reward and recognize staff for consistently using the right behaviors that result in high satisfaction scores. Recognized behavior gets repeated.

Pillars Affected by Measurement

Service—Understanding the measurement data, and using it to your best advantage, can help impact the patient's perception of the care delivered.

Quality—Measurement impacts the quality of care by identifying where improvement is needed.

Finance—HCAHPS measurement data is transparent, helping to drive admissions and improve the bottom line.

People—Measurement outcomes provide the opportunity to recognize and reward staff.

Growth—Increased admissions due to high performance metrics can result in new services and expansion of existing programs.

CHAPTER 19

A Culture of Safety

By Julie O'Shaughnessy and Rich Bluni

In 1999, the Institute of Medicine's report *To Err Is Human*[1] shined a spotlight on how medical errors have caused the death of tens of thousands of Americans. It also effectively placed the issue of patient safety and quality of care on the radar screen of the public. As a result, healthcare process improvements have received much attention in recent years.

Of course, the Institute of Medicine was hardly the first on the scene in promoting safety. Our own Florence Nightingale advocated for safe care by proposing nurses put the patient in the best condition possible. And while the values handed down by Nightingale drive nurses to provide safe care, there is something else very important to consider: changes in the external environment that impact every hospital from a financial perspective.

As of October 1, 2008, the Centers for Medicare and Medicaid Services (CMS) stopped paying for the following preventable conditions (referred to as Never Events):

- Foreign object retained after surgery
- Air embolism
- Blood incompatibility

- Stage III and IV pressure ulcers
- Falls and trauma
- Catheter-associated urinary tract infection
- Vascular catheter-associated infection
- Surgical site infection (Mediastinitis) after coronary artery bypass graft
- Surgical site infections following certain elective procedures (certain orthopedic surgeries and bariatric surgery)
- Certain manifestations of poor control of blood sugar levels
- Deep vein thrombosis or pulmonary embolism following total knee replacement and hip replacement

Each year, more than 650,000 patients experience one of these errors leading to needless pain, injury, and, for some, even death. Not only is the list of conditions expected to grow, other payers are expected to follow the lead of CMS in refusing reimbursement.

Never Events are costly in another way too: When they occur they sap caregivers' passion, purpose, and sense of worthwhile work. Most health-care professionals care deeply about their patients. Preventable errors are devastating to them in ways that go far beyond dollar signs.

Figure 19.1

Never Events
What's the financial impact?

Condition	Cases in 2007	$/stay
Stage III & IV Pressure Ulcers	257,412	$43,180
Falls & Trauma	193,566	$33,894
Deep Vein Thrombosis/Pulmonary Embolism	140,010	$50,937
Vascular Catheter-Associated Infection	29,536	$103,027
Certain Manifestations of Poor Control of Blood Sugar Levels	16,060	Range: $35k-45,989
Catheter-Associated Urinary Tract Infections	12,185	$44,043
Foreign Object Retained After Surgery	750	$63,631
Surgical Site Infections Following Certain Elective Procedures	747	Range: $63k-180,142
Infection After Coronary Artery Bypass Graft	69	$299,237
Air Embolism	57	$71,636
Blood Incompatibility	24	$50,455

Source: CMS Fact Sheet, "CMS PROPOSES ADDITIONS TO LIST OF HOSPITAL-ACQUIRED CONDITIONS FOR FISCAL YEAR 2009"

Creating a "No Never Events" Culture

As a nurse leader, you can use the Evidence-Based Leadership℠ framework (see "How to Use This Book" on page v if you're unfamiliar with EBL) to create a culture where these Never Events *never* happen. Here's how:

Tie leader evaluations to measurable safety goals.

Begin with defining the desired outcomes. The idea is to hold leaders and staff accountable for achieving measurable safety goals. Some examples are:

- Reduce the incidence of Never Events, resulting in a cost avoidance of $500,000 by the end of the fourth quarter
- Reduce the incidence of vascular catheter-associated infections by 30 percent
- Reduce the incidence of patient falls by 50 percent

Focus on development.

Once the desired goals are defined, identify what training and skills the staff needs for success. You will probably find when you introduce a new safety behavior that 20 percent of clinicians are already doing it intuitively; 60 percent will require positive recognition before consistently performing the new behavior; and the final 20 percent will need coaching to understand *why* the behavior is important, as well as how to integrate it into their practice. So when implementing a new behavior, recognize staff members who practice it and remember to connect the dots back to the "why." That way, you'll reinforce the efforts of the 60 percent who are on board with the behavior and motivate the 20 percent who aren't there yet.

A Thought-Provoking Question

Several years after I began coaching for Studer Group®, a nurse leader approached me and asked, "Knowing what you know today from your experiences with hundreds of healthcare leaders, what would you have done differently as a quality/risk management leader of a hospital?" My initial response was to list all of the Evidence-Based Leadership behaviors, tools, and tactics developed to create a safe environment for patients to receive care. But, after thinking more about this, I realized that the most important change I would make is to dedicate my energy and efforts to connecting staff and leaders to *purpose.*

—Julie O'Shaughnessy

Help staff connect to purpose.

Stop and think how many times you've said to your staff, "We have to do this because it's a regulatory requirement." Or, "This is a key item for calculating our liability premiums." Worse yet, "Hospital administration has made this mandatory." While these statements are probably accurate, they fall short on explaining the "why."

The most effective way to engage the hearts and minds of staff when it comes to patient safety is connecting to the *purpose* behind it. As a nurse leader, making this connection for your employees is most necessary to achieve full buy-in and engagement. How might you do this?

Ask yourself, *What's made me feel inspired about patient safety? What are the stories, from my own personal or professional experience, that moved me, motivated me, or encouraged me?* Start from there and find your story. Perhaps it was a patient who suffered needlessly due to a safety lapse. Or maybe it was the error *you* made, saw, or experienced that shook you as a nurse.

Then, once you've tapped into your own enthusiasm, tell your story. Gather the team, huddle, have a meeting. Use emotion, a powerful motivator that's all too often left out of patient safety and error prevention conversations. (Why is that, by the way? There is no higher calling than to protect your patients from harm—it's worthy of some genuine emotion.)

Next, ask the staff to share their stories. Maybe you'll hear about a time where someone prevented an error or learned from one. Maybe someone will relay a story that describes an individual experience or something that happened to a family member. When preventing errors becomes personal, total commitment follows.

> Connect-to-purpose messages resonate and increase compliance among staff much more effectively than a "do-this-because-I-said-so" approach. We find that staff members frequently thank their leaders for explaining *why* and role modeling behaviors themselves.

When you as a nurse leader round on staff, reinforce the purpose for certain practices; it will help hardwire℠ the actions. For example, make the care connection for hand washing: It decreases the number of infections, thereby saving lives, expediting discharges, decreasing re-admissions, and lowering the acuity of patients staff members are caring for!

In huddles, make note of individuals, departments, and units who have gotten great patient safety results. Explain that the steps they took to keep patients safe weren't to please a manager, but to save a patient.

Rounding on Staff

The first, and most far-reaching, safety tactic is very simple. Words. Yes, communication. Words can save lives. Use tactics such as rounding on staff, whereby you ask specific questions of your team to identify gaps in safety and to ensure that they have the tools and equipment to keep patients safe. Communicate with the staff about "near misses"; find out about best practices; and determine who should be recognized for preventing falls, skin breakdown, or infections.

—Rich Bluni

Leader Tactics for a Culture of Safety

After connecting to purpose, begin using specific tactics developed by Studer Group to achieve actual results. These are evidence-based practices that when practiced consistently lead to exceptional outcomes (which is why complete, detailed chapters are devoted to them in *The Nurse Leader Handbook*). And they can be cross-walked to prevent adverse events! Critical to success is training the staff to "always" use these strategies. The following table illustrates how specific actions can be used to reduce and eliminate Never Events.

Figure 19.2

Crosswalk of Never Events with Studer Group EBL Tactics

Hospital-Acquired Complication	Employee Engagement	Rounding for Outcomes	Key Words at Key Times	Hourly Rounding	Individualized Patient Care	Bedside Report	Pre/Post-Visit Calls
1. Foreign Object Retained After Surgery	√	√	√		√		
2. Air Embolism	√	√			√	√	
3. Blood Incompatibility	√	√	√		√	√	
4. Stage III and IV Pressure Ulcers	√	√		√	√		
5. Falls and Trauma	√	√		√	√		
6. Catheter-Associated Urinary Tract Infection	√	√	√	√	√	√	
7. Vascular Catheter-Associated Infection	√	√	√	√	√	√	
8. Surgical Site Infection (Mediastinitis) After Coronary Artery Bypass Graft	√	√	√		√	√	√
9. Surgical Site Infections Following Certain Elective Procedures • Certain Orthopedic Surgeries • Bariatric Surgery	√	√	√		√	√	√
10. Manifestations of Poor Control of Blood Sugar Levels	√	√					√
11. Deep Vein Thrombosis or Pulmonary Embolism Following • Total Knee Replacement • Hip Replacement	√	√					

Key Words at Key Times

"Key words" are used to help patients understand your actions as a caregiver. They also serve to reduce the fear factor, lessen anxiety, and facilitate relationship-building with the patient. You can use "key words" to reduce adverse events as well. Some examples follow:

To reduce infections: "At Chester Medical Center, we are committed to preventing our patients from getting infections. One of the best ways to do that is for all of us to wash or disinfect our hands before and after caring for you. Our goal is to do this 100 percent of the time. Will you please remind us if we ever forget, or if you're not sure we washed our hands?"

To reduce IV infections: "It is very important for us to assess your IV site. We'll do that regularly to prevent an infection. If you notice any redness, drainage, or burning at the site, please let us know right away."

Bedside Shift Reports

Bedside Shift Reports[SM] are an excellent opportunity to incorporate safety procedures into patient care. Done at the patient's bedside, the shift report process creates a partnership between the care providers and the cared-for. Essentially, the current nurse gives a verbal report to the next nurse who is assuming care of the patient. The off-going nurse includes the patient in the conversation by asking if anything was missed or if she has anything to add. As a result of hearing this handoff, the patient experiences less anxiety as she witnesses well-coordinated care.

With respect to patient safety and Never Events, Bedside Shift Reports create communications that may help catch potential medical errors in blood incompatibility, catheter-associated urinary tract infections, vascular catheter-associated infections, surgical site infections, and air embolisms.

A Bedside Shift Report conversation incorporating patient safety might go something like this: "Hello, Mrs. Smith. We want to go over your care today. Your nurse for the next shift is Marie. Marie's been working at Excellence Hospital for 15 years. She's an experienced and certified cardiac nurse. Mrs. Smith, we want to ensure that we provide you with the safest care. We also want to protect you from the risk of getting an infection so we'll ensure that we always wash our hands. One of the ways you can help is to let us know if you notice any redness, swelling, or drainage from the IV in your hand. Please let Marie know if you notice these symptoms. Mrs. Smith, do you have any specific needs or concerns we should discuss?"

Hourly Rounding

We so often leave the "patient" out of patient safety. Patients are your first line of defense. Involve them. Talk to them. Ask them what is going well and what could be better as it relates to the level of safe care they are receiving. Let your patients know when they are on fall precautions and what that means for them. Talk to them during rounds about the *importance* of safety interventions and what you are doing to ensure they have an error-free experience.

Hourly Rounding also prevents distraction. Distraction, you would most likely agree, is probably a direct or indirect cause of a lot of medical errors. When you decrease call lights, you decrease distraction. Making that connection for your staff will increase their buy-in for this lifesaving tactic.

Figure 19.3

Rounding on Patients Saves Lives

- How are we doing at managing your pain?
- Are your caregivers washing their hands every time before touching you? Who has asked you to remind them to wash their hands?
- Is there anyone I can recognize for making you feel safe? Please tell me how they did this.
- Does the hospital staff check your arm band or verify your identity verbally before administering medication or treatments?
- How did the staff check your site before the procedure?
- **You're on fall precautions. Can you tell me about them?**
- How are we doing at answering your medication questions?
- How are we doing at explaining your plan of care?
- Do you feel that the staff members provide a safe environment? **Can you tell me how we are keeping you safe?**

Reward and Recognize

People will respond most positively when prevention efforts yield positive outcomes, so develop a strategy to celebrate. Some ideas on how to celebrate include:

- Weekly celebrations for inpatient nursing units ***when there are no falls***
- Weekly celebrations for critical care units ***to celebrate the lack of central line infections***

- Handwritten thank-you notes to physicians ***who are observed washing hands***
- Sharing wins related to discharge phone calls, ***especially patient safety catches***
- Recognize Environmental Services ***when nosocomial infection rates drop***
- Acknowledge every department, leader, and staff member ***who identifies and reports errors***

For additional patient safety tools, visit www.firestarterpublishing.com/NurseLeaderHandbook.

Key Points in This Chapter

1. Understand financial impact. Never Events are costly; in fact, CMS has stopped paying for many preventable conditions and the list is expected to grow. And don't discount the fact that Never Events sap caregivers' passion, purpose, and sense of worthwhile work.

2. Engage staff. Be sure employees understand how their actions/behaviors impact the occurrence of adverse outcomes and Never Events. Connect to passion, purpose, and worthwhile work by sharing stories of missed opportunities and good catches on potential errors. Reward and recognition goes a long way with patient safety, so be sure to acknowledge those willing to speak up to create a culture of safety.

3. Harvest and share stories. Eliminating adverse events requires the full engagement of everyone in your department. Numbers don't engage people to act, but individual human stories do. Publicly celebrate when solid prevention efforts avoid harm from occurring. Also share stories when events occur causing harm; these lapses require everyone's attention in the future to ensure other patients don't experience the consequences.

4. Focus on your biggest opportunities. For most organizations these are falls, pressure ulcers, and infections. Use Hourly Rounding to reduce falls and pressure ulcers, Key Words at Key Times to engage patients in preventing infections, and Bedside Shift Reports to conduct visual assessments of catheters and wound sites.

Pillars Affected by Creating a Culture of Safety

Quality—Incidence of Never Events is reduced.

Finance—Bottom line is improved due to fewer medical errors for which there is no reimbursement.

Growth—Better patient experience promotes increase in admissions.

CHAPTER 20

Collaborating with Physicians

By Wolfram Schynoll, MD

Some things you never forget. The event in the story you're about to read—an event that underscores the importance of physician/nurse collaboration—is one of my unforgettable moments.

During my rotation on the Pediatric Intensive Care Unit (PICU), we took care of a baby who required open-heart surgery to correct a congenital abnormality. The surgery had gone well and at the time this event took place the child was post-operative day three. The nurse taking care of the baby on this particular dayshift was bothered by the trend of data showing mild but increasing strain on the heart. As she continued to monitor vitals, oxygenation, appearance, and cardiac output, she realized things just weren't adding up. Despite an outward appearance that said otherwise, the child's heart was slowly failing. Astutely, the nurse contacted the intensivist and informed him of her findings and suspicions.

I followed the attending intensivist to the bedside and observed the interaction between nurse and physician. Looking at the data myself, I could sense that something was wrong, but didn't have the experience or knowledge at that time to decipher the child's problem.

Things happened rather quickly. Within minutes after talking with the nurse and studying the data, the physician opened the child's sternotomy incision at the bedside. The cardiac tamponade was confirmed and quickly relieved through aspiration of the blood from the pericardial sac. The baby's life had been saved through the quick, efficient, and skilled teamwork of the nurse and physician.

I was impressed with the professionalism and respect that each party showed to one another. I saw firsthand the difference it can make when a physician and nurse work collaboratively. I have never forgotten this lesson. Saving lives...providing the best quality of care...acting as a team: This is how it's supposed to work!

The Patient Is Not the Only Customer.

As a nurse leader, it is your responsibility to educate and remind your staff who the customer is. And it's not just the patient! Regardless of whether nurses work in a clinic or hospital setting, they always have two customers: patient and physician. Likewise, physicians also have two customers: patient and nurse. Like any successful team, the two caregivers have to recognize that neither can function efficiently and effectively without the other. In order to provide the best possible care, we must "serve" the professionals who are helping us serve the patients.

> By consistently role modeling professionalism and good communication skills with one another, the nurse and physician function as a team. This enhances clinical outcomes, patient perception of care, and job satisfaction. Helping your staff understand this concept will promote the ongoing desire for them to work collaboratively with physicians. When done well, as it was on that memorable day in the PICU, quality of patient care is maximized and lives are saved. A nurse leader understands this concept and will work diligently to create it.

However, collaboration is not necessarily easy to achieve, and requires a well-designed plan that is properly executed. This chapter will focus on how a nurse leader can foster nurse/physician collaboration by implementing proven strategies and tactics in either an inpatient or outpatient environment. First, however, let's take a look at how doing so benefits the organization.

Three Good Reasons to Foster Nurse/Physician Collaboration

Creating and maintaining excellent nurse/physician collaboration brings about three very important results.

1. **It leads to improved patient care.** If the physician/nurse team is in sync, patient care and efficiency is maximized. Let's look at an example. In my specialty of emergency medicine, a patient history is usually the most important component guiding the work-up. Going down the wrong path based on flawed or incomplete information from the patient will lead to misdiagnosis. But patients don't always tell me everything. They may inadvertently leave out key information or hesitate to convey details for fear of embarrassment. However, they often *will* tell a nurse something they won't tell me—and it matters. In turn, the nurse communicates important points to me and many times it has changed the outcome. Hearing the nurse's perspective has led me to order additional tests I may not have ordered based on the history I obtained from the patient, and it has guided the correct diagnosis on many occasions. The nurse understands that we function as a team—a partnership—with each of us gathering vital information from the patient to efficiently and effectively render care. This collaboration has resulted in improved clinical outcomes and has saved lives.

2. **It creates personal and professional fellowship in an often stressful environment.** We all recognize that working in healthcare these days is not easy. Burnout is common. And when people do leave, it is often because they feel they are not supported by leaders or peers. Collaboration between nurses and physicians creates mutual respect for one another and often builds friendships. It makes you feel like you belong to a team that prides itself in providing great care to patients, communicating well, and appreciating one another. This kind of culture attracts the "best and brightest" in the industry and (not incidentally) creates an environment where people want to receive care.

3. **It results in decreased turnover.** Nurse leaders understand the importance of fostering nurse/physician collaboration as a means of maximizing nurse satisfaction and keeping turnover at a minimum.

From *Average to Exceptional:* A Collaborative Journey

In 2001, the Emergency Department (ED) I was working in had "average" everything—nursing turnover, patient satisfaction scores, and staff and physician satisfaction. We provided good care and had a solid reputation in the community. Then Studer Group® visited us, and we came to recognize we had the potential to do far better than our current 60 percent quarterly patient satisfaction marks. We also recognized that we could turn this *average* ED into an *exceptional* one.

About 15 months into our journey we achieved a quarterly patient satisfaction score of 99 percent! Our nursing turnover rate went to zero. A waiting list of nurses desiring to join the ED sprang up. Administration openly recognized our achievements. Morale soared. Professionalism flourished between the nursing and physician staff. New friendships were formed. We had created a new culture of operational and service excellence. I was proud to have been a part of it!

What was the key ingredient to our success? It started with the creation of solid nurse/physician collaboration. We recognized we could not achieve our goal without working together. Our nursing leader labored diligently to execute an effective team-building strategy between the nursing and physician staffs. She knew the importance of putting the physician voice into the process improvement plan.

We formed nurse/physician committees. We managed each other up to patients and administration. We broke down the "we/they" mentality. We pushed each other to perform better. Door-to-doctor times became best in class. And we sustained our results. Why? Because we hardwired patient care tactics, regularly rounded on nursing and physician staff to gather additional input, and acted upon their suggestions to create further wins. Our nurse leader worked to keep our newly created culture thriving and healthy.

That is the difference that effective nurse/physician collaboration can make.

—Wolfram Schynoll, MD

These efforts to ensure job satisfaction are appreciated, which in turn helps the nurse leader achieve a higher degree of respect and admiration amongst her staff. The resulting lower turnover is of course good for the organization's bottom line.

Creating a Culture of Collaboration

Designing a strategy to improve nurse/physician collaboration requires a nurse leader to understand and respond to the key physician drivers that impact their overall work satisfaction. There are four of them:

- **Quality:** Physicians want to know that their patients are receiving quality care and very good service.
- **Efficiency:** Physicians want to maximize their day-to-day efficiency due to the busy schedules they maintain.
- **Input:** Physicians want to be asked where they feel the organization should focus to make things run better.
- **Appreciation:** Physicians value a "thank you" and acknowledgment when things are going well.

A nurse leader can create an environment that successfully tends to these four drivers. Now, let's take a look at some tools that will help. (Some of these tools are covered elsewhere in *The Nurse Leader Handbook*. This chapter simply shows how you can use them to build stronger relationships with physicians.)

Nurse Leader Rounding on Physicians

This is a great opportunity to seek the input of physicians. Rounding is, in fact, the single most important tactic in creating a healthy collaborative nurse/physician relationship. Given the chance to contribute on a regular basis, doctors take greater interest in creating a best practice environment. The rounding concept is simple, and usually takes no more than five to ten minutes per physician. The four questions to ask are:

1. What is working well?

2. Do you have the necessary tools and equipment to take care of your patients?

3. What processes or systems need improvement in order to better serve your medical practice?

4. Would you like me to recognize anyone for a job well done?

After rounding, it's important that the nurse leader take the information and suggestions gathered from the rounding experience, and either problem-solve them successfully or pass them onto other hospital personnel to do so. The rounding process only gathers the data; success hinges on the ability of a hospital to act on the input received and deliver results back to the physicians. This greatly enhances nurse leader collaboration with the medical staff.

Physician Preference Cards

When is the first time a new nurse typically learns about a physician's preferences? It's usually on the nurse's first night shift after he's forced to wake her up at 3 a.m. to get information he needs to make a sound decision for a patient. (It should go without saying that the physician isn't happy about being woken up and the nurse isn't happy about having to call her!) Physician Preference Cards change all that.

How do the cards work? They typically capture contact information, the time the physician rounds, details preferred prior to rounding (such as lab work on charts, intake and output records available, and daily weights completed), support requests, and other preferences. So, for example, if nurses know a physician rounds between 7 and 8 a.m., they can make sure not to bathe patients during that hour and can get current lab results on the chart for review. Studer Group has an excellent toolkit that further outlines the exact steps necessary to implement this tactic. To download the Physician Collaboration Toolkit, visit www.firestarterpublishing.com/NurseLeaderHandbook.

A sample Physician Preference Card is shown on the following page:

Figure 20.1

Physician Preference Card Sample

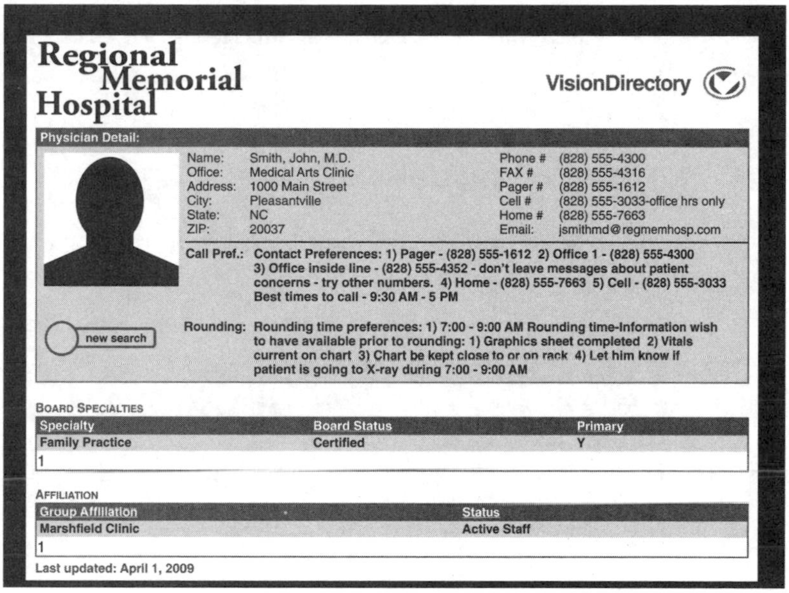

Regional Memorial Hospital

VisionDirectory

Physician Detail:

Name:	Smith, John, M.D.	Phone #	(828) 555-4300
Office:	Medical Arts Clinic	FAX #	(828) 555-4316
Address:	1000 Main Street	Pager #	(828) 555-1612
City:	Pleasantville	Cell #	(828) 555-3033-office hrs only
State:	NC	Home #	(828) 555-7663
ZIP:	20037	Email:	jsmithmd@regmemhosp.com

Call Pref.: Contact Preferences: 1) Pager - (828) 555-1612 2) Office 1 - (828) 555-4300 3) Office inside line - (828) 555-4352 - don't leave messages about patient concerns - try other numbers. 4) Home - (828) 555-7663 5) Cell - (828) 555-3033 Best times to call - 9:30 AM - 5 PM

new search

Rounding: Rounding time preferences: 1) 7:00 - 9:00 AM Rounding time-Information wish to have available prior to rounding: 1) Graphics sheet completed 2) Vitals current on chart 3) Chart be kept close to or on rack 4) Let him know if patient is going to X-ray during 7:00 - 9:00 AM

BOARD SPECIALTIES

Specialty	Board Status	Primary
Family Practice	Certified	Y
1		

AFFILIATION

Group Affiliation	Status
Marshfield Clinic	Active Staff
1	

Last updated: April 1, 2009

Physician Preference Cards say to physicians:

> *We respect your time.*
> *Your patients are in good hands. We care.*
> *We want physicians to work as efficiently as possible.*
> *More of your patients should come to our hospital.*
> *We value and appreciate physicians.*

Ultimately, these cards serve to facilitate customized, quality patient care. Physicians appreciate getting information when, where, and how they like it so that extra phone calls and unnecessary visits are eliminated. Nurses appreciate physicians who are courteous when they call. And patients appreciate very good coordination of their care.

Got Chart

What is a "Got Chart"? It's a tool first developed during Quint Studer's days as COO of Holy Cross Hospital in Chicago. Essentially, it's a checklist that helps nurses prepare all the information needed prior to paging a physician. For example:

Before you call:

- Ensure you are calling the appropriate physician (primary or consultant?).
- Check to see if there are standing orders to cover the situation.
- Review physician preferences for when and where to call.
- Check to see if anyone else needs to talk to this physician.
- Did you see and assess this patient yourself?
- Read the physician progress and nursing notes from the prior shift.

At the time of the call:

- Have in hand the chart, recent assessment, list of medications, code status, most recent vitals, and current lab results.
- Identify yourself, the unit, the patient, and the diagnosis.
- Be clear about the reason for the call.
- Document whom you spoke to, time of call, and summarize the conversation.

The result of the Got Chart is improved efficiency, better communication, and smoother, more effective professional relationships. It also leads to improved clinical quality with the potential to reduce errors.

Physician Performance Surveys

This tool allows physicians to understand how well they interact with nurses. Are they courteous...good communicators...efficient? Do they write legibly? Do they show caring and concern for their patients?

This tool is best used when one or two physicians stand out as low performers amongst their peers. A nurse leader can discuss the intent of this tool, its design, and approval with the group's physician leader prior to distributing the survey. Typically, the results of the survey are not released to the nursing staff, but are shared and discussed with the individual doctor and his leader. Once a physician is made aware of poor interpersonal performance, he often makes strides to improve.

Physician Recognition

Physicians typically do not look for recognition, but do appreciate it when it is bestowed upon them. And it can accomplish a lot in the way of relationship building! Here are a few things you can do to help recognize physicians:

- As the nurse leader, ask the staff which physicians should be thanked.
- Consider implementing a method by which your physicians are recognized for their excellent service or the exemplary way with which they interact with staff. Some organizations have created a "physician of the month" award, given to the doctor who role models desired behaviors during staff interactions.
- A handwritten thank-you note is an additional effective means of conveying appreciation. Make it a habit to write notes of appreciation each month to both nurses and physicians; sending these to their homes is an especially nice touch.

Patient Hourly Rounding

Because physicians respond most readily to quality improvement measures, nurse leaders should communicate the benefits of Hourly Rounding. Once physicians are aware of the added patient safety and quality of care that rounding brings, they will be supportive and commend the process.

Individualized Patient Care (IPC) and Notes at the Bedside

The purpose of IPC and Notes at the Bedside is to facilitate patient/physician communication, thus contributing to greater efficiency. Patients use both tools to record the most important concerns or questions they want addressed during their doctor's visit. In the case of IPC, a nurse writes the items for discussion on the whiteboard in the patient's room. In the case of the other tool, the patient receives a Bedside Notepad prior to seeing the physician. The completed form is then placed on the chart for the physician to read before entering the patient's room.

Consider also that patients don't like having to repeat themselves multiple times, so they appreciate it when nurses and doctors communicate. Implementing this strategy is relatively easy and rewarding for all parties: physicians, staff, and patients. However, prior to rolling it out, make sure that you gain the support of doctors, so it is actually used in the way it was intended.

Advance Knowledge = Better Care

As a practicing Emergency Department (ED) physician, I appreciate a nurse's efforts to gather and relay to me the most important questions a patient has for me during my visit. While I am in the room seeing and interviewing the patient, that person may be distracted or too anxious, thus forgetting to ask me these key questions. Having advance knowledge enables me to address concerns during our conversation, which also conveys a more team-centric approach to the care process.

—Wolfram Schynoll, MD

Tip: When considering all the tools and tactics to help you implement physician collaboration, it is better to pick one or two to start with, rather than to try to implement many simultaneously. When you have achieved the consistent and effective use of a tactic, move on to the next one. Understand that it may take six months to hardwire just one tool!

Engaging Staff in the Quest for Collaboration

The best way for a nurse leader to engage employees is to show them the value of working collaboratively with physicians. A wise and thoughtful leader promotes the concept as being in the staff's best interest as well as the patient's. This leader also makes it a priority to communicate and execute an effective plan that accomplishes collaboration.

Of course, like all healthcare professionals, nurses want to feel valued and respected. That's why it's important to emphasize that nurse/physician collaboration is an effort requiring participation on both sides. The following three tactics, designed to help a nurse leader engage her staff in the quest for collaboration, reflect the two-way teamwork nature of the journey:

1. Nurse Education: Organizing and providing regular educational offerings to nurses—classes and workshops presented by the medical staff—is a wonderful opportunity to build collaborative relationships. It is especially effective because nurses usually appreciate the chance to learn from physicians. Some organizations have arranged nursing Grand Rounds, given by a different member of the medical staff monthly, featuring a relevant patient care topic. Physicians can also give smaller, less formal presentations to individual hospital departments, such as the Intensive Care Unit or Labor and Delivery.

   As a nurse leader, you can recruit physician participation and organize these meetings, thereby managing up both the physicians and yourself.

2. Physician/Nurse Rounding: Across the country, more and more organizations are encouraging physicians to regularly round with the nurses who are taking care of particular patients. This allows a doctor to do some teaching, thoroughly outline the care plan for the day, and promote a more team-centric approach to patient care. The nurse will also welcome this time with the physician; it improves her understanding of the case, and often means that she can answer family questions later without necessarily having to page the physician. The practice also improves efficiency and communication.

3. Responses to Disruptive Physician Behaviors: There is nothing more frustrating and defeating to a nurse than being yelled at by a physician. Clinicians often feel helpless in correcting these behaviors, and repeated occurrences erode trust and destroy teamwork. Barriers start to form as communication breaks down.

   Disruptive behaviors also have the potential of negatively impacting patient care. As a result, organizations are implementing policies aimed at dealing with these occurrences on a case-by-case basis. They are taking actions that often bring about changed behaviors in offenders. As a nurse leader, it is vital that you support such policy changes. You also need to communicate the need to your supervisor or administrator for implementing a process to handle disruptive behav ior on all levels.

Breaking Down the We/They Barrier

The most damaging barrier that derails efforts to create effective nurse/physician collaboration is the formation of a "we/they" culture. When nurses or physicians are biased or mistrusting of each other, they create a negative work environment. It becomes very difficult to promote effective communication, teamwork, and efficiency. The nurse is left guessing about the plan of care, and the physician is kept in the dark on a patient's status or latest test results. As a result the quality of care suffers. No one wins.

Managing up is the method by which we break down the "we/they" culture. In essence, it is positioning the physician well by focusing on the positive. It is helping staff and patients see the physician in the best light and always striving to be supportive.

Skilled nurse leaders will promote the tactic of managing up throughout the areas that they oversee. Critical to building an environment of collaboration, it will result in mutual success for the physician and nursing staff—and that in turn will empower us to provide the best possible care to the patients we serve.

Key Points in This Chapter

1. Think of physicians as your customers. A significant part of their professional satisfaction depends on an organization's ability to execute on the four key drivers: quality, efficiency, input, and appreciation. A successful nurse leader understands that delivering on each of these points hinges upon creating nurse/physician collaboration as a foundational cornerstone.

2. Creating effective nurse/physician collaboration involves implementing a well-designed plan that tends to the needs of both nurses and physicians. Don't implement too many tactics at once. Hardwire one before moving on to the next.

3. Of all the strategies to implement, the one that most strongly impacts the nurse/physician relationship is rounding. A nurse leader should regularly round on physicians to gather their opinions and get input. Then act to problem-solve the identified issues and communicate the wins back to the doctors.

4. Achieving effective collaboration requires regular and meaningful interactions. Create ways that physicians and nurses can interrelate with one another to improve quality and operational efficiency, recognize each other's achievements, and provide feedback. Physicians are often receptive to meetings focused on improving the practice environment or the care delivered to their patients.

Pillars Affected by a Culture of Nurse/ Physician Collaboration

Service—Patient satisfaction and perception of care improves when patients experience a well-coordinated team approach to their care.

Quality—A strong nurse/physician team results in better patient care and safety.

Finance—Well-coordinated and efficient care results in decreased lengths of stay, which in turn decreases costs.

People—Nursing and physician turnover are reduced as a result of improved relationships between the caretakers.

Growth—A nurse leader who creates excellent physician collaboration will drive growth for the organization. Physicians will want to admit patients to your hospital, knowing their customers receive excellent care there.

SECTION 4: PROFESSIONAL DEVELOPMENT

Introduction

By Lyn Ketelsen

You're no doubt familiar with the phrase "It takes a village to raise a child." Well, in much the same way, it takes an organization's village to raise good leaders through education, coaching, and mentoring. But while organizational commitment to development is important, you must also understand the role of individual responsibility. As a leader, it's incumbent upon you to make sure you have the knowledge and skills to accomplish the goals of your area of responsibility. In other words, you *own* your professional growth.

All leaders want and need development. We are a "work in progress." Even the most accomplished leaders recognize their need to continue learning. But what differentiates high-performing leaders from their middle-performing counterparts is their willingness to take ownership for identifying and seeking development opportunities. High performers usually have good insight into what needs developing and require little to no intervention on the part of their bosses. Middle performers, however, need help in recognizing what should be improved or how to get the assistance they need.

High-performing leaders will not tolerate a culture that does not support development for long. Furthermore, their performance level gives them options, and they will leave if necessary. At the very least, they'll continue working for you while capitalizing on their talents outside of your facility or department—and this won't best meet the needs of the patients and family members with whom your first allegiance lies.

In this section, we discuss several areas designed to develop and enhance your skill set as a high-performing leader. We start, for instance, by showing you how to be as effective as possible in meetings. Understanding how to make the most of the tremendous number of hours you spend conducting and participating in meetings will set you apart from others and create discipline that will serve you well throughout your leadership career. You'll understand the importance of this when you take the time to calculate how much it costs to have everyone present in the next meeting you attend.

Let's say, for instance, that you have 12 leaders in the meeting, each of whom has an average hourly rate of $40. Each time you meet for 60 minutes, it will cost the organization $480. Ask yourself, *What did we do today in this meeting that will return $480 or more back to the organization?* Take it a step further. If you meet monthly for a year with this group, it will cost $5,760. What will this group accomplish that will give back at least that much or more to the organization? Remember, the higher the leadership level, and the longer the meeting, the more costly the experience will be. So my best advice is: Never enter or leave a meeting without thinking, *What did this cost and was it worth it?*

Leaders with this kind of mindset are already on the path to the type of learning and development that will not only demonstrate their ownership, but will benefit the entire organization and the patients and families it serves.

CHAPTER 21

Effective Meetings

By Lyn Ketelsen

I remember one of the first staff meetings I held as a nurse manager. It was quite a learning experience for me. I knew going in that I had to keep minutes for the meeting. After all, I would periodically read the minutes of meetings I hadn't attended. And that was pretty much *all* I knew on the subject of meetings.

Like many nurse leaders, I'd been promoted into a leadership position from a staff nurse status. I had been a charge nurse, but since that was only part-time on the second shift, I'd had no involvement with many of the daily administrative functions within the hospital or my department. Despite my prior leadership experience, my awareness of the specifics of operating in the healthcare environment wasn't very strong.

Anyway, after my first meeting I completed the minutes, which included a list of those who attended. I decided to save myself some time and show the staff my humorous side: In the area where I was to list those absent, I simply wrote, "Everyone who wasn't there."

Several weeks later, we were in the process of having our mock JCAHO survey, and the surveyors reviewed my department. When they saw my meeting minutes with that comment—well, let's just say they weren't laughing and certainly didn't appreciate my sense of humor.

I learned two important lessons that day: First, get up to speed quickly with regulations; and second, meetings have significance well beyond my initial understanding!

Good Meetings Matter.

If you read my introduction to Section 4 of this book, you know that meetings can be expensive. Sometimes *very* expensive (1 hour meeting with 12 leaders at $40/hour = $480). And that's one reason it's so important to get them right—and to make sure they accomplish the goals you want them to accomplish.

Understanding the impact running *effective* meetings can have on the ability to execute and drive change is an important nurse leader competency. No one likes a bad meeting experience, with issues such as:

- No agenda
- No clear purpose or objective
- A late start
- No leader or anyone taking charge
- Individuals monopolizing the conversation
- No closure or final decisions made
- Only laundry lists of information being presented (no discussion or decisions)
- Certain people barred from participating

As a nurse leader, your overall goal should be to create a healthy return on the investment of time put into attending the meeting. Not just your time, but the cost of the collective time for bringing everyone into the room. That requires gaining a thorough understanding of the components that make up an effective meeting:

1. Introductions/Review Objectives

2. Review Roles (facilitator, leader, timekeeper, etc.)

3. Review the Agenda

4. Work Through the Agenda Items

5. Review Decisions and "Next Steps"

6. Plan the Next Meeting

7. Gather Feedback on the Meeting

Let's take a closer look at each one.

The Seven Components of an Effective Meeting

1. Review Objectives: Each meeting should have a designated purpose. If you're conducting routine staff meetings, then the purpose of each agenda item should be designated. This is often done by simply using a code on the agenda format that identifies each item as "Action," "Discussion," or "Information." This allows everyone to understand the intended purpose of each agenda topic and to be prepared.

When you are leading multidisciplinary team meetings or peer-based leader meetings, then you should ensure that each group has a purpose statement developed during the very first meeting. It can be referenced occasionally to keep the team on track.

Sample Purpose Statement

Studer Group® Purpose Statement

We all have a purpose:

Studer Group believes the beginning of the journey from good to great must start with our values. In this way, we center or balance the Healthcare Flywheel®. In healthcare, we have great purpose, do worthwhile work, and have the opportunity to make a difference. This is our hub.

From here, the first step to creating movement is to connect the dots to our hub, so that people are inspired to truly believe they can make a difference. This inspiration allows organizations to implement initial changes. Each nurse, physician, housekeeper, transporter, transcriptionist, marketing executive, computer technician, and administrator in the healthcare industry is making a difference every day. When we truly understand and feel our purpose in this effort, the flywheel keeps turning.

A Studer Group coach who visited a hospital in California shared the following poem, written by a member of the outpatient satisfaction team. Because this hospital had experienced some difficult times, the poem had very special meaning. The hospital used the poem in an awareness campaign to remind staff of the importance of personal interactions. I hope it inspires you, as it did us, to remember we all can make a difference in healthcare.

One Voice

One voice spoke to my inner responsibility,
To realize I can be heard by many,
That the issues I discuss,
The words I use to express myself,
Provide a picture,
About me and where I work.
So, I've chosen to be professionally accountable,
To choose my topics carefully,
To realize not everything I feel should be said.
I want to make a difference.
I want to make the world, or my part of it, better.
I am one voice representing my medical center.

It's also very important that the template used for meetings serves as a useful tool to communicate the overall strategy of the organization. The institutions that use Studer Group's Evidence-Based Leadership^{SM} framework set up agendas by their pillars, the strategic areas of focus. Typically these pillars are Service, Quality, People, Finance, and Growth.

By using the pillar-based agendas, you also have the opportunity to continually reinforce a balanced approach to your leadership. This will counteract the common perception that leaders get too focused on one area—Finance, for instance—thus sacrificing another. By identifying which pillar the agenda item supports, you continually reinforce your balance as a leader.

2. Review Roles: During each meeting, there should be several positions assigned to help keep the meeting on track. (These can be rotated meeting to meeting.) The first one is the **facilitator/leader**. With staff meetings, this role is usually filled by the department manager. In other cases, it's assigned to the group's chairperson or co-chair. Regardless, everyone must be clear about who's in charge of the meeting.

Another role to be assigned is the **minute taker** or scribe for documentation purposes. This can be a permanent assignment of a team member or it can be changed out periodically. But either way, the scribe's role is capturing recommendations and documenting follow-up items resulting from decisions or actions taken.

Next we need a **timekeeper**. This person's responsibility is to let the facilitator or leader know when the time allotted for each agenda item has been exceeded.

The last position designated is called the **weed whacker**. This person assists in keeping the conversation on track with agenda items and their purpose. It's not unusual for the discussion to go astray or take off on a tangent. The weed whacker is assigned to identify such occasions and help the leader facilitate getting back on course—or if the discussion is pertinent, to determine if it needs to go into the "parking lot." This term, a part of the minutes template, refers to topics the group can't address in the context of the current meeting, yet which need to be included on future agendas.

3. Review the Agenda: Agendas should be distributed in advance of meetings, ideally with no less than 48 hours notice. Depending on the frequency of the meetings, an agenda may be distributed even further in advance. You want to ensure that everyone has time to review not only the agenda but also any preparatory information submitted. This lead time promotes meeting efficiency, as participants are prepared to discuss or make decisions as necessary.

Figure 21.1

Template: Meeting Agenda

			Meeting Agenda **Topic/Group:** Date: Time: **Call #:** **Action Designations*** **SG Process Improvement Step*****	**Attendees:** **Guests:** **Excused:** **Minutes:**
Time	**Pillars****	**Duration**	**Topics/Person Responsible**	**Desired Outcome**
00:00-00:00	**WINS**	0	•	•
00:00-00:00	**S, Q, P F, G, C**	0	Topic – Person – Action Designation* Process Improvement Step***	•
00:00-00:00	**S, Q, P F, G, C**	0	•	•
00:00-00:00	**S, Q, P F, G, C**	0	•	•
00:00-00:00	**Break**	0	**BREAK**	
00:00-00:00	**S, Q, P F, G, C**	0	•	•
00:00-00:00	**S, Q, P F, G, C**	0	•	•
00:00-00:00	**S, Q, P F, G, C**	0	•	•
00:00	**RATE**	5	Rate the meeting	
			Parking lot	

* FI=For Information; FD=For Discussion; FA=For Action
** Indicate by letter pillars impacted: S, Q, P, F, G, C
*** Process Improvement Steps: I (Identify Outcomes); D (Diagnose); T (Treatment); E (Evaluate)

4. Work Through the Agenda Items: This is a reminder to stay on task with the schedule. It can be very frustrating to participants when an agenda gets hijacked and suddenly changed. They feel their time has been wasted, and repeat offenses will eventually impact their level of engagement.

5. Review Decisions and "Next Steps": Have you ever been in a meeting where you felt as if team members were rehashing discussions and decisions over and over again? This most likely happened because previous outcomes weren't documented and communicated. Step 5 forces you to review decisions and put them in writing so the team has a historical record to refer back to.

The "next steps" component will make you decide how to implement any decisions made, and what communication is necessary to ensure the awareness of all involved stakeholders. When you have impeccable follow up, you will find that your reputation as someone who gets things done will enhance your success as a leader.

6. Plan the Next Meeting: Every time you have a meeting that takes place on a recurring basis, you should establish the agenda of the next one. Make this a standing agenda item. Doing this in the context of the current meeting creates efficiency. You not only save groundwork time later on, but you also prepare team members for what to expect at the next gathering.

7. Gather Feedback on the Meeting: One of the best ways to ensure an effective meeting is to measure it! Before you adjourn, you should have the participants rate each meeting on a one-to-five (or one-to-ten) scale telling you how they perceived its value. When a team member assigns a rating of less than four (or eight), have him suggest what would make it better. This provides you with immediate feedback on the value and effectiveness of your meetings.

Setting a Few Ground Rules

Even when you follow the seven steps to effectively structure your meetings and meet objectives, you can still run up against a barrier to success. For instance, have you ever been held hostage in a meeting peopled by participants who behave inappropriately or in ways not conducive to getting things done? Perhaps they try to strong-arm everyone else, or they withhold vital information, or they interject off-topic comments that get the meeting off track.

To address these kinds of problems, you must set ground rules that the participants *agree to abide by* during each meeting. Suggestions include:

- Notify the committee chair if you must miss a meeting.
- Come prepared for the meeting.
- Have assigned tasks done on time.
- Notify the committee chair or appropriate person ahead of time if you cannot honor an obligation or promise.
- Leave rank at the door.
- Keep communication focused on the issues of the meeting.
- All must role model the ground rules, structure, and behaviors.
- Have a sense of humor.
- Stick to the agenda.
- Encourage questions and discussions.

- No sidebar conversations during meetings.
- Don't text or check your email during meetings.
- Respect others' opinions.
- Make decisions based on good input and review options.
- Use straight talk and be honest and forthcoming.
- Do not hold a meeting "after the meeting."

When clearly identified and followed, ground rules are very helpful with promoting high functioning meetings. Have your team or department create its own set of rules—this will reinforce buy-in and is more likely to lead to strict adherence.

Great Meetings Pay for Themselves—and Then Some!

Remember, the primary objective for all meetings should be to maintain productivity and generate a return for the investment in time—and time *is* money! Now that you have the tools for managing both the process of effective meetings and the behaviors within the context of the meetings, you will be better prepared to lead effective ones. You and the team can efficiently accomplish the work necessary to be successful in your department and organization.

In addition, when meetings become more effective, everyone will experience a sense of individual involvement in the decision-making process. Communication will improve, and the group will end up being more creative in problem solving. Finally, your reputation as a nurse leader and great team builder will be enhanced when you become known as "the meeting guru"!

Key Points in This Chapter

1. Lack of competency for conducting effective meetings can derail your overall reputation as a leader.

2. Do the work necessary to keep your meeting process organized. The components of successful meetings are: Introductions/Review Objectives; Review Roles; Review the Agenda; Work Through the Agenda Items; Review Decisions and "Next Steps"; Plan the Next Meeting; Gather Feedback on the Meeting.

3. Establish clear ground rules and ensure that everyone adheres to them in every meeting.

Pillars Affected by Effective Meetings

Finance—Meetings are a productive use of staff's time.

People—Fosters teamwork; improves decision making and outcomes.

CHAPTER 22

Supervisory Meeting Model

By Bob Murphy and Lavonne Dwinal

Supervisory meetings are crucial. These one-on-one meetings between leader and direct report accomplish many things. They're the medium through which leaders evaluate staff members' performance, work with them to set new goals, and discover vital information that enables everyone to do their jobs better. Well-orchestrated, well-designed supervisory meetings—held once a month, ideally, or at least as often as possible—empower leaders to consistently convey their changing expectations to the men and women who carry them out.

Consistently is the key word here. As Quint Studer points out in his book *Straight A Leadership*, one major reason supervisory meetings exist is to standardize practices in order to make the organization better—yet, ironically, the meetings themselves are *not* always standardized. In fact, they are often quite inconsistent in terms of how often they're held and what happens in them.

Our goal for this chapter is to provide the structure for a productive and results-oriented meeting that can be held often enough to keep leader and supervisor in alignment regarding progress and priorities.

If you are a senior leader, follow this model when you meet with the nurse leaders you supervise. If you are a mid-level nurse leader, you might also consider asking your own boss to follow it in her meetings with you—and possibly even advocate for the model to be used organization-wide. It's been "road tested" in various healthcare organizations and it works well.

A Meeting Model That Works

The supervisory meeting model consists of a standardized agenda of all the elements that should be covered in a one-on-one meeting between leaders and those to whom they report. The agenda, designed to be used in direct supervisory discussions, does not apply to staff meetings. You may wish to include some of the model's elements as a means of updating staff; however, it's primarily designed for meetings within the leadership ranks—the monthly discussions are a very important component of a strong accountability system.

Figure 22.1

Studer Group Supervisory Meeting Model

Leaders bring the following items and results to their immediate supervisor:

1. Leader Evaluation
2. Monthly Report Card
3. External Environment / Industry Issues
4. 90-Day Work Plan
5. Linkage Grid from Leadership Development Institute (follow-up assignments)
6. Rounding Logs
7. Thank-You Notes
8. People Trends and Issues - Standards of Behavior

When you adhere to the supervisory meeting model described above, you cover updates on progress toward goals and specific actions that need to be taken; plus, you review the resources and assistance needed to be successful. You're also more likely to avoid the distractions that tend to pop up in the absence of a guiding structure.

In some organizations that have hardwired[SM] the agenda's usage, leaders have actually created a manual with tabs for each section of the meeting; it's used to collect data and information for discussion. This helps them stay on track, have the necessary resources to back up their supervisory report, and have verification of the information to be covered right at their fingertips.

> What's more, by standardizing the meeting model, they create an aligned organization—one in which leaders in all departments are communicating the same messages to the people they supervise. As Studer puts it: "Think of supervisory meetings as rehearsals for a play or timeouts during a game. You can't align the actors and actresses if everyone shows up at different times and if they all have different scripts. Likewise, in sports it's hard to make adjustments without calling a timeout."

Monthly Meeting Model

Leaders are required to report results to their immediate supervisor at least once per month and bring with them the materials that support the following meeting agenda:

1. Evaluation/Performance Appraisal: The first item on the agenda is a review of the leader's performance appraisal, which sets forth his annual goals. Studer Group® also recommends these goals be assigned values and weights (for more information read Chapter 15: Goal Management). The supervisor and leader prioritize what needs attention based on the weights of the various objectives. This monthly process also allows for early intervention to change course by adding, modifying, or deleting goals.

2. Monthly Report Card: The second item on the agenda is a summary of results for each goal and the identification of areas in need of the supervisor's support. Are priorities focused correctly? Are results in line with priorities? Does the goal still make sense in light of new regulations, marketplace changes, and so forth? In the ever-changing world of healthcare, flexibility is called for and sometimes goals must be revised mid-year. This assessment helps both leader and supervisor be confident they are not trying to hit targets that are no longer valid.

Leaders also use the monthly report card to update employees on progress towards goals. The card is reviewed at monthly staff meetings, and in some organizations it's posted on communication boards under the Quality pillar of excellence.

3. External Environment/Industry Issues: The external environment impacts many of the decisions an organization makes. As changes take place outside the organization, corresponding changes must take place inside it. Ensuring that all leaders in the organization are aware and on the same page regarding the impact of the external environment allows for better execution of initiatives. (For an in-depth look at this subject, please check out Quint Studer's *Straight A Leadership*.)

4. 90-Day Plan: The fourth step of the model calls for a review of the leader's 90-Day Plan, with specific tactics and updates. Leaders create this plan at the beginning of each calendar quarter as a means of assuring *incremental* progress on annual goals. It is also a communication tool to help employees engage in the goals, action steps, and outcomes of their leader/department. The 90-Day Plans are often shared openly with staff; some organizations even post them on the communication board under the Quality pillar of excellence.

During the review, if the plan's tactics are lacking, the supervisor can drill down by asking:

a. Are the action items focused on getting results or are they just busy work?
b. Are there best practices included in the action items (for example, Must Haves® as defined by Studer Group, or other research-based methods)? Are there any best practices from your own organization that could be incorporated into your area? Remember to look for opportunities to gain best practices from other leaders.
c. What barriers exist that must be worked through or eliminated?

5. Linkage Grid from Leader Training: Linkage grid discussion provides supervisors with the opportunity to review the learning that leaders have continued from the last Leadership Development Institute (LDI). Many organizations hold LDIs quarterly to provide training to leaders. The linkage grid takes these learnings and builds out opportunities to help leaders connect them to execution. <u>Supervisors may ask:</u> *Tell me how you are progressing on your linkage items. Are there areas where you need my help?*

This step assures implementation of new knowledge, organizational improvement, and return on investment. It's also a great time to review documentation that LDI learning and information have been cascaded to staff. The cascade process is critical to employees' realization that the leader's time away is not just for fun and games, but instead is a source of valuable learning that will impact *their* work environment.

Figure 22.2

Leadership Development Institute Linkage Grid					
Key Learning	**Activity**	**Person Responsible**	**Due Date**	**Completed Y or N**	

6. Rounding Logs: In addition to looking at and verifying the logs, supervisors should also engage in a meaningful conversation around finding out what the leader is doing differently as a result of staff, patient, and/or support department rounding. Asking the following questions validates the "heart" of rounding, and that it is not just another task or checklist:

- *Since our last time together, what have you learned about our organization by rounding?*
- *What is working well for your direct reports/staff?*

- *What are the tough questions you are getting and how can I help you answer them?*

For those at the bedside or those who provide direct patient care: *What is the one thing our patients have been saying consistently in your area?*

The logs provide an opportunity to learn what's going well; who should be recognized; what tools, equipment, and physician issues may be hindering staff; what process improvements might be needed; and what safety opportunities have been discovered. If leaders are harvesting bright ideas around cost savings or profitability, supervisors can also reap those nuggets and apply across their division, or even across the entire organization.

7. Thank-You Notes: Many organizations hardwire[SM] staff reward and recognition through the use of thank-you notes. The leader documents these in a log reviewed during the monthly meeting. Questions the supervisor might ask are:

- *Help me know you better. Why did you write these notes the way you did?*
- *Help me know your staff better. What has been recent reaction to these notes?*

8. People, Trends, and Issues: Staff information and other issues are covered under this agenda item. Examples of questions the supervisor should ask are:

- *How many staff members attended the last employee forum? What is your plan for improving that number? How can I help?*
- *Who have you hired since our last meeting? Tell me about the peer interview process for each person.*
- *Tell me how you are using the Standards of Behavior to improve performance in your department.*
- *What evaluations are due for your direct reports/staff?*
- *Tell me about your last 30- and 90-day meetings with new staff. What are one or two things you learned?*
- *I want to spend a few minutes talking about your high performers. How can I assist you with helping them advance in our organization?*

Hardwiring the Supervisory Meeting Model

Okay, now how do you hardwire this model? If you are an upper-level leader, first have a meeting with your direct reports to talk about your new and improved meeting process. Share the model format and your expectation as a supervisor that they will come prepared to discuss each item with their documentation. Second, make sure leaders have access to all the items you'll be covering. If not, don't wait for perfection—just start and add the other items as they become available.

(If you are a nurse leader implementing this with your supervisor, explain the process to him. Let him know that you would like to use it to standardize your meeting process and feel it will help you better manage his expectations.)

An additional way to ensure a more meaningful meeting is to hold it in the direct report's office. At the conclusion of your structured get-together, shadow the leader doing rounding either on patients, staff, or an internal customer. This accomplishes visual confirmation of the leader's ability and skill, gives you a chance to reward and recognize what's going well, and provides an opportunity to coach for improved performance. The additional time spent on rounding shows leaders you are invested in their success.

> You may have one or two leaders who, from time to time, do not follow this model, or fail to bring all of the items you have agreed upon. When that happens, simply cancel the meeting. Tell them you will come back next month when they have everything you expect. You'll probably have to do that only once—word will quickly get back to other direct reports that "you mean it."

Overcoming Objections

In some cases, leaders will complain about having to meet with their supervisor each month. They'll say, "We always talk every day. Why do we need a special meeting each month?" The supervisor should respond with, "Nurses say the same thing about patients, 'I am always in their room.' And yet we know the reality is that they're not there as much as they perceive."

Yes, leaders and supervisors probably do have frequent contact, but those conversations are likely not as purposeful as this process demands, and the results probably are not as predictable. The discussion you currently have can occur alongside this model, so advocate for the structured time.

If you report to someone who doesn't typically schedule a monthly meeting with you, then arrange one yourself with the supervisor. Bring your binder containing the model's agenda and proactively review your information. The supervisor will find value in your presentation, plus you'll impress that leader with your organizational skills and high-performing, proactive nature. In the event you are unable to get a scheduled time, simply e-mail an update of the progress you're making to your supervisor—and be sure to ask how you should keep that leader informed in the future.

Implementing This Model Pays Off in Many Ways.

Most obviously, the supervisory meeting model results in consistently productive meetings. When hardwired throughout an organization, it helps leaders, and those who work for them, stay aligned in the pursuit of big picture goals.

The meeting model also helps keep leaders on track by discouraging everyday distractions that can hinder results. The agenda is comprehensive, ensuring the most important topics are covered on a monthly basis. In addition, the interaction between the supervisor and leader is dynamic, fostering innovative solutions to problems.

Bottom line: Organizations that desire to achieve results and take better care of patients will hardwire the monthly meeting model; it's a process underscored by every leader's accountability for taking the actions necessary to make successful outcomes happen.

Key Points in This Chapter

1. The monthly meeting model is an expectation format for your monthly meetings. If your leader doesn't introduce it, you may want to suggest it to her.

2. Organizations that hardwire the meeting model go a long way toward achieving alignment and consistency from one leader to another—and one department to another.

3. The model's list of items ensures you are talking about the right things every month and helps you stay accountable for meeting your goals. It also helps reduce the distractions that invariably creep into meetings and make them less than successful.

4. Be proactive in getting time with your boss each month. If you absolutely can't get a meeting with her, e-mail her with the progress you've made.

Pillars Affected by the Supervisory Meeting Model

Service—Review of the rounding log ensures the process (which improves the patient's perception of service) is actually happening.

Finance—Allows leaders to see where desired financial outcomes are lacking, so that necessary changes can be implemented on a timely basis.

People—Provides the opportunity to reward and recognize; helps leaders be more successful by fine-tuning goals and implementing new tactics to reach targets on a monthly basis.

CHAPTER 23

How to Delegate

By Regina Shupe and Jill Ellis

As far back as the 1800s, delegation was identified by Florence Nightingale as one of the most critical skills nurses must understand and practice. Today, the American Nurses Association (ANA) defines delegation as "the transfer of responsibility for the performance of a task from one individual to another while retaining accountability for the outcome."[1] It's a core competency that's extremely important to the efficient use of nursing staff.

For new nurse leaders, however, learning how to delegate can be most challenging as they struggle with the level of trust required. In this chapter, we will discuss how to overcome this hurdle and shorten the learning curve associated with delegation. We will also give some pointers on how to choose the right staff member when delegating specific tasks.

Why is delegating so important? The most obvious reason is a simple one: Nurse leaders can't be in two (or ten!) places at once. They must make the best possible use of their time while accomplishing a tremendous amount of work.

Plus, when it's done properly, delegation benefits the staff members being delegated to. It provides meaningful work—which is tremendously important in job satisfaction—and helps them improve their skills sets.

First Things First: What Does It Mean to Delegate?

The ANA states that in order to be successful with delegation, a leader should understand *The Five Rights of Delegation*, which include:

1. Right task
2. Right circumstances
3. Right person
4. Right directions and communication
5. Right supervision and evaluation[2]

Let's consider an example of how this can be achieved:

Fullfilling *The Five Rights*

At one point in the past, I served as the director of Emergency Services for a new hospital being built. One of the first tasks was building my staff, and I knew that hiring the right people for this department was essential. The first person my team chose (utilizing peer interviewing) was a nursing educator. Not only would I delegate the huge task of planning the extensive orientation process to her, I would also assign the coordination of unit-specific policies. During one of the first conversations we had, I set clear expectations of exactly what I wanted her to do. Over the next few months, we met to review the accomplishments of the previous week and where she stood with her assigned tasks. Thus, I made sure I had the right person in the right position; assigned the right tasks for her skill set as an educator; held daily huddles with her; and evaluated her progress on a weekly basis. I ensured that *The Five Rights of Delegation* were fulfilled.

—Regina Shupe

In addition, clear communication when delegating is essential. It has to be *two-way* communication so the staff can ask for clarification. For example, when you delegate a task, have a conversation with the employee regarding what needs to be done; also, give suggestions on how it can be accomplished and in what time frame you need it completed. Then always ask if he understood or has any questions.

Why is setting clear expectations the first step to delegation? It eliminates performance barriers and fosters staff and physician buy-in to what must be done. It makes the delegation process much, much easier because everyone knows upfront what's necessary to achieve goals.

As a new nurse leader, you may have difficulty with delegating and tend to micromanage. However, at some point you must learn to *trust but verify*. For example, as post-visit (discharge) phone calls are implemented, develop a process for how they will be done, by whom, and in what time frame. Then, train the staff to fill out a discharge phone call log, a tool that helps you ensure the calls are made as per instructions. You

A Few Tasks to Delegate:

- Standardization of a process or report Having a standardized process orreport that the entire team is aware of makes the team more efficient. A staff member can research and provide a recommendation of the best way to standardize and implement.
- Job assignments. Each member of the team can take turns performing a rotating job assignment. One of the assignments on the rotating chart would be verifying that the task is complete and up to standard. For example, an assignment could be checking the crash cart and making sure it has all the supplies and is ready for use. Another team member is responsible for verifying that this occurred. (The verification could also be a rotating assignment.)
- Researching tactics to improve patient outcomes or achieve goals. Let's say as a leader you want to decrease decubiti on your unit. You can ask a member of your team to research the best tactic to implement to accomplish this goal.
- Taking minutes at staff meetings and posting communications for staff.
- Creating and developing the format used for shift reports and handoffs or other unit-based activities that require hands-on awareness of patient care.
- Organizing the unit supplies and nurse station materials.
- Participation on hospital or organization teams that would benefit from staff-level feedback.

are trusting staff to do the calls correctly, but the log helps ensure they *are* being made.

This holds true for Hourly Rounding as well. You trust but verify using the rounding log.

Laying the Groundwork

Let's say, as a nurse leader, you have a group of 40 direct reports. How do you decide the right fit as you delegate tasks?

First, you become a sponge. You learn about your staff, become an active listener in all situations, and take notes every step of the way. Second, you let employees continue in their work while you gain a clear understanding of your responsibilities as the leader. Third, as you are learning the functions of the unit, you start rounding on staff. As a leader, it is critical to build a strong foundation with your employees. And since you will be the one who completes the annual performance reviews, it is paramount you know as much about the staff and its performance as possible. Begin building that personal relationship through rounding.

Another tool that will assist you in choosing the right staff members to delegate to is the highmiddlelow® performer conversation. Through this process, you may have opportunities to entrust another to act on your behalf for professional growth and development or simply fulfillment.

A Priceless Skill Discovery

At one time, I had a direct report who was very detail oriented. I had discovered during staff rounding that this nurse loved completing puzzles—they were a challenge that gave her a great sense of fulfillment when she worked out the problems. I had found a talent that could assist the unit and me as a manager, so I delegated the scheduling function to her!

I had already set the expectations for staff as to how the scheduling process would work and timelines. I asked her to assist me in creating a schedule for the staff on an eight-week basis. I met with the nurse every day at first to make sure she understood the rules of the scheduling process. I approved the schedule once completed prior to posting it.

After four schedules and a few minor adjustments, I no longer needed to approve it. The time I gained back in my day by delegating to this nurse who had a unique skill set was priceless!

—Jill Ellis

Rounding on Staff: The Opportunity to Follow Up on Delegated Tasks

Let's say you've asked a nurse to review the end of shift report process to standardize what should be included. As you round on your staff, use this as an opportunity to check in on projects you've delegated to her: *Can you tell me how you are doing on standardizing the end of shift report? Remember we set a deadline of Oct. 12 for your recommendations. Are you on track to hit that deadline? Is there anything you need from me? Is there anyone who has been particularly helpful? Thank you for your work on this; once it's implemented it will save our team time by ensuring we have just the information we need all in the same place.*

This rounding conversation allows you to verify that the staff member is on task and aware of the deadline. It gives you the opportunity to thank her for her work. It also gives you the opportunity to manage up the nurse as you recognize the staff member she mentioned was helpful.

But what happens if you discover that the staff member is *not* on task? Well, the rounding conversation gives you the opportunity to ask what barriers might be impeding her progress. Then, you as the leader may be able to remove those barriers—or, if they really do take priority over the shift report process, to modify the timeline accordingly.

The Pay-Offs of Delegation

How does delegation pay off? Let us count the ways! As we mentioned earlier, the biggest benefit of successful delegation is the fact that it frees up the nurse leader's time. By handing off a task to someone else—perhaps someone far better suited for it than you are—you have more time to devote to areas in which you can have maximum impact.

It also helps staff members grow in their skills and reach new levels of performance development. This is good for the organization, obviously, but it also benefits individual nurses. All good employees want to be challenged. They want to feel that their work is meaningful and makes a difference...and delegation fosters that condition.

Finally, as employees carry out the delegated tasks, they are better able to connect the dots between the action and its impact on achieving goals. Delegation is an important offshoot of accountability—and increased accountability leads to better results and, in the end, a more successful organization.

Key Points in This Chapter

1. For new nurse leaders, learning how to delegate can be most challenging as they struggle with the level of trust required.

2. In the beginning, micromanaging may be necessary; but as new leaders become more comfortable in their roles, this tendency will lessen.

3. When delegating, take the different skill sets of individual staff members into consideration.

4. Successful delegation involves verifying that the tasks are done. Rounding for outcomes is one valuable tool for achieving this.

Pillars Affected by Delegation

Quality—With successful delegation, the nurse leader is able to devote more time to quality improvements.

People—Delegating nursing tasks frees up time for nurse leaders; it helps develop staff and hardwires accountability.

CHAPTER 24

How to Talk to the C-Suite

By Jackie Gaines

It's 7:50 a.m. and you are on the 8:00 a.m. agenda for the executive team meeting to discuss a new nursing model for the hospital. Because you are the chief nursing officer, the nurse management group is counting on you to sell this idea because it will offer a career ladder that is long overdue.

As the hour draws near, your palms begin to sweat and you wonder if you have prepared well enough. Will the C-suite understand the importance of its support for your nurses? That chief financial officer (CFO) is tough, and you can never tell which way the chief executive officer (CEO) will go. It's a safe bet that the vice president of human resources (VPHR) will have something to say—she's known for wanting to explore both sides of any issue raised. The rest of the team will defer to those three people since the proposal is not directly linked to their work. Welcome to the dynamic multiple personality executive team. **Are you ready?**

For many nurse leaders, this scenario may sound familiar. Presenting to and communicating with the organization's top leaders can be a scary proposition. As nurses, we are expert in the clinical arena and sometimes feel out of sorts when asked to translate that expertise and wisdom into a business proposal. Our inherent "fear" of those sitting in the top slots is often related to feelings of being incompetent in their world. Many nurse leaders have advanced degrees, but few are in business or healthcare administration. The skills we use to create a care plan or a model for patient safety are not quite the same as those deployed in the corporate world. Or are they?

Communicating and engaging with senior leaders to set and execute the strategic direction of the organization is an essential part of being a nurse leader. The entire leadership team, from the senior suite on down, needs to be united and aligned in its vision and also welcoming of the members' differing talents. Remember, it takes all those components to be the best for your patients, physicians, and workforce. The CEO and CFO cannot run that hospital without you! So embrace what you bring to the table. Nurses are master communicators with a diverse group of patients and their families; use that talent as you prepare your discussion points for those on the executive team.

Think of that business proposal you are about to make as one big plan of care—this time for the organization instead of the patient. Both have the same goal of making healthcare better. You may need to add some more bells and whistles, but structurally it can follow the same format.

Getting Ready for the Big Meeting

So, where does a nurse leader begin to prepare for that meeting with the C-suite?

It should come as no surprise that before presenting any idea to senior leadership it's important to **DO YOUR HOMEWORK.** The senior officers are expecting a well-thought-out proposal with a road map of tactics designed to achieve the desired results. They'll also want to know the value added for the organization, as well as the impact on existing resources (enhanced revenue, additional expenses, cost avoidance, and manpower). A good starting point may be to read Chapter 16: Understanding Financial Impact (From ROI to Revenue Creation).

Follow the five-step planning process: Evaluation, Assessment, Planning, Implementation, and Evaluation (yes, again).

Evaluation

Start with what you are trying to achieve and how you define success. Be able to articulate ROI and measurable results over a specific time frame. **Senior leaders want to know the targeted outcomes at the beginning of a proposal**. Don't string them along. They'll be more attentive to the rest of the story if you start at the end. Aligning the sought-after results with the organization's strategic priorities (service, quality, finance, people, and growth) will score you more success points in your presentation. Having some forethought about the fiscal implications will certainly gain the respect of the CFO!

Assessment

Research best practices from similar organizations and build the foundation of your proposal on evidence-based models. Be able to articulate the relationship between the research and current operations. Be concise, using language that cuts across all disciplines and beware of acronyms: Everyone at the table is not a nurse or clinician. Use current market data as appropriate. For example, if you're considering career ladders, what are the competitor hospitals offering to their nurses?

Planning

Take time to be fully prepared for the meeting. Anticipate questions that may be asked and work through how you intend to answer them. Also, prepare any background documents that may be needed to make your case. **Arrange all materials in an organized fashion so you can efficiently grab what is requested. The more prepared you are the more confident you will feel—and the more likely it is that your requests will be met.**

Implementation

Outline the tactics you are recommending to achieve the desired results. Again, focus and brevity are critical in your presentation or you will lose the attention of the executive team. Identify the person(s) who will be accountable for the tactics as well as the time frame for implementation. Discuss rollout and communication plans to maximize employee engagement.

Evaluation

You started out your meeting preparation by evaluating what you're trying to achieve. You'll end it here as well, but with a focus on follow-up. (You'll also want to re-state your ROI projections as well.) **Communicate how you will follow up post-implementation and method of accountability. Assure the executive team of a reporting structure back to them and employees (if appropriate).**

Remember, whether you are presenting to the entire C-suite or a single member, you must be able to present all the above in 10-15 minutes. Keep it short and to the point.

Additional Tips for Success

- **Know your audience.** Each member of the executive team receives and interprets information differently. Some may be very detail-oriented while others desire "CliffsNotes." In a mixed crowd, you may want to provide handouts with specifics for those who would like them. But hold back from distributing material until the end; otherwise the Type A personalities will flip through the documents looking for the end of the story and not be attentive to you. In a one-on-one meeting, ask the executive his or her preference; have both details and an abbreviated version available.

  Pre-meetings with stakeholders on the executive team may help to clarify direction, foster a sense of inclusion and ownership in the proposal, and solidify acceptance in the larger group. It would be very wise for a nurse leader to have a pre-meeting with the CFO for proposals that may have significant financial implications, or with the VPHR for proposals significantly impacting the organizational structure.
- **Follow up every meeting with written communication.** Document your interpretation of the meeting's outcomes, the next steps, and who is accountable. Place the proposal on the agenda for the next meeting with your supervisor.
- **Don't write a book.** Tables and charts work well in a presentation. Use one-page documents that are compelling and get to the point. Put yourself in the executive's place—what would ring your bell and what information is needed to make a sound decision?
- **Think of the hospital's financials as you would your personal checkbook.** If you had to make a decision about something your household or family member needed and it required unplanned resources, how would you decide to take on that additional expense? How would you prioritize, what has to be placed on hold, and how would you communicate the decision to your family? These are the same questions members of the C-suite ask themselves about the organization's priorities. Thinking through

ahead of time how your proposal might fly in light of these issues may help you frame your presentation.

- **Think ahead.** Try to envision likely questions and scenarios and be prepared to respond to them. Anticipation and thoughtful preparation are the keys to success.
- **Listen with an open mind.** The beauty of the executive team is its depth of experience and wisdom. Even if your proposal is declined or delayed, what you learn can be hugely valuable if you're open to it. Welcome constructive criticism—sometimes a hard pill to swallow—because it will help you grow as a leader. Follow up with your supervisor on your presentation and delivery; look for opportunities to improve the next time you're up at bat.
- **Seek to understand and then be understood.** Try to gain an understanding of why decisions were made. Push back respectfully on issues you feel strongly about, but watch for those non-verbal signals that tell you to stop. You can always reframe or clarify your position in your follow-up communication. Or maybe on re-examination, your position on an issue may need to change for the good of the organization or the patients served.
- **Don't fall victim to the we/they mentality.** Be cognizant of how you communicate the executive team's decisions to the nurses who report to you. Negative words/behavior are not appropriate.
- **Have faith in yourself and the special gifts you bring to the organization.** Nurse leaders play an essential role in the success of any organization!

As a nurse leader, when you take all the steps required for successful interaction and engagement with the C-suite, you become an integral part of the team. The group is better able to align its goals through open and effective communication. Your talents, as well as those of each team member, are leveraged to achieve a culture of excellence and execution.

Big and Little Buckets

Russ, the regional CEO for the health system, was my boss. I worked hard over a two-year period to get into a rhythm with his leadership style. He was very detail-oriented, similar to my own approach. I learned that giving him sufficient background information would be essential to successful communication and to our working relationship. As a result, my documentation to Russ was always thorough, and agendas were packed for each one-on-one session. Fast-paced meetings included a multitude of topics. And then, just when I thought I had successfully mastered the tempo of working with him, I got a new boss—Rick.

Rick had a very different leadership style—visionary and extremely social. As I transitioned from one leader to the next, I struggled with the best way to communicate. For the first three months, I used the same format. Every meeting I had lots of information, packed agendas, and back-up documentation. Rick graciously listened and offered feedback…that is, until the fourth month.

At that meeting, Rick began by taking out a blank sheet of paper and drawing two buckets, one big and one small. I must admit, I was a bit confused because I knew I had only one hour and lots to share. He told me he was very impressed with the depth of information I wanted to share with him each month, and proceeded to put my name on the big bucket he had drawn. He went on to describe his leadership style and how he preferred to receive information. He asked that I bring him only the executive summary, keeping the back-up information in my office in case he would need it. He then put his name on the smaller bucket. He said when I tried to dump my large bucket's contents into his small one each month, much of the content never made it.

I got it! Our meetings changed dramatically, including smaller agendas and an executive summary on the most important issues. From then on, when I got a new boss or engaged with a senior leader in an organization, I would start the relationship by asking how that person liked to receive information. In my mind I would think, *Are you a big bucket or a little bucket?*

—Jackie Gaines

Key Points in This Chapter

1. Communicating and engaging with senior leaders to set and execute the strategic direction of the organization is an essential part of being a nurse leader.

2. Executive officers are expecting well-thought-out proposals with a road map of tactics to get the desired results, the value added to the organization, and the impact on existing resources (enhanced revenue, additional expenses, cost avoidance, and manpower).

3. Follow the five-step planning process: Evaluation, Assessment, Planning, Implementation, and Evaluation.

4. Remember, whether you are presenting to the entire C-suite or a single member, you must be able to present in 10-15 minutes.

5. Consider these tips to enhance communication with your executive team:

    - Know your audience.
    - Follow up every meeting with written communication.
    - Don't write a book.
    - Think of your hospital's financials as you would your personal checkbook.
    - Anticipate and thoughtfully prepare   the key to success.
    - Listen with an open mind.
    - Seek to understand and then be understood.
    - Don't fall victim to the we/they mentality.
    - Have faith in yourself and the special gifts you bring to the organization. Nurse leaders play an essential role in the success of any organization!

Pillars Affected by C-Suite Communication

Service—The nurse leader communicates a well-thought-out proposal with a road map of tactics to achieve service-related results.

Quality—The nurse leader researches best practices from similar organizations and builds the proposal's foundation on evidence-based models.

Finance—Value added and impact on existing resources are a significant part of the proposal.

People—The focus and brevity of the nurse leader's presentation is respectful of the group's time.

Growth—The anticipated, measurable results (growth) over a specific time frame are communicated.

CHAPTER 25

How to Manage Change (Nursing Evolution Required)

By Jackie Gaines

Evolution has been defined as the change in the traits of a population of organisms from one generation to the next. These changes are caused by a combination of three main processes: variation, reproduction, and selection. Traits helpful for survival are retained from one age group to the next, while those that are harmful (or irrelevant) become rare. Over many generations, adaptations occur through a combination of successive, small changes in traits and selection of those best-suited for their current environment.

What does this have to do with nurse leadership? Quite a bit, actually. The concepts of evolution can be applied to our thinking about the changes we have experienced over many generations in healthcare. Nurses have had to adapt over time, because advances in technology, changes in treatment protocols, and even the uniforms we wear have changed. Today, unless a nurse wears a badge with credentials clearly visible, it is hard to distinguish nursing from another profession. No longer does the crisp white uniform with the matching cap define us!

Nursing has responded to a consumer demand for a risk-free environment by focusing on tactics that eliminate Never Events. We have embraced the creation of a diverse culture upon seeing our community and work-

> "There is nothing more difficult to take in hand, more perilous to conduct, or more uncertain in its success, than to take the lead in the introduction of a new order of things."
>
> —Niccolo Machiavelli

force demographics change. Multiple generations of nurses are now working side by side with differing ideas, skills, and work ethics.

Some of us have accepted the changes necessary to provide the best healthcare possible for our patients. Others have come along kicking and screaming because the past is what we know; how we were trained just feels more comfortable. It's like trading in those well-worn shoes for a new pair—we never enjoy the break-in period. And new shoes are really hard to dance in.

Today, keeping up with the volatility of the external environment (such as fiscal constraints and tightened regulations) is forcing nurses to change again. Staying competitive requires organizations to adapt at much higher rates than ever before. Waste in healthcare is unacceptable. Efficiency and effective and appropriate models of care are required…and nursing must evolve.

Breaking Down the Barriers to Nursing Evolution

Introducing change in an organization requires a blend of good technical and organizational skills. Most leaders find that the real challenge to successful implementation is on the behavioral side. Remember, resistance to change is very personal. Many people do not resist the change itself; however, they do resist change being imposed *on them*. Change (real or perceived) is viewed as a personal loss—of either job security or of an established routine.

Employees may even see the long-term value but cannot get over the short-term impact. Mark Twain said, "It's not the progress I mind; it's the change I don't like." How many of you remember things your parents tried to instill in you as a child? We may have known they were imparting wisdom, but at the time all we could see was the removal of something we enjoyed. Yet as adults, we are grateful for their guidance, even passing it on to the next generation who challenge the value just as we did in our youth.

Change requires the will and effort to learn new things. In the beginning, one must have tolerance for the time and energy it takes to learn. In today's world of instant gratification, however, patience is at a premium. A heightened level of intolerance could lead to resistance and sabotage.

Understanding the potential roadblocks is a key to successful implementation, and should be top of mind when planning for any organizational change, large or small.

So What Kind of Change Are We Talking About Anyway?

Organizational change nurse leaders may need to facilitate could be:

- **Operational**—Affecting ongoing operations, like medical records going paperless.
- **Strategic**—Reflecting a change in business direction, like a recent merger with another health system or hospital.
- **Cultural**—Reflecting a change in an organization's core values, philosophies, or beliefs. (This could include areas like a focus on cultural diversity, or incorporating work/life blend into standards of behavior.)

The direct impact the change has on nursing will be dependent on type and scope. For example, strategic realignment with a new partner may be virtually invisible (except in new name badges) at the bedside. However, senior nurse leaders will need to learn how to work with a new governance model and by-laws. By comparison, implementing a paperless medical record requires nurses to be computer savvy and change the way they interact with patient data. Resistance may be high in those nurses who are not a part of the tech movement and who don't embrace computer technology. Their new shoes must be really uncomfortable!

Four Communication Tools to Help You Drive Change

Tough Questions Exercise. No doubt about it: Any major change inspires many questions from staff members. And sometimes those questions aren't easy to answer: *Why are we being asked to do so much more with fewer resources? This is too heavy of a workload—how can we do it and still take good care of our patients? Since all pay increases have been frozen, how can the hospital afford this new initiative?*

The key to answering tough questions is preparation and training. By anticipating possible questions (and also harvesting them from staff members during rounding and other communications) you and your leaders can work together to prepare "standardized" answers. The "Tough

Questions Exercise" provides a structured method for doing so. (Visit www.firestarterpublishing.com/NurseLeaderHandbook for more information.)

Not only does the Tough Questions Exercise allow all leaders to speak in a unified voice, it forces them to think about how they can connect staff to the "why." When people understand *why* they're being asked to make a change, they are more likely to buy into it and go the extra mile to make it successful.

Rounding for Outcomes. You've likely already read about rounding in other parts of this book. These regular, purposeful conversations with staff members are great vehicles for increasing their job satisfaction and also boosting patient perception of care. And they can also help you implement change smoothly and successfully.

The questions asked in the rounding process naturally lend themselves to driving the change process. For example, when you ask a staff member if he has the tools and equipment he needs to do the job, you have the opportunity to remove any barriers that might be hindering the implementation of the change. And when you ask who should be recognized for doing a great job, you can specify that you're seeking an answer regarding the change. Then, when you recognize that person, you reinforce her efforts—and remember, what we reinforce we get more of!

Communication Boards. What is a communication board? Basically, it's a physical display board that presents an ever-changing snapshot of the organization's "big picture." Organizations typically post a board in every unit, in a highly visible location. Often, they structure their boards around the Pillars of Excellence—Service, Quality, Finance, People, Growth, and Community—or whatever organizing system they use in their goal-setting efforts. (Quint Studer recommends adding a section for the External Environment as well.)

It's easy to see how these communication boards can help support your change efforts. When you make progress toward a change goal, you can post it on the board. When you fall short of an incremental goal, post it on the board. The idea is to keep the status of the change in front of staff members at all times so that they stay aware of what they need to be doing. Oh, and it never hurts to post heartfelt "thank-yous" from people who have been positively impacted by the change!

Newsletters. Does your organization have a newsletter? If so, it's a wonderful tool to help you manage change. Even if you're not in charge of the newsletter, you can almost certainly influence the editorial calendar and even submit articles that deal with subjects related to the change effort. (Most organizations are hungry for newsworthy material!)

A few hints to help you create good articles:

- Always focus on *why* staff are being asked to make the change.
- Be transparent. Share the facts and figures that necessitate the change as well as projected ROI.
- Provide action steps. Tell readers what they can do to move the change forward and smooth its implementation.
- Share mini-success stories. Also, if you get glowing thank-you letters from patients or employees, include them in the newsletter as well. This will boost morale and reinforce their efforts.

Nine Helpful Hints for Orchestrating the Dance

So, what can nurse leaders do to maximize their potential for success in change management? Here are some tips for successful execution.

1. **Know your dance partners!** Identify those who may be affected by the change you're trying to implement. Who are your stakeholders? Who will block your moves? Ahead of executing the change, think about the tough questions staff may have and identify your barriers to success.

2. **Be aware of others on the dance floor; develop your peripheral vision.** Often leaders who are managing change will focus on their area of responsibility and lose sight of the implications across other departments. Map out the ripple effect of your actions.

3. **Identify who will lead the dance.** Who could serve as a champion for the change? Engage someone who's passionate about it and possesses enough internal influence to help deliver the message(s).

4. **Carefully plan the dance steps.** A poorly executed plan for change is sometimes worse than the change itself. However, a well-thought-out plan will buy you credibility for the next change you need to implement.

5. **Make sure you have adequate resources before you dance.** You cannot be successful without adequate tools and people power.

6. **Group dancing is great!** Include as many stakeholders as possible from beginning to end. This builds a sense of ownership, commitment, and accountability for successful implementation.

7. **Sing loud before, during, and after the dance.** Communication is a must-have. Answer the questions of, *Why this change? Why now?* Don't dodge the tough inquiries—transparency is your friend. Your visible commitment as a nursing leader during the change process is critical. Do not rely 100 percent on the champion to sing, but instead perform a duet. As you build enthusiasm, start a choir. Enthusiasm is contagious!

8. **Create a souvenir of the past.** With significant organizational changes, consider having a ritual to mark the change with tokens that reflect the value of the past or the perceived loss. This is particularly important in a strategic change like closure of services. A small transition ceremony can go a long way in offering a bridge from the old to the new.

9. **Celebrate small dance steps.** Don't wait until the entire change has been implemented before you celebrate. Show you appreciate incremental change, as this will generate more enthusiasm along the way.

It's Time to Embrace Change.

Change is always going to be a constant in our professional and private lives; evolution is inevitable. But the more you're on the innovative end of change instead of the reactive end, the more palatable it becomes. Nursing must be a vital and proactive part of the evolution to make healthcare the very best for the patients served. We must learn new dance steps and love our new shoes.

As a nurse leader, you must get comfortable with navigating others through these volatile times and facilitating their development for what's required of them in today's environment. Some of their basic skill sets will be retained, but many will need alterations or improvements. The evolution of nursing directly impacts the quality of patient care, and moves an organization forward toward a necessary culture of excellence and execution.

Take a hard look in the mirror and determine if you are wearing your new dancing shoes! You also need to decide if you even like the dance. Sometimes, as leaders, the changes required of us do not resonate with our passion, values, or beliefs. We attempt dancing with the new shoes, but they are killing our soul and that translates to the workforce. Leadership self-awareness is always the critical first step. **You cannot lead successfully what you do not believe in, including leading nursing through change.**

Closing Obstetrical Services: A Portrait in Change

After three years of declining obstetrical volume in a hospital where I worked, the executive leadership team decided closure of this service was the best decision in the interest of patients and future viability. Delivering only one to two babies a day on a 10-bed unit was financially challenging to say the least. In addition, the low volume of births did not offer nurses enough daily experience to maintain their skills, therefore increasing the risk potential for patients.

Obstetrical services had been a core service line for this hospital since its inception and many of the staff had been born there. However, less than a mile away another hospital had developed a modern, comprehensive set of obstetrical and newborn services, drawing anchor physicians and patients through its doors. Even many of the current nurses had left for what was perceived to be greener pastures. Community access for care was not an issue; this competitor hospital had enough capacity for all.

Now came the difficult part of developing the plan for closure.

The executive leadership team explored who initially needed to be involved in developing the action plan. A core group of senior leaders, physicians, and key stakeholders formed a workgroup to create the plan; from that team came nursing and physician champions. This group met frequently throughout implementation to assure a smooth transition. A representative from Public Relations and Marketing was also included to facilitate a sound internal and external communication plan from beginning to end.

The nursing leader and chief executive communicated the decision for closure—and why—to the staff in a variety of formats:

employee forums and unit-by-unit meetings for more intimate dialogue. The thought process was clearly outlined with the impact on quality; staffing and financial viability were also defined. Transparency was the key. The physician champion and chief executive repeated the same message to the staff doctors. Although a tough message to deliver, the connection to quality and staffing made sense to everyone, even the community. Focusing on finance would have been a PR disaster.

The transition was not completely flawless, as staff and physicians who lost their jobs personalized the closure and tried to engage others in a negative spiral. Our saving grace was that we had been extremely transparent in the "why," included the next steps, and communicated on a variety of fronts. The message was also delivered in a compassionate way in line with the core values of the health system.

To honor the history of obstetrics in that hospital, the nurses and staff held a closure service after the last baby was born. Prayers, reflections, and stories were shared as a big ribbon was tied around the unit doors. In remembrance of this cherished unit, each participant walked away with a small card printed with a poem about the beauty of birth. The ladies' auxiliary also purchased a plaque so that no one ever forgot the special service this hospital once provided to the community.

As a footnote, many of the nurses remained with the hospital and retrained for other jobs that fueled their purpose. *They evolved.*

—Jackie Gaines

Key Points in This Chapter

1. Introducing change in an organization requires a blend of good technical and organizational skills. Most leaders find the real challenge to successful implementation is on the behavioral side.

2. Remember, resistance to change is very personal. Many people do not resist change; they resist change being imposed *on them*.

3. Understanding the potential roadblocks is a key to successful implementation, and should be top of mind when planning for any organizational change, large or small.

4. Tips for success:
   - Identify all those who may be affected by the change you are trying to implement.
   - Map out the ripple effect of your actions.
   - Identify champion(s) for change.
   - Plan carefully.
   - Make sure you have adequate resources.
   - Include as many stakeholders as possible from beginning to end.
   - Communication is a "must-have."
   - Create a souvenir of the past.
   - Celebrate along the way!

5. Change is always going to be a constant in nurses' professional and private lives. Evolution is inevitable. The more you're on the innovative end of change instead of the reactive end, the more palatable it becomes. Nursing must be a vital and proactive part of the evolution to make healthcare the very best for the patients served.

Pillars Affected by Effective Change Management

Service—Good change management techniques allow the organization to stay competitive in providing service.

Quality—The connection between quality and change is clearly defined, which in turn fosters staff and physician engagement.

Finance—When managed efficiently, financial outcomes do not suffer as the change takes place.

People—Barriers to change on the part of employees are successfully navigated.

Growth—Community perception of the organization is enhanced due to effective communication of why the change is necessary.

CHAPTER 26

Walking Life's Tightrope

By Jackie Gaines

The circus is in town and you have front row seats with your two children, ages five and seven. It's been a long week at work, chasing one crisis after another. All the nurses in your department seemed to be in an uproar about something. As their manager, your office has been a revolving door with staff members seeking counsel, respite, or just an ear. You have looked forward to this day with your children as a way to release some of the week's tension. And you absolutely love the circus.

The lights go down and the spotlight is on the act high above the center ring. The tightrope walkers are up first. As they begin their perilous journey across the tense wire, you suddenly are struck with how walking the tightrope is so reflective of your life. Each day there is tension pulling you between your work life and your personal life. *You* are the tightrope walker trying to make it from one end of the rope to the other without falling—most days without a safety net to catch you or a pole to help maintain your balance.

In a single day, you might be a parent, teacher, disciplinarian, cook, housekeeper—you fill a multitude of roles. But you are also a nurse, belonging to a profession whose members, unfortunately, just might be the *worst* in caring about their own well-being and living a balanced life.

Women in Healthcare: A Work/Life Blend Snapshot

In 2008, Studer Group® conducted a study on Work/Life Blend Among Women in the Healthcare Industry. Here are just a few of the results…

Many of the women who responded are caregivers: Fifty-two percent have children under 18 and 23 percent have the caregiver responsibility for a dependent parent or other relative.

They work more than 40 hours per week: The average number of hours per week was reported as 47.7.

Seventy-five percent would choose healthcare all over again.

Seventy-three percent would recommend a career in healthcare to a friend.

They rarely dedicate time to their personal or emotional needs—only 46 percent report treating themselves "rarely" (no more than a few times a year).

Forty-five percent of the respondents reported they experienced work-family conflicts at least one day or more per week. Only 6 percent notes they experienced family interference with work.

Figure 26.1

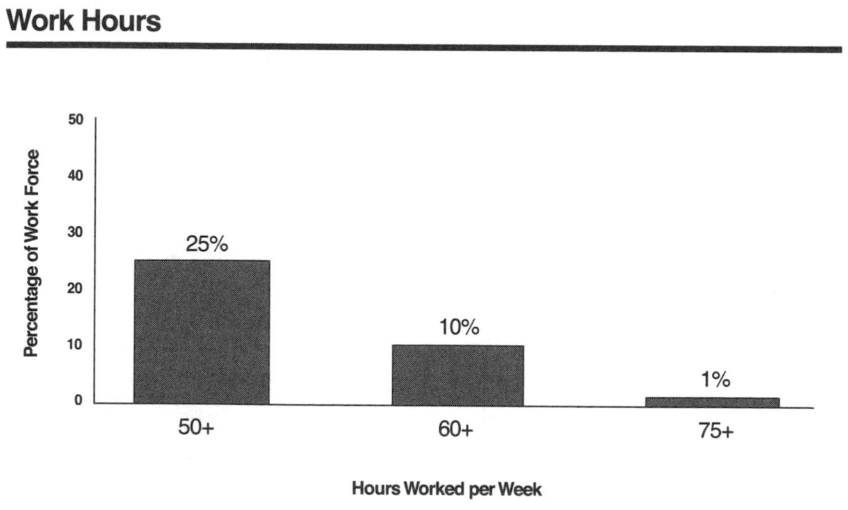

To download an overview of this study, go to www.firestarterpublishing.com/NurseLeaderHandbook.

And as much as nurses think they can separate their lives into neat boxes for work and home...they bring their whole selves to work. Daily worries or lack of rest (or both!) impact performance and ultimately the quality of care for patients. In reverse, nurses carry home the stress of work, affecting family members or significant people in their lives and sometimes even their own health. The reality is that without balance, a nurse leader runs the risk of **falling off the tightrope**, hitting hard, and perhaps even impacting someone else.

But you do not have to fall victim to this scenario. There are several tools available to improve work/life balance or at least strengthen your safety net for those times when despite your best efforts you slip off the rope. If staff members observe your commitment to balance and you integrate it into a standard of behavior for them, everyone wins—especially the patients who are counting on exceptional care. Their lives literally depend on you and those you lead.

Four Simple Steps for a Healthier Work/Life Blend

Step 1: Recognize the need for balance and commit to addressing it in your life.

The first step to successfully getting across the tightrope is self-awareness. On a scale of one to five, where do you rate yourself with regard to balance? If one is the least balanced and five is the most, what's your number? Any number from one to three means you are at risk of falling. A rating of four means you have a shot at getting across the wire, and five means you are the master of work/life balance!

If your number is one to four, keep reading! Those with a rating of five should reach out to others and be their safety net; teach them what you have learned along the way.

Step 2: Set realistic goals for yourself.

Studer Group coaches recommend that organizations identify their priorities in a balanced scorecard referred to as pillars of excellence. They include: service, quality, finance, people, and growth. The goals outlined under each pillar help you to run a great business through organizational alignment.

Consider creating pillars of excellence for your personal life. They could include life goals around work, family, self-health, or spirituality. For example, you might set a goal of:

- Getting certified in a different area of healthcare if the one you work in now isn't fulfilling
- Trying out places of worship until you find one you're comfortable with
- Volunteering for a charity that's meaningful to you
- Joining a gym and working out three days a week

This process will help you obtain personal alignment with what's important to you. Moreover, the "right balance" is a very personal thing and will change for each individual at different times in his or her life. What you need as a young adult is very different from what you need as a senior…and it also may be very different based on your culture, gender, or any variety of factors.

As a nurse leader, you may find that a life pillar dialogue is a great agenda item for a department meeting. It says to staff members that you care about their whole person and their well-being. In doing so, you expand the safety net for all involved.

Step 3: Engage and take back your life!

The journey to a balanced life is in your hands. No one can do it for you. Consider scheduling your new goals on a calendar (there's great power in simply writing things down!) or ask a friend or family member to hold you accountable.

Step 4: Track your progress and readjust your life pillar goals each year.

You will be amazed at the results at work and at home. You will be happier and better equipped to maneuver life's daily challenges.

Your To-Do List for a Balanced Life

As a nurse leader, you need to lead a more balanced life. And your staff does, too! Practice the following tips yourself and help the people you lead to do so as well:

Figure out what works for you. Spend some time thinking about the things that make you feel better and more balanced and create a game plan for making them an integral part of your life. For instance, if you aren't spending enough time with a friend who always inspires and revitalizes you, create a standing "date" once a month to have dinner with her or (at the very least) to talk on the phone. The point is to be honest about what really, truly creates the kind of life you want to live.

Beware of the technology chains that bind. Cell phones and computers blur the distinction between work and personal time…don't fall victim to the temptation to stay "connected" 24/7. We all need a break from emails, phone calls, and the constant bombardment of bad news. For instance, if one of your goals is to give your family uninterrupted time, schedule several hours a day that your computer and phone are off limits (unless of course there is an emergency).

Use your faith to help put life into perspective. Faith makes all things possible and can be a rock to stand on in this crazy world. It also offers many a healthy way to balance personal, interpersonal, work-related, and community responsibilities.

Get organized. The most important issues related to having a good work/life balance are organization, planning, and time management. This could mean planning meals a week in advance, laying out clothes the night before, and spending as much evening time with young children as possible.

Enjoy life. Focus on what is going well, not what is stressful. Take time to play, laugh, love, work, cry together, and respect one other. We all make mistakes at home and at work, so learn to forgive yourself and others. Take time for yourself and smile.

Find a job you enjoy. We spend more waking hours at work than we do with loved ones. It's imperative to be in an environment that brings you joy. How miserable to spend most of your waking hours unhappy and stressed out. If your workplace is "toxic" for whatever reason, you might need to make the tough choice to find a different job.

Remain fit and use exercise as a way to deal with stress. People who exercise regularly are better able to handle stress. Whether you do so at 5 a.m. or 6 p.m., exercising can improve the quality of your day.

Make a date with yourself. Many of you have probably heard about the trend for married couples to have a date night actually scheduled. It's very important to have quality time with the important folks in your life and having a pre-set date is not a bad idea. However, consider starting a new trend: Schedule a date night, morning, lunch, or weekend—with yourself! You can start small, blocking out 15 to 30 minutes a day. During that time, do something that makes you happy...exercise, read, meditate, pray, shop, get a massage...whatever gives you just a small break. You'll be surprised by the change you immediately start to feel in the quality of your life.

Stay connected to the difference you make. Do you feel as passionate about what you do for a living as you did on your first day as a nurse? If not, it's time to reconnect with the difference you make in the lives of others. Rich Bluni's excellent book, *Inspired Nurse*—along with its companion, *Inspired Journal*—can help you remember why you chose this profession and how you can fully integrate its spiritual and emotional gifts into your daily life.

Key Points in This Chapter

1. As a general rule, nurses struggle with taking care of themselves and living balanced lives.

2. Use the four simple steps to a healthier work/life blend:

   Step 1: Recognize the need for balance and commit to addressing it in your life.
   Step 2: Set realistic goals for yourself. Consider creating pillars of excellence (life pillars) for your personal existence.
   Step 3: Engage and take back your life! The journey to a balanced life is in your hands—no one can do it for you.
   Step 4: Track your progress and readjust your life pillar goals each year. You'll be amazed at the results at work and at home.

3. There are various tips to help you stay balanced. Loosen your "technology chains," get in touch with your faith, exercise regularly... and always strive to stay connected to the difference you make.

Pillars Affected by a Healthy Work/Life Balance

Service—Without balance, patient care can suffer.

Quality—Without balance, errors and safety lapses due to stress can occur.

Finance—Without balance, burnout affects retention, leading to staff replacement costs.

People—Without balance, job satisfaction and home life behaviors are impacted.

SECTION 5: STORIES FROM THE FIELD

Introduction

By Lyn Ketelsen

In this final section, you will have the opportunity to hear from nurse leaders who are currently out there working in the healthcare "trenches" every day. Each of these leaders has made an impact not only on the patients served by their unit and their organization as a whole, but also in the lives of their staff, their families, and their community.

Strong nurse leaders aren't nurses just for the 50 or 60 hours they are at work every week. Certainly they have a deep and life-shaping commitment to caring for their patients and the family members who love them. But they are also nurses and leaders in every aspect of their lives—in their children's schools, their church groups, their neighborhoods and book clubs. Their passion for caring and sharing reaches far beyond the bounds of their healthcare organizations.

In the following pages, four strong and successful leaders will share their individual paths to nursing, along with some of the lessons they've learned along the way. You will hear some common themes in each of their stories: adapting to change, communication, accountability, mentoring. All of these are important skills, reflecting the insights you've gained in previous chapters.

These leaders are representative of the thousands of nurse leaders out there every day making healthcare organizations better places for employees to work, physicians to practice, and patients to receive care. Your story could just as easily go here, too. To all nurse leaders past, present, and future...thank you.

Linda Deering: The Journey Is Never Complete

Where I Belong

I never had a lifelong dream to be a nurse, but I do know that my godmother had an impact on my decision to enter into the nursing profession. She too was a nurse, and I remember her coming home in that striking white uniform. She just seemed so important and so passionate about her work.

Still, I didn't really know what nursing was about until I got further into my education. I was what was known as a "diploma nurse"—I attended a three-year hospital-based program that doesn't even exist anymore. During those three years, however, I was still wondering where I belonged. I found the answer during the last semester of my education during my critical care rotation.

I just fell in love with caring for the critically ill patients, with the machinery, and with the complexity of the work. Being able to actually save a life each and every day gave me a sense of purpose. This was the time during which nursing and my path really came alive for me. As a new graduate, I ended up going into critical care and have had a vibrant career ever since.

Helping Other Nurses

After working as a critical care nurse, I decided to continue my education and get a master's degree because I wanted to be a clinical nurse specialist in the critical care arena. I wanted to be that top clinician who was helping other nurses learn and grow in their skills and critical competence.

It took me several years of continuing education to get my bachelor's degree and finally my master's. Along that trajectory of education, I continued working, and during this time I kept getting pulled into various leadership positions. First I was a charge nurse, then a nursing supervisor, then a nurse manager, and eventually I got into director of nursing. By the time I actually got my master's degree, I had been in leadership for so long that it was evident I had a talent for leadership. I loved being a leader.

Love, Satisfaction, and Focus: A Recipe for Success

If you gain a position in nurse leadership, you will find that in order to survive you have to love what you do—that's the bottom line. Be comfortable making decisions even when it's not popular. You have the opportunity to make a great impact on your hospital and to change your work environment for the better.

Next, never be satisfied. Leading means that you are constantly making things better, so you should never tolerate a "good enough" attitude or solution. You have to be tenacious and seek out improvements to make patient care and the professional practice better.

Finally, as a leader you must always be focused on results because measuring them offers tangible proof that you're making a positive impact. Don't fixate on the process or on what other people will think about you. All that matters is that you are making a difference and making things better for your patients.

As a leader I have learned that respect is worth more than being liked or being popular. Initially, I think (especially for women) we have a desire for approval. Being able to give up that longing and learning to value respect and results above my popularity was a turning point for me.

Always Evolving—and Always Improving

My career choices have put me in a pivotal position to help make a difference in the success of my organization, the quality of patient care, and the quality of the nursing profession. Nurse leadership is a unique position that can make a difference in healthcare, and it's hugely satisfying.

The journey of becoming a better leader is never complete. I often think of careers in which you start your job and not much changes for the next 30 or 40 years. But nurse leadership is different. There are so many opportunities to try new and exciting methods to improve our effectiveness.

My organization, for example, is going above and beyond each day. In the four years that I have been here, our patient satisfaction has improved from the 45th percentile to the 65th percentile; employee satisfaction has increased from the 40th percentile to the 63rd percentile; physician satisfaction has increased from the 50th percentile to the 93rd percentile; and turnover has decreased from 20 percent to 11 percent. Furthermore, my organization's operating margins went from -9 million dollars to -1 million dollars annually. Soon, we'll be moving forward.

Based on those numbers alone, I think we are definitely moving in the right direction—and I have to give a great deal of credit to two Studer Group® professionals: CEO Quint Studer and coach Dan Collard. I know that my monthly coaching calls with these folks have really driven my personal performance. Without them, I wouldn't have been able to make nearly so big a difference!

Jeanny Platt: Fostering a Successful Staff

Old School to New School

I have been a professional nurse for 30 years. Over the course of my career, so very much has changed in the nursing industry—especially in the realm of nurse leadership. Earlier in my career, I practiced old school leadership; it was my way or the highway. Now, however, nursing is all about helping the staff become more successful; e.g., resolving conflicts, coaching and counseling employees, cultivating their self-esteem, and maintaining flexibility with work schedules (because nurses are, of course, people too!).

I've been a nurse leader for 14 years now, and everything I have learned has come by trial and error. I never had a mentor as a new nurse, so it took me much longer to reach my full potential. For this reason, I highly recommend leadership classes and mentoring programs to all new nurse leaders. In that same spirit, following are some of the things I've learned about being an effective and respected nurse leader:

Relationships for Nurse Leaders

The very first lesson I learned is that there are always two sides to every story. (By the way, I definitely learned this one the hard way.) It is very important not to jump to conclusions too quickly after hearing only one side of an issue. Always talk to everyone involved in situations that require a closer look.

If counseling or a reprimand is required, always find a way to correct the person in question in private. Remember that in order to maintain healthy self-esteem, staff members must know that they are important members of the team and therefore will be held accountable for their actions if they are not following hospital policies and procedures. Likewise, if recognition or praise is to be given, always do so in public. Well-deserved praise also fosters healthy self-esteem—and the promise of receiving it for a job well done will act as a strong motivator.

Change for a Reason.

As all nursing staff knows, change is an integral part of the medical profession; however, change is not always easy, welcomed, or accepted. When you are ready to institute a major change, try selling it to the staff by putting a positive spin on things.

Here's an example: When we instituted Hourly Rounding^{SM}, it was met with much negativity and frustration. *I don't have time to see each patient every hour. Are you crazy?* But when we explained to the staff how Hourly Rounding decreases the number of times the patient uses the call light, everyone understood that this change would minimize the constant interruptions of their workdays. Ultimately, what caught the staff's attention was the realization that Hourly Rounding would give them *more* control of their patient care, and that it would benefit them *and* their patients. Sometimes you just have to find ways to illuminate the hidden benefits of reform and change.

I've also seen how effectively campaigns can be used to drive initiatives. After all, they inject a "fun" element into what might otherwise be a dry effort to reach certain standards or benchmarks. When we were trying to instill more teamwork in our units, we launched a campaign with an "I've got your back" theme, and every Friday the unit that had the most staff wearing their "I've got your back" t-shirts won a pizza party.

Communication Counts.

Of course, being a nurse leader is about more than t-shirts and pizzas. It is important that teams increase the communication between RNs and

PCTs. For example, the RN asks the PCT for help and the PCT says, "I'm busy. Get someone else." The RN takes it personally, gets angry at the PCT, and feels as though the PCT is lazy or just doesn't want to help.

In my own efforts to solve this problem, the PCTs were educated about not saying "no." Instead, they were instructed to tell the RN what they were doing and to give a time frame of when they could help. Another good option is to get together at the beginning of the shift and plan the workload for the day. Set up a time when the two of you can get together to bathe that total care patient or complete other difficult tasks.

It might not surprise you to learn that miscommunication is responsible for about 90 percent of all staff conflicts. Successfully resolving them requires coaching staff members to better communicate with each other. After all, effective communication between staff members leads to increased teamwork. This directly influences staff work satisfaction, which ultimately increases patient satisfaction—and isn't that one of our ultimate goals?

You must continuously hold staff accountable and validate what they do on a daily basis. Remember to listen to what your staff has to say, because it is essential that they know their voices are being heard. Ask them what they need you to do in order for you to be a better leader. And last but not least, if you say you're going to do something, well, you had better do it.

Results Make the Work Worthwhile.

These are just a few of the elements that can help a nurse leader drive results to meet organizational goals. What makes all of these tactics worthwhile is the knowledge that your leadership skills have contributed to the overall well-being of your department, and most importantly, the positive effect your leadership can have on elevating the quality of patient care delivered.

So how can you tell if you're doing a great job? Effective nurse leadership is indicated by decreased staff turnover, fewer med errors, more positive patient outcomes, and fewer falls. It is also indicated by increased employee, physician, and patient satisfaction.

Kris Powell: Lessons Learned Along the Way

Becoming a Compassionate Caregiver

Like most managers, I learned the majority of what I know from a number of different resources and experiences, including role models, mentors, business and management books, conferences, and life experiences (that includes mistakes along the way!).

Early in my career—during my first year as a nurse, in fact—I found myself standing in the corner of an ED treatment room not knowing what to say to a distraught woman who had been raped.

I was so afraid of saying the wrong thing that I chose not to say anything at all. I assisted with the forensic exam and evidence collection, went through the motions of education and discharge, and never really connected in a meaningful way with this patient who needed a confident and compassionate caregiver.

Later, I realized that this was not the type of nurse I wanted to be. From that time on, I committed to learning as much as possible about emergency nursing so I could be confident in my knowledge and skills.

Ultimately, I became a SANE (Sexual Assault Nurse Examiner) nurse and began to teach others about the care of this vulnerable population. I soon realized that I enjoyed teaching what I had learned to other nurses, and I went about seeking as many teaching opportunities as possible. I eventually moved into education positions in the Emergency and Trauma Departments.

From Teacher to Manager

Several years later, I transitioned from education into a management role. In my early days as a new manager of a trauma program, I learned several important lessons. First, I learned the value of understanding, organizing, and presenting data in order to effect change. Second, I learned that in order to advocate for patients, I needed to sit at the table and engage as an equal with physicians, administrators, consultants, and colleagues. Third, I learned that delaying or avoiding conflict usually results in bigger problems later on. Learning that particular lesson came at a high cost: I lost a valuable member of my team because of my delay in managing a problem staff member.

It has been my experience that most staff will rise to the expectations that are set for them if they believe they can and if they have the tools and resources they need. The last thing they need is a team member who does not buy in to the goal.

A Challenge...and a Triumph

During the first year in a two-year contract with Studer Group®, the Emergency Department had a 25 percent controllable turnover rate. While some staff were terminated for practice or performance issues, most of the turnover was comprised of staff members who voluntarily left because they were not committed to the team or its goals and who were feeling the pressure that comes along with accountability.

While the high turnover was a huge challenge to overcome, the staff who remained and the new staff members who were hired came together as a team and achieved more than they had ever expected, culminating in the Press Ganey Success Story and Compass Awards for patient satisfaction in the following year.

The Benefits of Buy-in

It is worth all of the work you put in and all of the difficult decisions you have to make to see individual team members (and the team as a whole) take pride in their work when they have achieved something they did not think possible. Once the staff has seen that their efforts result in success, they are much more open and adaptable to other changes, and they will face challenges head-on.

Staff also become protective of this culture and hold each other accountable to the standards that have been set. When I saw this happening, I realized that the culture in the department had truly changed. Now staff are more satisfied, retention is high, nursing vacancies are almost nonexistent, and several staff members commented that their jobs are easier now than they were two years ago.

Lessons to Live By

I still have much to learn in my journey. I am still learning to better balance work and life. I am working harder to be fully present in the moment. I am still learning to be a leader, and I hope that I can inspire others to have the confidence to reach for higher goals. Some of the more common pearls I like to pass on to young leaders are:

- The answers come easily if you put the patient at the center of the issue.
- Be firm, kind, and respectful. You can adhere firmly to standards and hold people accountable while still being kind and respectful.
- If you feel uncomfortable in a situation, it means you are pushing your own boundaries, learning new skills, and growing professionally and personally.
- Stand strong and exude confidence (even if sometimes you don't feel it).
- You'll never be bored if you keep learning.
- Always find a way to laugh at yourself.

Mark Quirin: A Passion for Service

An Unlikely Path to Nursing

The path that led me to a career in nursing took me in directions I never could have imagined. My desire to help others first became evident in high school when I became a ski patroller. Although I had enrolled in ski patroller school mostly for the unlimited free skiing, I realized that I enjoyed responding to accidents and emergencies on the slopes. That adrenaline rush was the first indication that my afterschool job was giving me more fulfillment than just the recreation for which I had signed on.

After high school I still wasn't sure what I wanted to do with my life, so I ended up joining the military for a few years as an infantryman—which had nothing to do with the medical field. However, it did give me four free years of schooling after my military tenure.

I had my sights set on something related to the medical field, and I started taking classes toward a future in physical therapy. As it turned out, though, the physical therapy field was flooded and there were just not enough jobs for physical therapists. So I did a little research about job security and found some articles stating that nursing was one of the most secure and in-demand jobs out there. I really didn't know what being a nurse actually entailed, so I did some more research.

Luckily, I had a few more years of free school available to me, so I applied to the school of nursing at my college. My GPA was good, I did well in the interview, and I was accepted.

Recognizing a True Calling

As I got into my clinicals and started understanding what nurses actually did each day, I enjoyed what I was doing more and more. It wasn't the diagnosing and treatment that I enjoyed so much as the communication with the patients. I enjoyed getting to know people and helping them through moments of fear and complete dependency in some cases.

One particular clinical showed me that I was on the right path. I was on a critical care unit and was taking care of an 86-year-old woman who had actually been a World War II nurse. I didn't realize this until we started talking. You learn a lot about someone when you open the doors of communication.

Since I had just gotten out of the Army, we started telling our stories to each other. She talked about the soldiers she had seen, and I was able to relate her stories to my recent experiences. During this time I had an epiphany. I, the infantryman-turned-nurse, was repaying her for her protection of infantrymen all those years ago.

It was a really cool feeling for me to realize that you can impact someone's life as a nurse by just talking to them and helping them through their most difficult times. I have loved my job ever since, and I look for that opportunity with every patient I treat. I'm always trying to figure out what people do and what their lives are like. It just gives me a neat perspective of where they are now and why they're in a particular situation. This enriched perspective helps me better understand what we at the hospital can do to help.

The Right Man for the Job

Although I stumbled into my nursing career, it has led me toward wonderful opportunities. Right now I am a clinical nurse manager in charge of a 30-bed cardiac telemetry unit at Advocate Good Samaritan Hospital. I came here after I had only one year's nursing experience. I realized that I didn't want to do bedside nursing forever, so I looked into practitioner school in hopes of being able to diagnose and treat patients in a doctor's office. Eventually, I was offered a job as primary nurse practitioner at a doctor's office that I greatly respected—but I was simultaneously asked to take over as the manager on the very unit I for which I currently worked!

I knew nothing about management and had been planning to go in a totally different direction. However, my colleagues, with whom I had worked side by side for five years, came to me and said, "We want you to be the manager. We will support you in whatever you decide. We'll work our butts off for you, and we think you're the right person."

I was touched by their support, and I was nervous about such an unfamiliar and difficult position—but I know I made the right decision. Yes, becoming a nurse leader can be scary at times. It consists of new and unfamiliar responsibilities, along with the many branches of patient care and comfort you've already been practicing. My advice to new nurse leaders consists of what I learned when I started out.

Active Leadership

The first thing I would say is to practice what you preach. It isn't enough to give orders and then just sit back and watch. If I said, "You guys need to do your rounding," then obviously I need to do my rounding as well. If I say, "You guys need to hold each other accountable," then I need to be doing the same.

Secondly, you can never recognize good work enough. In fact, I think I could still do a better job of patting my nurses on their backs. I am sure there have been times when I've shied away from giving positive reinforcement when things have gotten hectic, but the results are always the same. If you catch people doing great work, you realize how important it is to acknowledge a job well done. A kind word of congratulations goes a long way, lifts people's spirits, and keeps performance up.

Finally, empower the people working for you. Give them ownership. If you give them the power to help you make decisions, they will make the right choices 99 percent of the time. I've found that one of my top assets is my ability to find the people able to handle that kind of responsibility, and then encourage them to keep up the good work. This motivates them to help guide your whole team. Call it delegation, but I think it's empowerment as well.

The Power of Positive Change

A big lesson I have learned as a nurse leader is that change is going to happen no matter what you do. Positive change consists of a lot of work. You have to set a goal, follow up, check accountability, and make sure that your goal is met. It's a whole lot of work! On the other hand, negative change happens when you sit back and do nothing. I've seen both sides of change, and I know that it isn't enough to get things running and then sit back and watch. Goals are achieved only when you follow through all the way.

My hospital has come a long way even in the five years I've been in a management role, in large part thanks to Studer Group®. When I took over, our patient satisfaction year-end results were in the 10th percentile. Now they're in the 70th percentile—and we still have work to do. I know we're not in a perfect place, but I'm proud to see that we're working toward our goals.

I understand that in order for any healthcare establishment to be the best it can be, people have to care. Healthcare workers must care about the service they provide, and I'm not just speaking clinically. We want the families in this community to feel good about coming here, and we want them to be proud of this hospital. We know that change begins in every branch of hospital care, starting with the bedside nurses and going all the way up the chain of command. We are all a part of this hospital, and we are all a part of its continued success.

REFERENCES

Chapter 1

[1] Bruce Tulgan, Competing for the Future, Harvard Management Update, Mar. 2003.

Chapter 2

[1] Studer, Quint. *Hardwiring Excellence: Purpose, Worthwhile Work, Making a Difference*. Gulf Breeze, FL: Fire Starter Publishing, 2003.

[2] Buckingham, Marcus, and Curt Coffman. *First, Break All the Rules: What the World's Greatest Managers Do Differently*. New York: Simon & Schuster, 1999.

[3] Studer, Quint. *Hardwiring Excellence: Purpose, Worthwhile Work, Making a Difference*. Gulf Breeze, FL: Fire Starter Publishing, 2003.

Chapter 3

[1] Studer, Quint. *Hardwiring Excellence: Purpose, Worthwhile Work, Making a Difference*. Gulf Breeze, FL: Fire Starter Publishing, 2003.

[2] Rath, Tom, and Donald O. Clifton. *How Full Is Your Bucket?: Positive Strategies for Work and Life*. New York: Gallup Press, 2004.

[3] Studer Group, ed. *What's Right in Health Care: 365 Stories of Purpose, Worthwhile Work, and Making a Difference*. Gulf Breeze, FL: Fire Starter Publishing, 2007.

Chapter 7

[1] Bozeman, B., and M. K. Feeney. "Toward a Useful Theory of Mentoring: A Conceptual Analysis and Critique." *Administrative and Society* 39, no. 6 (2007): 719-39.

[2] Ibid.

Chapter 9

[1] Clark, Paul Alexander. *Patient Satisfaction and the Discharge Process: Evidence-based Best Practices.* Marblehead, MA: HCPro, Inc., 2006.

Chapter 19

[1] Kohn, Linda T., Janet M. Corrigan, and Molla S. Donaldson, ed. *To Err is Human: Building a Safer Health System.* Washington, DC: National Academies Press, 2000.

Chapter 23

[1] American Nurses Association. "Principles of Delegation." *Nursing World.* 2005. (28 February 2009).

[2] National Council of State Boards of Nursing. *Concepts and Decision-Making Process National Council Position Paper.* 1995. Quoted in American Nurses Association. "Principles of Delegation." *Nursing World.* 2005. (28 February 2009).

RESOURCES

Accelerate the momentum of your Healthcare Flywheel®.
Access additional resources at www.firestarterpublishing.com/Nurse-LeaderHandbook.

STUDER GROUP COACHING:

Studer Group® coaches hospitals and healthcare systems providing detailed framework and practical how-tos that improve bottom lines, clinical outcomes, and the patient experience. Studer Group coaches work side-by-side establishing, accelerating, and hardwiring the necessary changes to create a culture of excellence. In our work, Studer Group has identified a core of three critical elements that must be in place for great organizational performance once a commitment is made to the pillar approach to goal setting and the Nine Principles® of Behavior.

Emergency Department Coaching Line
Is a comprehensive approach to improving service and operational efficiency in the Emergency Department. Our team of ED coach experts will partner with you to implement best practices, proven tools, and tactics using our Evidence-Based Leadership℠ approach to improve results in all five pillars: People, Service, Quality, Finance, and Growth. Key deliverables include decreasing staff turnover, improving employee, physician, and patient satisfaction, decreasing door-to-doctor times, reducing left without being seen rates, increasing upfront cash collections, and increasing patient volumes and revenue.

To learn more about Studer Group coaching, visit www.studergroup.com.

BOOKS: categorized by audience

All Leaders
Hardwiring Excellence—A *BusinessWeek* bestseller, this book is a road map to creating and sustaining a "Culture of Service and Operational Excellence" that drives bottom-line results.
Written by Quint Studer

Results That Last—A *Wall Street Journal* bestseller by Quint Studer that teaches leaders in every industry how to apply his tactics and strategies to their own organizations to build a corporate culture that consistently reaches and exceeds its goals.

Hardwiring Flow: Systems and Processes for Seamless Patient Care—Drs. Thom Mayer and Kirk Jensen delve into one of the most critical issues facing healthcare leaders today: patient flow.

Eat THAT Cookie!: Make Workplace Positivity Pay Off...for Individuals, Teams and Organizations—Written by Liz Jazwiec, RN, this book is funny, inspiring, relatable, and is packed with realistic, down-to-earth tactics leaders can use to infuse positivity into their culture.

"I'm Sorry to Hear That..." Real-Life Responses to Patients' 101 Most Common Complaints About Health Care—When you respond to a patient's complaint, you are responding to the patient's sense of helplessness and anxiety. The service recovery scripts offered in this book can help you recover a patient's confidence in you and your organization. Authored by Susan Keane Baker and Leslie Bank.

What's Right in Health Care: 365 Stories of Purpose, Worthwhile Work, and Making a Difference—A collaborative effort of stories from healthcare professionals across the nation. This 742-page book shares a story a day submitted by your friends and colleagues. It is a daily reminder about why we answered this calling and why we stay with it—to serve a purpose, to do worthwhile work, and to make a difference.

101 Answers to Questions Leaders Ask—Written by Quint Studer and Studer Group coaches, offers practical, prescriptive solutions to some of the many questions he's received from healthcare leaders around the country.

Frontline Heroes: A Story of Saving Lives—Written by Kurt Larson, reveals top-of-the-line actions and tactics well-led fire and emergency service agencies use to bring order out of chaos—and shows readers how they can develop standardized leadership practices at their own organizations.

Senior Leaders & Physicians

Straight A Leadership—A leadership resource that helps identify obstacles and reveals how to overcome them to execute and lead in 21st century healthcare, written by Quint Studer.

Leadership and Medicine—A book that makes sense of the complex challenges of healthcare and offers a wealth of practical advice to future generations, written by Floyd D. Loop, MD, former chief executive of the Cleveland Clinic (1989-2004).

Engaging Physicians: A Manual to Physician Partnership—A tactical and passionate road map for physician collaboration to generate organizational high performance, written by Stephen C. Beeson, MD.

Physicians

Practicing Excellence: A Physician's Manual to Exceptional Health Care—This book, written by Stephen C. Beeson, MD, is a brilliant guide to implementing physician leadership and behaviors that will create a high-performance workplace.

Nurse Leaders & Nurses

Inspired Nurse and Inspired Journal—By Rich Bluni, RN, helps maintain and recapture the inspiration nurses felt at the start of their journey with action-oriented "spiritual stretches" and stories that illuminate those sacred moments we all experience.

Emergency Department Team

Excellence in the Emergency Department—A book by Stephanie Baker, RN, CEN, MBA, is filled with proven, easy-to-implement, step-by-step instructions that will help you move your Emergency Department forward.

For more information about books and other resources, visit www.firestarterpublishing.com.

ARTICLES:

Quint Studer on 5 Important Issues Facing Healthcare Leaders
The Hospital Review
November 14, 2008

Unlocking the FEAR Foothold
Quint Studer
March 2009

Evidence-Based Leadership
Projects@Work
Quint Studer

How to Achieve and Sustain Excellence
Healthcare Financial Management

To read these articles and view other resources, please visit www.studergroup.com/StraightALeadership.

SOFTWARE SOLUTIONS:

Leader Evaluation Manager™: Results Through Focus and Accountability
Studer Group's Leader Evaluation Manager is a web-based application that automates the goal setting and performance review process for all leaders, while ensuring that the performance metrics of individual leaders are aligned with the overall goals of the organization. By using Leader Evaluation Manager, both leaders and their supervisors will clearly understand from the beginning of the year what goals need to be accomplished to achieve a successful annual review, can plan quarterly tasks with completion targets under each goal, and view monthly report cards to manage progress.

To learn more, please visit www.firestarterpublishing.com.

INSTITUTES:

Taking You and Your Organization to the Next Level with Quint Studer
Learn the tools, tactics, and strategies that are needed to Take You and Your Organization to the Next Level at this two-day institute with Quint Studer and Studer Group's coach experts. You will walk away with your passion ignited, and with Evidence-Based Leadership℠ strategies to create a sustainable culture of excellence.

What's Right in Health Care℠
One of the largest healthcare peer-to-peer learning conferences in the nation, What's Right in Health Care brings organizations together to share ideas that have been proven to make healthcare better.

To review a listing of Studer Group institutes or to register for an institute, visit www.studergroup.com/institutes.

For information on Continuing Education Credits, visit www.studergroup.com/cmecredits.

Visit www.firestarterpublishing.com/NurseLeaderHandbook to access and download many of the resources, examples, and tools mentioned in *The Nurse Leader Handbook*.

ABOUT THE AUTHORS

Stephanie Baker, RN, CEN, MBA

Stephanie Baker has 20 years of clinical nursing and administrative experience in the areas of emergency, trauma, flight, and critical care medicine and proven results with her partners around the country. Her consistent achievement of organizational and Emergency Department results speaks to her ability to motivate senior leaders and staff, implement evidence-based tactics, drive accountability, and create a culture of "always."

Prior to joining Studer Group® in 2005, she was the director of emergency services at Paradise Valley Hospital in San Diego, CA. In her role there, Stephanie moved the Emergency Department from the 4th to the 98th percentile in patient satisfaction, reduced patients who left without treatment from 8 percent to 2.9 percent, and implemented a new "Wipe Out Waiting" bedside registration that contributed to a 20 percent patient volume increase over 18 months.

Rich Bluni, RN

Rich Bluni is a Studer Group expert coach assisting healthcare organizations in implementing the Evidence-Based Leadership℠ framework, a national speaker, and the author of *Inspired Nurse* (Fire Starter Publishing, 2009). He brings a strong knowledge base in healthcare operations coupled with the ability to articulate the passion partners expect from Studer Group.

As a coach Rich achieves outstanding results working with his partner organizations and in 2008 was awarded Studer Group's Pillar Award for these outcomes. As a speaker he scores an average 4.95 out of 5 for his presentations.

Rich has more than 16 years of clinical, legal, risk management, patient safety, and nursing management experience. With clinical experience in a broad range of areas such as pediatric intensive care, trauma intensive care, behavioral health, and emergency medicine, Rich understands the challenges, joys, and value of purpose, worthwhile work, and making a difference in healthcare.

Debbie Cardello, RN, MSN

A Studer Group coach and trained examiner for the Malcolm Baldrige Quality Award, Debbie Cardello works with healthcare leaders to focus, align, and accelerate their performance excellence journey. She is the former chief operating officer (COO) of New Jersey-based Robert Wood Johnson University Hospital-Hamilton. Under her leadership, the organization won the prestigious Malcolm Baldrige Quality Award in 2004. In addition, the hospital achieved bottom-line results in the nation's top 10 percent in quality outcomes, as well as patient, employee, and physician satisfaction.

Upon beginning her career as a staff nurse in the Critical Care and Emergency Departments at RWJ Hospital-Hamilton, Debbie realized her desire to make a difference as a nurse leader. Subsequently, she held several leadership positions, including Emergency Department director, nursing supervisor, assistant vice president-nursing, and chief nursing officer. The last five years of her hospital career were spent serving as that organization's COO.

Debbie is the author of "Improving Patient Satisfaction with a Bit of Mystery" and "Monitoring Daily Staffing Variances, Productivity, and Length of Stay in the Emergency Department," both published in *Nursing Management*. She also wrote "Implementation of a One-Hour Fast Track Service; One Hospital's Experience," which appeared in the *Journal of Emergency Nursing*.

Lauren Charles, RN

A coach with Studer Group for the past five years, Lauren Charles has worked with partners ranging from small rural hospitals to large medical systems. Her strength and passion is focusing on areas of nursing leadership and quality improvements. Particular areas of expertise include coaching leader rounding, Hourly Rounding^{SM} by staff, and individualizing patient care.

Lauren received her diploma of nursing from St. Elizabeth School of Nursing in Youngstown, Ohio. Her bachelor's degree in nursing was awarded by the University of Akron, and she earned her master's degree in nursing from Kent State University. She served at Akron General Medical Center for nearly 20 years in various positions ranging from staff nurse to director of patient care services cardio/thoracic/vascular surgery. Prior to joining Studer Group, Lauren worked at the Cleveland Clinic Foundation as the director of nursing: medicine, oncology, and psychiatry.

Karen Cook, RN, BSN

Karen Cook is one of the most senior coaches at Studer Group. With more than 30 years of experience in the industry, she has been involved in coaching some of the largest healthcare systems in this country. Her nursing and administrative background provides the expertise necessary to help organizations favorably impact quality patient care, employee loyalty, efficiency, and profitability.

During her ten years with Studer Group, Karen's partner hospitals have achieved numerous accolades including designations as Top 50 Hospitals and Top 100 Places to Work, as well as patient satisfaction achievements such as Client Success Story and Summit Award winners. Demonstrating her passion for quality patient care, she was the primary author of the Studer Group HCAHPS toolkit and has helped hospitals implement the HCAHPS survey since 2005, including participating in early focus groups with the Agency for Healthcare Research and Quality.

Her engaging style has made her a popular speaker at events like What's Right in Health Care℠ and IHI Expeditions and for organizations like the Healthcare Financial Management Association and the North Carolina Hospital Association.

Davy Crockett, RN, FACHE

Davy Crockett has served as a Studer Group coach and account leader with a proven track record of success since June 2005. His expertise includes such diverse areas as service excellence, creating a culture for employee engagement, process improvement, and leadership development. He coaches organizations to create strong cultures focused on Evidence-Based Leadership. He also enjoys mentoring emerging leaders.

Davy possesses over 30 years of experience in acute hospital/health system operations. Previously, he acted as vice president for patient care services in a large multi-hospital system. In addition, he held numerous leadership positions in tertiary and community hospital environments. He is certified as a black belt in Six Sigma.

Lucy Crouch, BSN, MSN

Lucy Crouch joined Studer Group as a coach in 2002 after serving as a nurse for more than 25 years. During that time, her experience included both staff and leadership positions. She excels at implementation and in getting results. Having worked at Baptist Hospital, Inc., with both Quint Studer and Gail Boylan, she is a skilled coach.

Lucy's management background encompasses quality improvement, nursing education, and case management. This experience gives her the unique ability to understand the challenges of balancing the business of running a hospital with the necessity of providing the highest possible care for the patient.

She has worked with a wide variety of nursing and ancillary departments to help improve processes, streamline procedures, and facilitate the development of new services, always with a focus on employee and patient satisfaction. This experience was also one of the reasons she was selected to serve as an examiner on the 2002 and 2003 Malcolm Baldrige Board of Examiners.

Lucy has consistently produced results and has the unique perspective of having served on almost every area of the service teams and in the leadership development process.

Linda Deering, RN, MSN

Linda Deering has 30 years of experience in nursing, leadership, and hospital operations. She is also an entertaining and articulate speaker.

In her current role as the chief operating officer for Sherman Health in Illinois, she is leading the organization to great outcomes. Prior to her work at Sherman, Linda served as the vice president for patient services and chief nurse at Delnor-Community Hospital in Illinois, where she was their champion for excellence. In that role, she helped move inpatient satisfaction to the 95th percentile and Emergency Department patient satisfaction to the 99th percentile. Additionally, Delnor won awards for employee and physician satisfaction, both at the 99th percentile for four consecutive years.

Through her participation in Studer Group, Linda fulfills her passion for improving healthcare environments across the nation by making hospital cultures healthier for patients and clinicians. Her presentations at Froedtert Medical Center, Eastern Maine Medical Center, Cleveland Clinic, Intermountain Health, and more have resulted in the highest praise from her audiences.

Lavonne Dwinal, RN, BS, MOL

Lavonne Dwinal acts as a Studer Group coach for acute and rural hospitals. She is highly accomplished in the field of critical care, having worked in an Intensive Care Unit (ICU) for 14 years. Lavonne also served as nurse manager of a Cardiac, Neurological, and Surgical ICU for nine years. She was one of the first clinicians in her hospital to obtain critical care registered nurse (CCRN) certification in 1982.

As an information technology senior analyst, she developed and implemented the point of care documentation system for two Obstetric Units. Lavonne also managed the clinical staff in a 22-physician cardiovascular practice for five years.

Before joining Studer Group, she held the position of service excellence coordinator for a 5,000- employee health system in the Quad Cities region of Iowa and Illinois. There Lavonne initiated call light rounding; as a result, within nine months, a Rehabilitation Unit saw call lights decrease by 25 percent and falls by 20 percent, while pain scores on the patient satisfaction survey improved 8.3 points.

Jill Ellis, RN, MA

Jill Ellis, a registered nurse, joined Studer Group as a coach in 2008. In her work, she routinely uses the Nine Principles® and enjoys proven results. In addition to a bachelor's degree in nursing, Jill holds a master's in health services administration.

Jill worked in healthcare for 25 years, with more than 12 years of experience as a nurse leader. As a staff nurse, she served in the Intensive Care Unit (ICU), Neonatal ICU, Emergency Department, Post-Anesthesia Care Unit, Pediatric Medical/Surgical Unit, and Urgent Care.

As a manager, Jill led two Pediatric Med/Surg Units, multiple Urgent Care/Primary Care centers, and Adult Critical Care. She also served as the director of nursing for Med/Surg and Critical Care Services. In that role, she had oversight of five nurse managers and over 300 full-time employees.

A native of Georgia, Jill has lived in the Atlanta area for more than 20 years.

Bonnie Forsh, RN, BSN, MBA, CNA-BC

Bonnie Forsh joined Studer Group in 2008 and brings with her a wealth of knowledge from both her educational background and work experience. Her background in emergency medicine allows Bonnie to excel in specialty coaching with Emergency Departments around the country. Bonnie received her BS in nursing from Olivet Nazarene University, received her MBA from the University of Phoenix, and is a certified nursing administrator (CNA).

Bonnie has held a variety of positions in the hospital setting, ranging from a nurse clinician at the Greater Southeast Community Hospital to the administrative director of emergency and outpatient services at

Washington County Hospital in Hagerstown, Maryland. While serving as the administrative director of emergency and outpatient services, Bonnie led teams in initiatives that decreased ED wait times by 60 percent, improved ED throughput times by 10 percent, and decreased order-to-discharge time for admitted patients by 40 percent. Additionally, Bonnie implemented a successful one-year internship program to recruit and retain graduate nurses into a busy Emergency Department and has expanded emergency services to include two Urgent Care centers, an Observation Unit, and a SAFE (Sexual Assault and Forensic Examiner) program.

Bonnie's experience and leadership skills allow her to consistently improve organizational results and drive accountability in the organizations she coaches.

Tonya Fuller, RRCP

Tonya Fuller, a registered respiratory care practitioner, has worked with Studer Group since 2007, coaching organizations around to country to achieve sustainable service excellence.

Utilizing process improvement methodologies, Tonya has coached nurse leaders how to drill down into measurement analysis and AIDET℠ execution. As a result, one partner hospital in Jacksonville, Florida, moved its inpatient satisfaction scores from the 54th percentile to the 78th percentile in half a year. Currently sustaining the 85th percentile ranking, the hospital has earned the Sterling Award and several Professional Research Consultants (PRC) nursing unit awards.

In healthcare more than 20 years, Tonya is the former director of respiratory care services at St. Alexius Medical Center in Hoffman Estates, Illinois.

Tonya earned her bachelor's degree in respiratory therapy at Tennessee State University, Nashville, Tennessee. Her master's in continuing education and training management was awarded at the University of St. Francis in Joliet, Illinois. She currently resides in Nashville.

Jackie Gaines, MS, BSN

Jackie Gaines is an executive coach and senior leader for Studer Group. A high-performing senior executive, she enjoyed a progressive career encompassing more than 30 years of leadership and accomplishments.

Jackie served in a variety of roles including management, health education, and program coordination. She started her career as a nurse working for Johns Hopkins Medicine. After graduating with a master's degree, she went to work at Health Care for the Homeless, Inc., in Baltimore, Maryland, serving as a nurse practitioner. In 1987, she was appointed that organization's first president and chief executive officer (CEO), going on to develop the business into a national model.

In 1999, Jackie was appointed vice president of community health systems integration for Bon Secours Baltimore Health System. There, Jackie led an effective $15 million turnaround initiative called Transformation 2000. A year later, she joined Providence Health System in Oregon as chief executive for Providence Milwaukee Hospital and regional chief executive for ancillary business. She took Providence Milwaukee to 100 Top Hospitals® status three times and implemented the organization's family practice residency program. In 2007 Jackie left Providence to become the president and CEO of Mercy Health Partners (Northeast Region), where she had oversight of two hospitals and 15 free-standing clinics and diagnostic centers.

Liz Jazwiec, RN

Liz Jazwiec is a nationally renowned speaker, strategist, and consultant who has shared her passion for customer service, employee satisfaction, and leadership development with audiences across the country.

She's also been a longtime hospital officer who helped raise service scores at Chicago, Illinois' Holy Cross Hospital from the 5th to the 99th percentile in just a few years. Her work as vice president of patient care and as the director of emergency services was one of the key reasons Holy Cross won *Fortune* magazine's Enterprise Award for Best Business Practices in 1996.

Today, she uses that expertise as well as humor, enthusiasm, and memorable anecdotes to inspire other organizations interested in building a culture where employees deliver superior service as a matter of routine. Audiences love her inspirational, motivational style—but they appreciate her practical, no-nonsense, easy-to-implement ideas even more.

Liz is the author of *Eat THAT Cookie!: Make Workplace Positivity Pay Off…For Individuals, Teams and Organizations* (Fire Starter Publishing, 2009).

Beth Keane, MA

Since 2002, Beth has spearheaded the training programs and resource materials that are the backbone of Studer Group's highly successful path to success. She has literally written the book on creating and sustaining excellence for dozens of the country's premier healthcare organizations.

Prior to joining Studer Group, Beth spent 20 years as a corporate trainer, providing course training and development for organizations in diverse industries such as healthcare, manufacturing, aerospace, wood, and petroleum. She also served as president of the Gulf Coast Chapter of the American Association for Training and Development and received key certifications from some of the country's foremost training organizations. Beth is an expert on communication skills and the Studer Group process for both peer interviewing and highmiddlelow* performer coaching. Beth has worked with hospitals, long-term care facilities, medical groups, and Emergency Departments.

Julie Kennedy-Oehlert, RN

Take 18 years of clinical experience as an Emergency Room trauma nurse and proficiency as a forensic nurse examiner and combine it with an energy level that draws in chief executive officers, physicians, and nurses—and you get Julie Kennedy! She commands a national presence in sharing her passion for excellent patient care with the next generation of "difference makers."

As a Studer Group expert in coaching physician practices and Emergency Departments, Julie led the prestigious study "The Effects of Emergency Department Staff Rounding on Patient Safety and Satisfaction." The results were included in an electronic edition of the *Journal of Emergency Medicine* in 2009. She has worked closely with healthcare leaders, nurses, and physicians across the U.S. and Australia, sharing strategies that positively impact service and quality outcomes and make a big difference in professional growth and satisfaction.

Julie is a five-time winner of the Studer Group Pillar Award for outstanding partner outcomes. She's highly valued for her no-nonsense presentation style that's at once passionate, entertaining, and prescriptive. While Julie appreciates all that's right in the healthcare arena, she has the confidence to say what needs to be said to make it a better place for staff to work, physicians to practice, and patients to receive care.

Lyn Ketelsen, RN, MBA

Since joining Studer Group, Lyn Ketelsen has worked with over 100 organizations. She helps leaders put prescriptive elements in place to build a culture of operational excellence and improve the level of patient, employee, and physician satisfaction. Several of Lyn's partner organizations have won the coveted Studer Group Fire Starter of the Month award.

During her 24 years as a registered nurse, Lyn experienced healthcare in a variety of settings from Neonatal Intensive Care Units to managed care to Emergency Departments.

She coauthored a study with the Alliance for Healthcare Research on reducing frequency of call lights through Hourly Rounding. After it was published in the *American Journal of Nursing* in September 2006, hundreds of organizations across the country adopted hourly rounds.

Consequently, they realized marked improvements in quality and patient satisfaction, along with enhanced nursing efficiency and fulfillment. In December 2007, the Institute for Healthcare Improvement officially recommended that healthcare entities implement the Hourly Rounding process.

In December 2008, Lyn was honored with the coveted Flame Award, Studer Group's highest award for employees. She is the mother and stepmother of six children and nine grandchildren.

Bob Murphy, RN, Esq, FACHE

Bob Murphy, a well-known operations leader and international healthcare presenter, joined Studer Group in 2006. A true difference maker, he speaks to and coaches organizations on a wide variety of leadership and accountability topics, working with directors and senior leaders. He is frequently called upon to speak at conferences and seminars.

Having worked in healthcare more than 24 years, most recently Bob served as the senior vice president and administrator for Baptist Hospital in Pensacola, Florida. His efforts contributed to Baptist's ranking in the top 1 percent of healthcare customer service organizations for over eight consecutive years, according to Press Ganey. During his tenure, Bob also played a significant role in Baptist's being awarded the Malcolm Baldrige National Quality Award in 2003, and being named six times as one of *Fortune* magazine's 100 Best Companies to Work for in America.

Bob's diverse experience includes work as a phlebotomist, registered nurse, department leader of emergency/trauma services, quality leader, chief operating officer, and hospital administrator. Bob is also a paramedic, healthcare risk manager, attorney, and forklift operator. He's board certified in healthcare administration and is a Fellow in the American College of Healthcare Executives.

Julie O'Shaughnessy, SS, MHA, CHE, CPHQ

Julie O'Shaughnessy has 14 years of experience as a leader of Quality Management Departments. She also has extensive coaching experience and is the author of numerous articles. Julie has a master's of health administration from Duke University and a bachelor of science from Cornell University and is a certified professional in healthcare quality.

Since Julie joined Studer Group in 2004, over 90 percent of the organizations she's coached have achieved their goals for employee, physician, and patient satisfaction. By designing and implementing an integrated model for quality, risk, and case management, she helped one organization achieve a 41 percent reduction in operating expenses and an increase in employee satisfaction from the 48th percentile to the 92nd percentile.

Julie is adept at coaching CEOs, senior leaders, physicians, middle managers, and staff on not only interpreting results but also defining actions to improve performance.

Jeanny Platt, BS, RN

Jeanny Platt is the director of nursing for five Medical/Surgical Units as well as a 31-bed Emergency Department at North Austin Medical Center in Austin, Texas. She has held various positions throughout her career, ranging from staff nurse in both critical care and emergency nursing to various leadership roles in medical/surgical and emergency nursing.

Jeanny's passion for providing exceptional care and service for the patients and families she serves is the cornerstone of her success. Over the years, she has created innovative nursing campaigns, such as "I've got your back," aimed at fostering teamwork and a positive work environment for her staff.

Her employee satisfaction scores continue to be excellent as do her physician satisfaction scores. She has mastered the fiscal management for five Medical/Surgical Units as well as the Emergency Department, and has done exceptionally well by eliminating all contract labor usage on her Medical/Surgical Units with considerable annual cost savings, unit expense costs, and overall operational costs within all her departments.

Kristine (Kris) Powell, RN, BSN, CEN

Kris Powell is the director of nursing for a 29-bed Emergency Department and two Medical/Surgical Units at Baylor Regional Medical Center in Grapevine, Texas.

She has been in emergency and trauma nursing for over 23 years. She has held a variety of positions including staff nurse, educator, injury prevention outreach coordinator, trauma program manager, director of emergency services, and more recently director of emergency and medical/surgical services. She is active in the Emergency Nurses Association at the local and state levels, has served as an elected officer in local and state chapters, and has also served many years as a national delegate at the Emergency Nurses Association annual meeting.

Kris has been a guest speaker at numerous local, state, and national conferences and also coauthored the education chapter in the sixth edition of the *Emergency Nursing Core Curriculum*. As a result of patient satisfaction improvements implemented by the Emergency Department staff and physicians, the Emergency Department at Baylor Regional Medical Center was the recipient of two national Press Ganey Awards in November 2008—the Compass Award and Success Story Award.

Mark Quirin, RN, MSN

Mark Quirin is currently the clinical nurse manager of a 30-bed Telemetry Unit and the Centralized Telemetry Department at Advocate Good Samaritan Hospital, in Downers Grove, IL.

A nurse since January of 1998, Mark has worked in telemetry his entire career. He started working at Advocate Good Samaritan Hospital after having one year of experience as a nurse and has stayed with the organization ever since. He started on the Telemetry Unit as a staff nurse, then moved into the charge nurse role, then unit educator, and now the clinical nurse manager. During this time he completed his master's of science in nursing.

He helped implement a new Shared Governance format for Advocate Good Samaritan Hospital and has helped improve customer service scores. His leadership has contributed to Advocate Good Samaritan Hospital's earning accolades such as Magnet recognition, Top 100 Hospital by Thompson Reuters, and the Lincoln Silver Award for progress towards excellence.

Brian C. Robinson, MHSA, Executive Vice President, Studer Group

During the past 25 years, Brian Robinson has led several hospitals and has a successful record of improving patient satisfaction and clinical and operational outcomes. A 20-year CEO veteran, he has led small rural hospitals, large urban teaching facilities, and most recently Las Vegas's busiest system of hospitals and clinics. Under his leadership, his facilities have had the distinction of being named in America's "Top 100 Hospitals" eight times.

Brian takes great pride in his ability to build meaningful relationships with employees and physicians—and for ensuring their needs are heard and understood. His focus on patient, employee, and physician satisfaction have allowed him to increase patient access to care, improve clinical outcomes, and improve the overall delivery of patient care.

Brian is known for his knowledge and understanding of healthcare in America. He is often called upon for his expertise in Washington, D.C., where he has been appointed by the secretary of health and human services to serve as a technical advisor to CMS. He has served as a member, board of directors, of the Federation of American Hospitals and as chair, CEO

Committee, Federation of American Hospitals. He has also been a member of the American College of Healthcare Executives for over 20 years.

Terry Rose, RN, MHA

Terry Rose has 31 years of experience in the clinical arena. Prior to joining Studer Group, she was the executive director of emergency services at a large community hospital, including oversight of the Emergency Department and EMS, as well as Service and Operational Excellence. Terry also has experience in Surgery and was director of endoscopy for 11 years.

Terry has a master's in healthcare administration that balances perfectly with her experience in clinical operations and service excellence.

Wolfram Schynoll, MD, FACEP

Dr. Wolfram Schynoll is a practicing emergency and occupational medicine physician in his 19th year of practice and resides in Eau Claire, Wisconsin. In 1998 he founded a hospital-based occupational medicine program for which he continues to serve as medical director.

In 2001, under Dr. Schynoll's leadership as president of his medical group and Studer Group's guidance, the Emergency Department attained a quarterly patient satisfaction score in the 99th percentile at the end of the first year. Over the next six years, the Emergency Department's results stayed above the 95th percentile.

In 2007 Dr. Schynoll joined Studer Group as a physician coach, and since then has coached hundreds of physicians on the principles of creating organizational service excellence.

Regina Shupe, RN, MSN, CEN

Regina Shupe is a full-time coach with Studer Group and has more than 20 years of nursing experience. She began her career as a registered nurse at Mercy Health Partners, Cincinnati, Ohio. In 1994, she transferred to the Emergency Department, where she rose to the role of assistant nurse manager, and eventually, manager. During her years as manager, she moved the ED to the 93rd percentile for patient satisfaction and decreased the door-to-doc time from 45 minutes to 30 minutes.

Regina has also worked for the Health Alliance in Cincinnati as a staff nurse in the Surgical Intensive Care Unit/Trauma Center at University Hospital. Prior to joining Studer Group, she was the director of emergency services and the Central Monitoring Unit at Cincinnati's West Chester Medical Center, which opened in the summer of 2009. This ED currently ranks in the 99th percentile for patient satisfaction according to Press Ganey and has a door-to-doc time of 16 minutes.

She holds a master of science degree in nursing administration from Indiana Wesleyan University and a certification in emergency nursing (CEN). She is a member of Sigma Theta Tau International, Greater Cincinnati Nurse Executives, and the Emergency Nurses Association.

Quint Studer

Quint Studer is founder and CEO of Studer Group, a coaching company that implements Evidence-Based Leadership systems and practices that improve organizations' bottom lines while improving clinical outcomes and patient experiences. He spends much of his time creating, harvesting, and sharing best practices from his company's "national learning lab" of hundreds of organizations and thousands of leaders.

Inc. magazine named Studer its Master of Business, making him the only healthcare leader to have ever won this award. Twice *Modern Healthcare* has chosen Quint as one of the 100 Most Powerful People in Healthcare.

In addition to his latest book, *Straight A Leadership*, Studer has written two bestselling books. His first, *BusinessWeek* bestseller *Hardwiring Excellence*, is one of the bestselling leadership books ever written for healthcare. More than 450,000 copies have been sold. His second book, *Results That Last*, hit the *Wall Street Journal's* bestseller list of business books.

Faye Sullivan, RN

As a registered nurse with 30+ years in healthcare, Faye has cared for patients in a wide variety of care settings. She started her career in emergency nursing and this is her first love. She has cared for patients in a broad spectrum of settings ranging from outpatient clinics to ICUs. Additionally, she has led teams to drive significant financial and operational results in her role as project manager for systems redesign and post merger system integration.

While director of service excellence, her organization achieved top decile performance and was named Press Ganey's Compass Award winner in 2004 and Success Story winner in 2005.

Faye has twice been named as winner of the prestigious Studer Group Pillar Award for partner outcomes. She views coaching with Studer Group as an opportunity to share her outcomes-oriented philosophy with leaders—supporting them as they take the next step in their journey to achieve and sustain excellence across all pillars within their organizations.

Colleen Thornburgh, MSA

An experienced healthcare, training and leadership executive, Colleen Thornburgh brings over 20 years of learning knowledge to Studer Group. She coaches organizations to create and implement results-oriented leadership development and human resource processes. She also acts as the principle coach for Selecting and Retaining Talent and highmiddlelow performer conversations. In addition, Colleen serves in the area of research and development for Studer Group, working on new products and webinars.

Prior to joining SG, Colleen was the chief learning officer for Children's Healthcare of Atlanta, Georgia, one of the country's foremost and largest pediatric systems. Under Colleen's leadership, Children's was recognized as one of the country's Top 100 learning organizations for five consecutive years!

Pat Treiber, MA, MPH

Pat Treiber has over 25 years of experience in non-profit operations and service excellence. She is results-oriented, self-motivated and experienced in large system redesign. She has a personal and unique understanding of service and quality through her continuing work as a practicing Speech Language Pathologist, educator and published author. Pat has helped many departments develop systems and processes that are customer focused and training staff in sensitivity to customer needs—and has won national recognition in the process.

She has worked in multiple aspects of an integrated healthcare delivery system and she has successfully spearheaded corporate efforts to affect a cultural renewal across the various disparate entities. Her management experience has embraced staff, physicians and senior leadership. Understanding the importance of community, she has consulted on several projects working with community members to prioritize health resource needs.

Pat has a master's degree from Seton Hall University in public health administration. She also has a bachelor of sciences degree from Marquette University and a master's degree from Temple University in Speech and Hearing Science. She has also served as an examiner for the New Jersey State Governor's Quality Award and was a member of the American College of Healthcare Executives.

How to Order Additional Copies of

The Nurse Leader Handbook

The Art and Science of Nurse Leadership

Orders may be placed:

Online at:

www.firestarterpublishing.com

www.studergroup.com

By phone at: 866-354-3473

By mail at: Fire Starter Publishing
913 Gulf Breeze Parkway, Suite 6
Gulf Breeze, FL 32561

(Bulk discounts are available.)

The Nurse Leader Handbook
is also available online at www.amazon.com.